Raising the Bar

Crime Science Series

Series editor: Gloria Laycock

Published titles

Superhighway Robbery: Preventing e-commerce crime, by Graeme R. Newman
  and Ronald V. Clarke
Crime Reduction and Problem-oriented Policing, by Karen Bullock and Nick Tilley
Crime Science: New approaches to preventing and detecting crime, edited by
  Melissa J. Smith and Nick Tilley
*Problem-oriented Policing and Partnerships: Implementing an evidence-based
  approach to crime reduction*, by Karen Bullock, Rosie Erol and Nick Tilley
Preventing Child Sexual Abuse: Evidence, policy and practice, by
  Stephen Smallbone, William L. Marshall and Richard Wortley
Environmental Criminology and Crime Analysis, edited by Richard Wortley and
  Lorraine Mazerolle
Raising the Bar: Preventing aggression in and around bars, pubs and clubs, by
  Kathryn Graham and Ross Homel

Raising the Bar
Preventing aggression in and around bars, pubs and clubs

Kathryn Graham and Ross Homel

WILLAN
PUBLISHING

Published by

Willan Publishing
Culmcott House
Mill Street, Uffculme
Cullompton, Devon
EX15 3AT, UK
Tel: +44(0)1884 840337
Fax: +44(0)1884 840251
e-mail: info@willanpublishing.co.uk
website: www.willanpublishing.co.uk

Published simultaneously in the USA and Canada by

Willan Publishing
c/o ISBS, 920 NE 58th Ave, Suite 300,
Portland, Oregon 97213-3786, USA
Tel: +001(0)503 287 3093
Fax: +001(0)503 280 8832
e-mail: info@isbs.com
website: www.isbs.com

First published 2008

ISBN   978-1-84392-318-3 hardback

British Library Cataloguing-in-Publication Data

A catalogue record for this book is available from the British Library.

Project managed by Deer Park Productions, Tavistock, Devon
Typeset by GCS, Leighton Buzzard, Bedfordshire
Printed and bound by T.J. International Ltd, Padstow, Cornwall

Contents

List of tables, figures and boxes

Tables

Figures

Boxes

Acknowledgements

We are indebted to many people who greatly assisted us as we prepared this book. We are especially grateful to Samantha Wells who most generously provided detailed constructive feedback on draft versions of every chapter as well as general intellectual and emotional support throughout. Alasdair Forsyth very kindly allowed us to draw on examples from his rich research database from Glasgow, in addition to our own examples from Canada and Australia, helping us to illustrate that particular features of bar aggression cross national boundaries. Tim Stockwell, Steve Tomsen, Lorraine Mazerolle, Phil Hadfield and Paul Gruenewald kindly supplied references and copies of papers, commentaries and reports. We are also grateful to James Roberts who kindly sent us copies of his Masters and PhD theses and clarified citation details. Matt Manning endured constant interruptions to his PhD project to compile lists of references and locate elusive documents. Sue Steinback provided similar help in finding documents and references as well as help with formatting, figures and other details that required her technical expertise. Richard Wortley and Ron Clarke provided very valuable feedback on our idiosyncratic treatment of situational crime prevention theory, while Russell Carvolth and Gillian McIlwain checked the accuracy of our account of the Australian research and commented more generally on early drafts of several chapters. Carmel Connors assisted hugely by copy editing the penultimate manuscript and by checking, correcting and consolidating references. Many thanks are also owed to Sharon Bernards who provided insightful editorial suggestions on the final version.

We are very grateful to Rich Allinson, publisher at Criminal Justice Press, for permission to reproduce Figures 5.1, 5.2 and 7.1 from *Crime Prevention Studies Volume 7*, and to Professor John Saunders, editor of *Drug and Alcohol Review*, for permission to reproduce Figure 8.2 from Volume 23(1) of the journal.

In some chapters we drew heavily on the *Safer Bars* observational research which was supported by a grant (RO1 AA11505) to Kathryn Graham from the US National Institute on Alcohol Abuse and Alcoholism (NIAAA), although contents of this book are solely the responsibility of the authors and do not necessarily represent the official views of the NIAAA or the National Institutes of Health (NIH). The book also draws on the multi-level analyses and other contributions to the *Safer Bars* project made by co-investigator, Wayne Osgood. The Australian research conducted by Ross Homel and his colleagues was supported by a range of grant programs: the National Campaign Against Drug Abuse; the New South Wales Directorate of the Drug Offensive; the Criminology Research Council; and the Queensland Department of Health (National Campaign Against Drug Abuse Law Enforcement Fund; and Drugs of Dependence). As with the funding of *Safer Bars*, the interpretations of the Australian studies presented in this book do not necessarily represent the views of the funding organisations.

Finally, Kathryn Graham would also like to express her appreciation to Cindy Smythe and especially to Reg Quinton for their personal support throughout this process. Ross Homel is equally grateful to his wife, Beverley, for her generous and stoic support during a long project.

Kathryn Graham is a Senior Scientist and Head of Social and Community Prevention Research at the Centre for Addiction and Mental Health, Toronto/London, Ontario, Canada; Adjunct Research Professor, Department of Psychology, University of Western Ontario, London, Ontario; and Adjunct Professor, National Drug Research Institute, Faculty of Health Sciences, Curtin University of Technology, Perth, Western Australia.

Ross Homel is Professor of Criminology and Criminal Justice; Director of the Strategic Research Program in Social and Behavioural Sciences at Griffith University, Brisbane; and Director of Research and Development for the Pathways to Prevention Project.

Foreword

Alasdair Forsyth
(Glasgow Centre for the Study of Violence)

The link between alcohol and violence can often seem straightforward, unmodifiable and can easily be taken for granted. In Western cultures a great deal of violent or otherwise disorderly behaviours can be described as 'alcohol-related'. This relationship soon becomes apparent when either observing the behaviours of intoxicated consumers or by comparing the times and places where violent incidents occur in relation to when and where most alcohol is sold. The arena where alcohol-related aggression would appear to be the most obvious, and also the most public, is the barroom environment. Although it does not necessarily follow that the most serious alcohol-related disorder takes place in or around bars, it does indicate that here lies an opportunity for researchers to investigate this association in order to formulate strategies which can successfully modify such harmful behaviours. This book compiles evidence from a growing body of research into the problems associated with the barroom environment, highlighting the complex nature of alcohol's association with aggression, and proposes a range of strategies which have the potential to foster the creation of safer bars.

People visit bars or other premises where alcohol is sold for many reasons. Although the provision of alcohol may at first seem to be the prime, perhaps only, reason to visit barrooms, the variety of such premises and the mere fact these are chosen in preference to drinking in the comfort and safety of the consumer's home are indications that there are other motivators at play here. However, as this book reveals, these other motivators can also be demonstrated to lead to problems in barrooms, especially when combined with alcohol. Nevertheless, despite the potential risks or discomforts, so important is bar culture to a large section of the adult population that they are prepared to spend a considerable amount of their disposable income or leisure time inhabiting this environment. This leisure-time drinking activity is long-standing and would appear to be becoming more important, in both social and economic terms, at the present time.

In line with an expansion in leisure culture generally across the developed world, recent decades have witnessed a period of rapid growth and change in barroom provision and culture, particularly in city centres, spawning what has become known as the night-time economy. This has involved a change from the traditional bars, pubs or taverns, which were often small, family-owned, locally run, male-dominated spaces, towards large-scale, corporate-owned, cosmopolitan, 'feminised' venues. This evolutionary process in premises type has been coupled with a trend towards increased deregulation within the drinks market, as economic rather than socially motivated policies have become dominant, resulting in a greater provision of alcohol outlets, serving more customers, with a greater range of beverages, over longer opening hours (that is, towards 24 hours). This has created a barroom 'brandscape' involving the conspicuous consumption of global brands from branded vessels in branded premises which may have chameleon-like, hybridised, functions from licensed cafés/restaurants during the day, to bars/pubs in the evening, to nightclubs/dancehalls after midnight.

Although these changes have been most marked in some English-speaking countries, most notably in England and Wales, these trends would appear to be global, witnessed for example by the proliferation of Irish-themed pub premises in many quite different countries. This trend towards a homogenised globalising drinking pattern can be characterised by greater levels of patronage, and 'binge drinking', by young adults, including women, at the weekend, often to the exclusion of other city centre users. At the same time, there has been increased heterogeneity in the products being consumed. For example, young adults in traditional wine-drinking nations are consuming more beer, as illustrated by the rise of 'el botellon' in Spain, while wine consumption has increased in traditional beer-drinking nations, a process contemporaneous with the advent of new drinks (for example, 'shots') and techniques to market these (for example, the internet).

This timely book takes an international perspective and draws upon insights from research conducted across the English-speaking world in recent decades. As the authors of the book point out, in terms of levels of alcohol-related disorder in public space, the recent changes in bar culture have the potential to be either positive or negative or both. Barroom gentrification may have led to the demise of skid-row type establishments and the rise of up-scale clubs; however, there has also been a continuation in the permissiveness of behaviours and uncomfortable settings which are known to increase the likelihood of disorder, by which the new feminised environment has retained the old hyper-masculine culture. The demise of smaller, family-run establishments, where serving staff had more scope to monitor patrons' behaviours, means that today's bar servers are less likely to know their clientele, who may now also be more mobile both within and between licensed premises. This is a far cry from the traditional view of bartender and 'regular' (patron) interaction, one where lasting personal relationships could be formed, with the former taking on the role of informal counsellor or therapist in a scene reminiscent of the TV show, *Cheers*. This control vacuum has been filled by an ever growing, ever professionalised, 'private army' of bouncers, door-staff, stewards and other security operatives. In position above these new recruits, there also appears to be an increasing number of stakeholders taking an interest in or being charged with managing this barroom order, including dedicated police officers, policy-makers, premises managers, licensing authorities and alcohol/hospitality trades' staff trainers. This book should become essential reading for all such stakeholders.

Both of the authors of this book have been at the forefront of research into the relationship between alcohol and violence for the past three decades and their work has been instrumental in formulating policies aimed at creating safer bars. Their expertise has come from observing alcohol-related disorder in this naturalistic setting, and also from making risk assessments of the physical environments within barrooms. These observations have been supplemented by interviews with barroom patrons and staff, who may themselves have been affected by alcohol-related violence, including as the perpetrators. Their approach goes further in attempting to explain, and reduce, barroom violence than could ever be possible from either the mere analysis of official statistics, where the context of incidents remains unknown, or from the findings of highly controlled unnaturalistic laboratory experiments where stooges may be given alcohol before purposively being aggravated by the experimenter in settings which can never replicate aggression in the real uncontrolled world of the night-time economy.

This book details many real-life incidents of barroom aggression by describing them in graphic, sometimes shocking (even comical) detail, including their precursors, triggers, escalation factors and outcomes. The research detailed in this book is brought together in an objective fashion, as opposed to the sensationalised reporting of the media, or the partial explanations of the drinks industry and those with an opposing moral agenda. The authors emphasise the consistently high degree of cross-validation of findings between studies, conducted on different continents, at different times and using varied yet complementary methods. The chapters of this book mainly focus on the micro situation, at individual barroom, patron or server level, but set this against the macro situation of regulatory change over time, across jurisdictions, and of local and national drinking cultures.

The book begins by explaining the importance of research into barroom violence. Why should premises licensed for the sale of alcohol be associated with violent disorder? Alcohol is more evidently linked with aggression than any other drug. Not only does the mere presence of alcohol (or not) predict the likelihood of violence, but levels of consumption and disorder are also clearly interrelated. However, these relationships are neither inevitable nor linear. Yet they are modifiable, by the manipulation of mediating factors such as those found in the barroom environment. Some people do not become aggressive, no matter how much they drink. Some drinking cultures are more violent than others, and some bars may record more violent incidents than ostensibly identical premises. This can only be because, as well as the effect of the drug, there are also the effects of social interaction and the physical environment to be considered. Indeed, in accordance with the rules of the bio-psycho-social model of controlled intoxicant use ('drug, set and setting'), the desired effects of alcohol (such as 'time out', 'risk taking' or a 'moral holiday') and especially patrons' motivations for visiting barrooms (such as meeting new sexual partners, engaging in competitive games or team bonding) are as likely reasons for any resultant conflict as mere pharmacology. The authors describe some of the many theories which attempt to explain barroom violence, but in doing so acknowledge that no single theory is sufficient, and that often in aggressive situations there may be more than one operating simultaneously.

The book continues by examining the factors which are predictive of barroom trouble. These include patron types (the young, single, male, or those from less advantaged backgrounds being consistently found to be associated with an increased likelihood of trouble), poor service (including irresponsible drinks promotions) and environmental factors (such as higher levels of crowding and permissiveness). Each of these mediating factors can be modified at premises level. However, this may not be possible in all premises. For example, although an individual bar can easily change its clientele, based on age, gender or social background, this clientele will inevitably have to be catered for somewhere else. Similarly patrons' reasons for attending barrooms may be difficult to change. Nevertheless, the chapters of this book identify ways in which more easily modifiable mediating factors can be changed, such as promoting safer barroom design or more responsible beverage service.

The relationship between alcohol and violence is conditional, and the authors go on in the later chapters of this book to investigate ways of breaking this link by removing mediating factors or triggers. This task is not easy as many of the indicators of violent bars may be spurious rather than causative, with some features actually indicating that positive action has been taken to lessen trouble on the premises. Among these 'chicken and egg' situations are staff security measures. On the one hand, a bar with a large number of security measures, such as high staff numbers, large tough-looking bouncers, CCTV, metal-detectors, plastic drinking vessels and strictly enforced house rules, may have these features because it has a history of trouble. On the other hand, whether or not it has a history of trouble, the presence of a large number of security measures may also indicate a high level of management responsibility in taking action to prevent trouble. To some, these security measures may send a signal that troublemakers will not be tolerated, while to others these security measures may act as a challenge or even a signal that trouble is to be expected.

Another consistent theme throughout the book is the question of why there should be such tolerance of disorderly behaviour in barroom environments, or alternatively why 'normal trouble' is not tolerated in other public arenas, such as in the workplace, in other retail environments, in the day time (leisure) economy or elsewhere. This is highlighted by exploring the levels of acceptable behaviour (decorum or rowdiness) between different bars, or types of bar. Orderly premises do tend to have orderly patrons, but is this down to better standards (for example, of customer service or comfort) alone or is this (also) down to the message about behavioural expectations which higher standards send out? Similarly, premises with orderly staff tend to have orderly patrons, but could this be down to the effect of staff training or due to underlying greater levels of management responsibility in those bars which choose to train their staff to a higher degree?

The final chapters of the book outline ways of preventing or reducing violence in bars, whilst acknowledging that the total elimination of these problems may be an unachievable goal. For example, the variation in levels or types of trouble which can be accounted for by patron type are often dictated by a bar's geographical location (for example, local or rural versus central or urban), social catchment (mainstream or affluent versus minority or disadvantaged) or market segment (for example, young or campus versus mature or employed). These socio-economic and cultural factors lie beyond the scope of bar managers or even alcohol-policy makers. Therefore the policy objective of fostering safer bars is a more realistic goal than a trouble-free night-time economy. In the extreme, the enforced closure of bars with a high level of trouble may only displace their problems elsewhere, perhaps to premises where the staff are less able to cope, or perhaps even on to the street, with obvious consequences for policing. Thus, having a relatively high crime rate need not be a reflection on a bar's management practices or staff, as these other factors need first to be taken into account. This same principle, of 'value added', also applies to other venues, for example schools in poor areas can have the best performing, most dedicated teachers, but this is unlikely to be reflected in league tables of grade averages.

This book therefore paints a picture of the barroom environment as one with ambiguous boundaries of behaviour in a contested public space, one in which no one-size solution fits all, but where the local knowledge of servers, bar managers and other stakeholders can be as effective as large-scale policy initiatives to reduce violence. The authors highlight the difficulties in evaluating initiatives in this challenging environment, where natural experiments can easily become contaminated by uncontrolled factors ranging from changes in national legislation to individual bar staff mobility. Nevertheless, the authors describe a range of violence/disorder reduction programmes and risk assessment strategies implemented around the English-speaking world (as well as Sweden), including both community-based approaches and more general regulatory approaches such as stricter or more liberal national licensing schemes, each with their own mix of successes and shortcomings.

Ultimately, *Raising the Bar* is an apt title for this book. It provides a unique international summary of research into barroom violence and as such offers us the best available evidence for making interventions in this area of growing concern.

For Reg and Bev

Chapter 1

Why a book about bar violence?

21 dead in Chicago night club stampede (18 February 2003). *Hundreds of people stormed the exits of a crowded Chicago night club after a disturbance broke out early on Monday, killing at least 21 people and leaving many more injured, police said.*[1] *Authorities said they are investigating what occurred at the E2 club on the city's South Side. Based on information they've gathered so far, it seems a stampede in the club began when a security officer sprayed pepper spray into the crowd, presumably to break up a fight.*[2]

Two men beaten in Sydney hotel[3] *(23 May 1989).* *Mark and his 23-year old brother, Danny, went to a large Sydney hotel to celebrate Mark's 21st birthday. When they refused to buy drugs from a young man who approached them, they were badly beaten with cue sticks by about 12 men, known to some patrons as 'a bad bunch'. Hotel staff and patrons refused to help, and the police when they arrived didn't want to know anything about the incident. Police advised that the attack 'had nothing to do with them, and that the young men should not go to that hotel again'. Later, when the men went to the local police station to make an official complaint, they were, according to station staff, 'ranting and raving and getting very stroppy'.*[4]

Fight in bar leads to street brawl in downtown Toronto (2 February 2001). [The following incident was documented by two observers on the *Safer Bars* evaluation study (Graham *et al.* 2000–04)]. *Two men were trading insults because one man was pestering the other man's girlfriend to dance. The argument escalated as friends of the two men became involved. Security staff told them to 'take it outside'. About 20 men were outside arguing when a punch was thrown. Then, everyone began to fight, punching, kicking and wrestling on the ground. Some men fell into the street forcing traffic to stop to avoid hitting them. One man had blood running down his face, and another was seen waving his leather belt in the air. Two of the security staff came outside and told them to 'break it up' but it was too chaotic for them to have any impact. At this point, the female observer called the emergency police line. As the fight moved down the street, one of the men came back to get his jacket. One of the security staff saw the jacket lying on the sidewalk, picked it up and threw it on the road, saying 'Go and get it! Get the fuck out of here!' One man who was lying on the edge of the sidewalk and being tended by his girlfriend had a bloody nose (possibly broken), bleeding lip, an open wound on the back of his head and was semi-conscious. The girlfriend was crying and explaining to a bystander who was helping her that the man had had his head bashed against a metal pole. The police and ambulance arrived about 10 minutes later and the police officer questioned the observers about what took place. The observers were later informed by one of the officers that the man who had been bashed on the head was unwilling to press charges so there was nothing the police could do.*

(Toronto *Safer Bars* evaluation study, Graham *et al.* 2000–04)

People go out to clubs, bars and pubs to have a good time. However, as the incidents above illustrate, violence that occurs in drinking establishments can lead to dire consequences that were not part of the original plans for an enjoyable evening out. In the Chicago example, violence, combined with poorly trained staff, was the immediate trigger that led to deaths and injuries. The example of the two young men who were beaten at a hotel in Sydney also shows poor management of patron behaviour as well as more systemic problems in the form of accepting attitudes of police and others toward bar violence. Similarly, the Toronto incident illustrates how poor management can contribute to street violence. The Toronto incident also demonstrates how, even when injury occurs and police are involved, perpetrators of bar violence do not necessarily receive punishment for their actions. Thus, these incidents highlight the fact that bar violence cannot be viewed purely as a function of the characteristics of patrons and the ways that patrons interact with one another, but must also be understood in terms of broader societal attitudes and regulatory systems. Poorly trained staff, ineffective enforcement of municipal codes, a 'blame the victim' attitude, police difficulties in gathering evidence from intoxicated and uncooperative people, and many other factors can both increase the risk of violence and increase the risks that such violence may lead to injury.

It has to be acknowledged that these examples are quite extreme. Many people never experience violence when they go out drinking. And, despite the large numbers of mainly young people who frequent licensed premises, violence is rare to non-existent in many drinking establishments. Nevertheless, although for most individuals the risk of involvement in violence during any one visit to a drinking establishment is low, when this risk is multiplied across all venues and patrons, the cumulative number of violent incidents over a year can be large and the potential for serious consequences high.

In the next section, we examine the research evidence suggesting that licensed drinking establishments are high-risk settings for aggression and violence. This is followed by a discussion how the problem of bar violence and societal responses to this violence have been framed in terms of individual patron responsibility in the context of overall market deregulation. We conclude with an outline of the rationale of this book and the subsequent chapters. At the end of the chapter, we provide a glossary and explanation of key terms in order to define a common language that encompasses the many different terms related to licensed premises that are used in different English-speaking countries.

Licensed premises as hot spots for violence – what is the evidence?

Although the 'night-time economy' has become a major feature of life and leisure in many cities around the world (Grazian 2008; Hobbs, Lister, Hadfield, Winlow and Hall 2000; Hobbs *et al.* 2005; Hadfield 2006), and problems with violence in entertainment areas and in and around certain types of drinking establishments have received considerable media attention recently, the linking of violence and crime with bars and clubs is not new (Kümin 2005). Studies conducted in the United States several decades ago found an association between the presence of licensed premises on a city block and a higher rate of crime, including violent crime, occurring on that block (Roncek and Bell 1981–82; Roncek and Maier 1991; Roncek and Pravatiner 1989). There is also research suggesting that the higher the number of drinking establishments within a particular geographic area, the greater the risk of violence (although this relationship has not been found in all studies as noted in the recent review by Livingston *et al.* 2007). In a time series analysis, Norström (2000) demonstrated a significant relationship between the number of drinking establishments per 10,000 inhabitants and criminal violence in Norway during the period 1960–95. Similarly, Gruenewald and Remer (2006) showed that an increase in alcohol outlets in local areas in California was associated with an increase in violence, especially in poor or socially disorganised areas.

Not only is there an association between the number of licensed premises in a geographic area and the overall level of violence in that area, licensed premises account for a substantial proportion of locations where crime and violent injury tend to occur. A study in Sydney, Australia (Ireland and Thommeny 1993) found that 44 per cent of assaults (excluding domestic violence) and 60 per cent of alcohol-related assaults occurred in or near licensed premises. A study in one Canadian city (Gerson 1978) found that licensed premises were the second most frequent location for alcohol-related violence, exceeded only by violence in the home. A New Zealand study of data on homicides and hospitalisations from assault (Langley, Chalmers and Fanslow 1996) found that 12.9 per cent of homicides and 18.4 per cent of assaults involving hospitalisation occurred in or near licensed premises based on cases where location was specified. The authors noted that these figures were probably underestimates given the large proportion of assaults for which the location was not specified. In a study of emergency room admissions at two Canadian hospitals, Macdonald, Wells, Giesbrecht and Cherpitel (1999) found that 37 per cent of those who were treated for a violent injury had been drinking in a licensed establishment prior to the injury, compared to 3 per cent for accidental injuries and 2 per cent for non-injury related admissions. Similarly, Roche, Watt, McClure, Purdie and Green (2001) found that about half of the injuries treated at an emergency room in Queensland, Australia, in which the injured person had been drinking during the preceding six hours, occurred on licensed premises. And, as found by Macdonald and colleagues (1999), injured persons who had been drinking prior to the injury were more likely than those who had not been drinking to have sustained intentional injuries.

General population surveys of non-criminal aggression provide further evidence that licensed premises are high-risk locations for aggression and violence. For example, the 1988 British Crime Survey identified that 28 per cent of incidents of violence against men occurred in or around a pub (Dowds 1994). In a general population survey of adults aged 18–60 in the province of Ontario, Canada, respondents were asked whether they had been personally involved in an incident of physical aggression in the past 12 months and, if so, where the most recent incident occurred (Graham, Wells and Jelley 2002). The most frequent location for aggression was in or near licensed premises (30 per cent of all incidents), and the proportion occurring in or near licensed premises was even higher for young adults, especially young males (Figure 1.1).

In a survey of young adults (aged 18–30) in Buffalo, New York (Leonard, Quigley and Collins 2002), respondents were asked how often they had (a) observed physical aggression, (b) been involved in verbal aggression where physical aggression might have occurred (experienced threat), or (c) experienced being the target or initiator

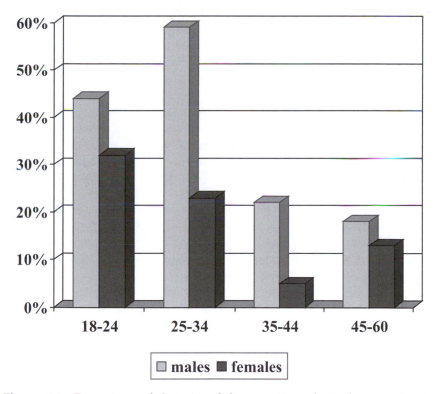

Figure 1.1 Percentage of Ontario adults reporting physical aggression in the past year who said that the most recent incident was in a drinking establishment, by age and gender of respondent

of physical aggression. Those who had experienced aggression were asked how often these types of experiences had occurred in various locations. Inside or outside a bar was by far the most common location for observing aggression, and bars and sports stadiums were the most common locations for experiencing aggression. Thus, the prominence of bars as locations for violence is significant, especially given that some respondents in the sample were under the US legal drinking age of 21, and approximately one-fifth of respondents in the sample never went to bars. When severity of violence was taken into consideration, the importance of bars increased, with almost half of male and female respondents reporting that the most severe violence they had observed had occurred inside or outside a bar. In terms of involvement in violence, about a third of males reported that the most violent episode they had experienced was at a bar (the most frequent location), while, for females, the most severe violence was experienced in the home (their own home and someone else's home), with bars the next most common location.

Other research has shown increased risk of aggression and other harms experienced by those who drink in bars compared to persons who drink in other locations, including being in a violent argument and receiving an injury (Stockwell, Lang and Rydon 1993), and being in a fight or being injured by an intoxicated person (Rossow 1996). Although the relationship between aggression and drinking in licensed premises may be attributable partly to people consuming more alcohol in public drinking establishments than in other locations (Demers *et al.* 2002; Martin, Wyllie and Casswell 1992), one study (Casswell, Zhang and Wyllie 1993) found that drinking in licensed premises was associated with alcohol-related problems even when demographic variables and measures of alcohol consumption were controlled. There is also research suggesting that greater frequency of drinking in licensed premises is associated with higher levels of hostility and greater acceptance of alcohol-related aggression (Treno *et al.* 2007).

Not only are patrons of licensed venues at heightened risk of involvement in aggression and violence, employment in licensed premises is also associated with a high risk of violence. In a study of workplace homicides in Chicago between 1965 and 1990, Hewitt, Levin and Misner (2002) found that workplace homicides occurred more frequently in taverns (22 per cent) than in any other workplace. A study of bar security staff and police in Halifax, Canada (Rigakos 2004) found that security staff in licensed premises were significantly more likely than police officers to report experiencing physical violence in the past year. Ethnographic research in the UK has also confirmed the dangers of working as a 'bouncer' or doorman (Hobbs *et al.* 2007; Monaghan 2003; Winlow, Hobbs, Lister and Hadfield 2001).

In summary, the link between licensed premises and violence and aggression has been demonstrated using a number of different research methodologies. It is important, therefore, to understand the reasons for the link in order to develop strategies for lowering the risk of violence.

Framing prevention of violence in and around drinking establishments

The creation of an environment in which people can let their hair down, have fun with their friends, and push the boundaries of acceptable behaviour has been the core function of licensed premises for hundreds, probably thousands of years (Kolvin 2005a). In many cultures, it is primarily young single adults who go to commercial drinking establishments in order to socialise, meet romantic/sexual partners, dance, play games and generally enjoy themselves. In addition, the pleasurable effects of alcohol, such as reduced anxiety, increased feelings of sociability and liveliness, and heightened feelings of attractiveness and mental acumen, are central to the appeal of drinking establishments. The combination of (a) the presence of large numbers of young adults, (b) under the influence of alcohol, (c) engaging in social and sexual competition, (d) in permissive escapist environments suggests that these settings will be riskier than other settings that do not involve this combination of factors. However, the ways in which these environments are structured and managed and the broader context of social policies and regulations can strongly influence the extent of this risk.

As we describe in the following chapters, there is much that can be done to reduce violence in and around drinking establishments, but whether such efforts will be made will be determined at least partly by societal framing of the problem. There is considerable evidence that fights, at least fights between men, have been considered normal and even part of the entertainment in some drinking establishments. For example, the lack of action on the part of the police in the Sydney incident at the beginning of this chapter is consistent with the argument by Room (2005: 872) that: 'The police have until recently regarded alcohol trouble as routine and everyday, and not something which could be affected by their policies and practices.'

However, it is not only the police, but often the population generally who tend to see violence in drinking establishments as an issue of young men 'sowing their wild oats'. It is often only when deaths or serious injuries occur or street violence becomes a public nuisance that steps are taken to address bar violence, and, even then, these efforts are often short-term rather than sustained. Even when the problem is widely acknowledged, community attitudes, as reflected in political rhetoric and police practices, tend to locate responsibility at the individual level rather than at the level of venue management or the regulation of the night-time leisure industry in the interests of public safety. For example, Room (2004: 1088) noted the following regarding the recent approach to social problems in the United Kingdom: 'Violence in pubs and outside them on the street tends to be seen as a matter of "drunken yobs" and the solutions are primarily individualistic ...' Consistent with this view, individual-focused solutions to pub-related violence such as 'pubwatch' or 'pub ban' agreements (where troublemakers are identified and banned from all drinking establishments in the area) tend to be popular despite the lack of evidence for their effectiveness as a means of reducing overall levels of violence (as we describe in Chapter 7). A similarly individualistic approach is evident in a contemporary Australian public education campaign directed at young men built around the slogan, 'Enjoy the night – not the fight.' The poster shows a young man being handcuffed by police with statements below of 'Know your limits' and 'No more – it's the law' clearly constructing the issue in terms of youth and excessive drinking with police enforcement used to punish offenders.

Fortunately, many police departments are experimenting with more innovative enforcement methods. As interest in community policing and problem-oriented and third-party policing has grown (Fielding 2005; Goldstein 1990; Mazerolle and Ransley 2006), police and other agencies are increasingly using community engagement, inter-agency partnerships and problem-solving strategies based on careful analyses of data to address problems related to drinking environments (see for example, Wiggers *et al.* 2004). A recent example of the power of community action, legislative resolve, and police and military enforcement comes from the Dominican Republic, where violent deaths and injuries appear to have been substantially reduced, partly as a result of the enforcement of a 'Last Call' law (described in Box 1.1). Although experience in the Dominican Republic was based on a broad policy approach (that is, enforcement of last call), the Secretary of the Interior and Police continued to frame the problem in terms

Box 1.1 A licensing and enforcement experiment in the Dominican Republic
(condensed from an AAP report, *'Last Call' Law Clears Dominican Streets*, Jonathon M. Katz, 14 October 2006)

Since July 2006 all bars, liquor stores and nightclubs must close at midnight on weekdays and at 2 a.m. on weekends. Armed soldiers and police, who also clear the streets in cities once known for all-night parties, enforce the rule. The new law stems from a backlash against violent crime in this impoverished country of nearly nine million. The day it took effect, hundreds of people marched with political leaders and media stars through Santo Domingo, shouting anti-crime slogans and carrying pictures of a teenage girl killed in Santiago, the country's second-largest city. Violent deaths were down in 2006, and although the trend began before the new law came in many believe the alcohol restrictions contributed to its continuation. Resistance to the new law has been sparse, with the National Hotel and Restaurant Association the most strongly opposed because their members have suffered a 25 to 30 percent reduction in sales. The Secretary of the Interior and Police, Franklin Almeyda, insisted the measures will remain until nights are safer and quieter. 'We are modifying a culture of Dominican youth', Almeyda said. 'If the culture changes, perhaps the measures will too.'

of 'modifying a culture of Dominican youth' rather than as an issue requiring sustained regulation.

The trend toward market deregulation

The emphasis of legislation in many countries in recent years has been toward market liberalisation, with control of alcohol supply and consumption largely restricted to public order issues and controlling underage drinking rather than being based on broader public health concerns (Babor *et al.* 2003; Romanus 2006). The growth of 'clubbing' at large capacity nightclubs has emerged as an important part of the night-time economy in a number of countries (see, for example, http://www.pubclub.com), contributing to the formation of entertainment areas that have major problems with violence and disorder, partly because markets have been deregulated with insufficient regard to the consequences for public safety and amenity.

Old-style regulatory controls have been dismantled and adequate mechanisms for maintaining order in and around licensed premises within this new context have not yet been developed.

Industry profitability has become a dominant theme in policies regarding drinking establishments in some areas because of the contribution of this industry to the success of regional and city economies (see, for example, http://www.audienceresearch.com/News/NightLifeEconomicImpact2003.pdf). In some cities, for example, derelict or declining areas populated by disused factories or warehouses have been transformed into entertainment districts. Underlying these trends is the belief that a marketplace free from the heavy hand of bureaucratic oversight will deliver consumer satisfaction and choice. Thus, one reason that it is so difficult to argue the public health and community safety agendas in the policy arena is that deregulation has become the norm for setting policies for licensed premises. It is assumed that in this liberated environment, all patrons will have a good time and consume alcohol in moderate quantities within a civilised, continental-style milieu of good food, quality entertainment, and hearty fellowship. Establishments that fail in these objectives, including those that are violent or disorderly, will fall by the wayside because consumers will vote with their feet. Grunge will be superseded by glitz in the city that never sleeps.

Changes in the regulation of alcohol, especially with regard to commercial drinking establishments, have been most publicised and documented in the United Kingdom where 'the most radical change in ... licensing laws for 400 years' (Kolvin 2005b: 2) was implemented in November 2005 when the Licensing Act 2003 was enacted in England and Wales (Newton *et al.* 2007; Plant and Plant 2005). The 2003 Act streamlined liquor and entertainment licensing into a single system, transferred administration from local justices to local authorities, and permitted the 24-hour sale of alcohol. Hobbs described the transformation in the UK as follows:

> We have entered a new era of urban politics, in which the ideological rationale of local government has shifted away from a 'municipal socialist' stance, whose central function axiom was the provision of local welfare services, toward a 'municipal capitalism' which seeks primarily to facilitate local economic growth and development. (Hobbs *et al.* 2000: 703)

There remains considerable controversy regarding the effects of this policy change. Scientific evidence generally points to the often negative effects of deregulation (Kolvin 2005b; Hadfield 2006; Room 2004), and a recent study of alcohol-related emergency admissions in the UK found strong evidence for a significant increase related to assault and injury following implementation of the 2003 Act (Newton *et al.* 2007). However, another study by Sivarajasingam, Moore and Shepherd using data from the National Violence Surveillance Network (NVSN) (http://www.cardiff.ac.uk/dentistry/research/phacr/violence/pdfs/Trends_violence_England_Wales_2006.pdf) led to the conclusion that the results were 'not consistent with the hypothesis that implementation of the 2003 Licensing Act in November 2005 would increase violence in England and Wales'.

Nevertheless, the reality on the street and inside bars is frequently very different from the planner's dream (Chatterton and Hollands 2002). Not only do violent establishments continue to exist, there are risks associated with the functions of all kinds of drinking establishments and with the characteristics of bar patrons generally, as we describe throughout this book. Moreover, the growing density of establishments in entertainment areas has resulted in thousands of intoxicated persons on the streets late at night, often creating noise, disorder and sometimes violent conflicts.

In summary, aggression and violence in and around drinking establishments is an important social problem that may be growing in importance in the context of the current trend toward deregulation of alcohol consumption. As argued by Babor and his colleagues (2003), alcohol is not an ordinary commodity, and the sale of alcohol imposes societal responsibility for limiting the negative effects of drinking and drinking contexts on public health. Yet, not only has bar violence met with mostly ineffective responses, the main policy initiatives related to licensed premises in the past two decades have included economic reforms that have dismantled most aspects of the old systems of regulatory controls (Craze and Norberry 1994; Hobbs *et al.* 2000). Therefore, we need to re-appraise old approaches and develop new ones to address the problem of bar violence in the current social and political climate.

'Raising the bar'

In order to 'raise the bar' in preventing violence in licensed drinking establishments, we need to have a full understanding of the factors that influence violence and the kinds of strategies that are likely to reduce the risk of violence and injury. In the following chapters, we draw on qualitative and quantitative research to identify the processes whereby bar aggression arises and the strategies that might be used to prevent it. As we describe in this book, aggression in drinking establishments is not solely the result of the effects of alcohol on a few aggressive individuals; rather there are clear and consistent relationships between violence and the physical and social barroom environment. We explore how patrons interact with each other and with the licensed environment and how those environments are shaped and maintained by management, staff and regulatory agencies. In essence, we put bar aggression and violence into a larger context so that we can gain a better understanding of the real nature of the problem on which to structure a foundation for the development of preventative practices that move beyond narrowly circumscribed and punitive responses to individuals. 'Raising the bar' involves, in particular, improving industry and regulatory practices. Licensed premises exist only because they are permitted to do so by law, and their contingent status, together with their need to make a profit, should be the starting points for efforts to promote safer public drinking.

In this book, we bring together the knowledge needed to raise the bar on the safety of operations of drinking establishments by examining, in turn, all aspects of the establishment and its relationship with violence. In Chapter 2, we look more closely at the function of drinking establishments in modern society, noting the diversity of forms of establishment and the manifold ways in which the 'time out' experience can be constructed. As part of a discussion of the many positive functions of licensed premises, we explore the concept of 'normal trouble' – the routine and supposedly unexceptional by-products of fun and sociability – as a starting point for our own analysis of aggression and violence, drawing on a variety of observational narratives. At the end of Chapter 2, we describe some theoretical perspectives that are useful in understanding why aggressive incidents occur in the licensed environment and how aggression might be prevented.

In Chapter 3, we describe how the various effects of alcohol on perceptions, emotions, thinking and risk-taking are related to aggressive behaviour. However, we also show that the relationship between these effects and aggression is very much a conditional one, dependent not only on the characteristics of the drinker but also on environmental and cultural factors.

Chapter 4 summarises the research on the relationship between aggression and patron characteristics. We describe how aggression is interrelated to the functions of the public drinking environment, including group solidarity and 'macho' concerns among young males, the risk associated with young men and women looking for sexual partners, and aggression related to violent subcultures.

In Chapter 5, we draw on results from 13 studies of the bar environment conducted over the past 25 years in Canada, Australia, the United States and the United Kingdom to identify consistent patterns between aggression and the social and physical drinking environment. We explore the implications of these studies for developing a public drinking culture that discourages aggression while maintaining an attractive and exciting environment for patrons and a sustainable business for owners.

Chapter 6 explores the role of staff in contributing to and controlling aggression and violence, arguing that the emergence in recent years of enormous 'club empires' with a concomitant differentiation, specialisation and gendering of staff roles has eroded informal social controls based on staff–patron relationships. We focus particularly on how bar staff enforce rules and the nature of interventions into patron conflicts, and conclude with implications for how staff and management can improve practices in order to prevent aggression.

Chapter 7 identifies the processes through which violence and disorder are frequently transferred from the inside to the outside environment. We then explore the ecology of public spaces using some concepts from environmental criminology, review available approaches for managing disorder and violence in the public spaces around drinking places and discuss some of the underlying governance issues.

In Chapter 8 we review evaluated approaches to preventing violence in and around drinking establishments, including voluntary training programs implemented by individual establishments, police enforcement, local accords and community action programs. We focus particularly on the *processes* through which positive changes were achieved, or in some cases, the reasons for failure.

In the final chapter, Chapter 9, we explore how regulatory systems could be reformed so that they deliver, on a routine basis, the critical ingredients of effective prevention programs. The concern is with moving from 'success in miniature' to large-scale, system-wide good practice that can be maintained indefinitely by police, liquor licensing departments and other regulatory players. We begin with a review of the key factors associated with bar violence and approaches to addressing these factors described in earlier chapters. We then describe how a responsive regulation framework can be used to implement a comprehensive long-term approach to preventing bar violence. We conclude with a discussion of future directions, including further development of evidence-based policies and practices, balancing targeted and universal prevention, modifying approaches to meet local needs and addressing the issue of sustainability.

Notes

1 http://www.smh.com.au/articles/2003/02/18/1045330550844.html.
2 http://www.cnn.com/2003/US/Midwest/02/18/chicago.nightclub/index.html.
3 'Hotel' is an Australian term for bar or tavern. The term is a relic from an era when most licensed premises were also required to provide accommodation.
4 Horrigan, D. 'Fight Victims Say Police Didn't Care', *Sydney Morning Herald*, 23 May 1989.

Glossary and explanation of terms

Aggression, violence. 'Aggression' and 'violence' are terms that overlap in meaning and are often used interchangeably. In research, the two terms tend to be associated with different research disciplines. A common way of defining aggression, especially for psychological research, is as: 'any form of behaviour directed toward the goal of harming or injuring another living being who is motivated to avoid such treatment' (Baron and Richardson 1994: 7). Aggression can be both non-physical and physical, and direct (for example, punching someone) or indirect (for example, harming someone by gossiping about him or her to other people). Criminologists, on the other hand, talk far more often about violence than aggression, violent crime being one of the central concerns of the discipline from its inception and the major concern of the public, legislators and the criminal justice system. In this tradition, violence is more often defined by its criminal impact than by a precise definition. Although the prevention of violence in drinking establishments is usually the primary policy objective, various forms of non-physical aggression such as verbal abuse, arguments, unwanted sexual overtures, irritating behaviour, provocations, and so on, heighten the risks of physical aggression and are important targets for prevention in their own right. Accordingly, when discussing specific behaviours, we typically use the term 'aggression' but will usually use the term 'violence' when discussing more general or societal level issues.

Drinking establishment. There is a variety of terms for licensed premises where people go primarily to drink and socialise, including bar, club/nightclub, cocktail lounge, discotheque/disco, hotel, pub and tavern. In the United States and Canada, the term 'bar' is commonly used and is well understood to refer to a drinking establishment as well as a counter where alcoholic drinks are served. In Australia and the United Kingdom, the term 'bar' tends to be restricted to the second meaning, although it can also refer to the whole establishment. Therefore, we tend to use the term 'drinking establishment' to distinguish places where people go primarily to drink (rather than eat) as opposed to 'licensed premises' which would include restaurants. However, other terms, including licensed premises, are used throughout the book according to the context – for example, prevention and policy approaches are often broadly focused on licensed premises. We chose the term 'bar' for the title of this book because it is short, can be used generically, and permits wordplay that indicates that the goal of the book is to improve drinking establishments and their environs (that is, 'raise the bar').

Bar staff. There are a number of staff functions in drinking establishments, including serving alcohol, clearing away debris and empty drink containers, screening entry at the door, managing other employees, addressing problems within the establishment, and so on. When no particular role is intended, we use the term 'staff' or 'bar staff' to refer to employees of drinking establishments.

Security staff. Staff who control who enters the establishment and have primary responsibility for addressing problem behaviour within are referred to as 'security staff', 'doormen', 'doorstaff', 'bouncers', 'crowd controllers' and 'stewards', depending on the country and context. Most often we use the general term 'security' or 'security staff' and, except when used as a direct quote, we avoid the term 'bouncers', which has pejorative connotations.

Entertainment areas. Areas (usually in the city centre) where there is a cluster of drinking establishments have been referred to by a variety of terms including: night-time high street (Hadfield 2006), night-time economy (Hobbs *et al.* 2003), entertainment districts (Graham, Bernards *et al.* 2006) or zones (Grazian 2008), city centres (Wikström 1995), downtown entertainment areas (Homel, McIlwain and Carvolth 2004), urban play spaces (Chatterton and Hollands 2002), and hospitality zones (Responsible Hospitality Institute 2006). We use or refer to all these terms at various points in this book, depending on the context.

Licensed environment. This is a general term that includes licensed premises or drinking establishments and the public spaces around them.

Night-time economy. This is a term used mainly in the UK (see for example, Hobbs *et al.* 2003) to refer to all aspects of the leisure, retail and alcohol industries and related aspects of city economies. Entertainment areas comprise an important part of the night-time economy.

Chapter 2

The culture of public drinking: normal trouble, violence and its prevention

Being with friends, engaging in romantic/sexual encounters, parading, dancing and experiencing altered states are all part of celebrating weekends and switching off from everyday realities. Most nights out go well but some, as we have seen, end 'in tears'.

(Parker and Williams 2003: 364)

In this chapter, we describe the overall social context and functions of drinking in licensed premises, including the many variations of such establishments. Within these contexts, a certain amount of trouble is generally considered 'normal'. However, as was evident by the examples in Chapter 1 and discussed further in this chapter, normal and harmless trouble can readily become serious and injurious violence. Therefore, in order to understand how and why violence occurs in drinking establishments, we need to understand normal patterns of social interactions in licensed premises, including 'normal trouble'. In the final section of this chapter, we describe theoretical perspectives that help explain the processes through which normal interactions can give rise to aggressive and violent incidents.

The heterogeneity of commercial drinking establishments

The English language is replete with words for places that are licensed by the authorities to sell alcoholic beverages for on-site consumption. Moreover, it is not just labels for licensed establishments that vary; these settings also vary in form and function, from the cosy pub with

20 or 30 patrons to the techno music dance club with thousands of patrons. The list provided on the 'alwaysout' website (http://www.alwaysout.com/bars-nightclubs/) shows the variability of venues, characterised by the main form of entertainment provided (for example, Comedy Club, Dance Club), the type of music (Piano Bar, Rock/Pop), type of alcoholic beverage (Brewery, Martini Bar), or clientele (Gay/Lesbian Bar, Neighbourhood Bar, College Bar). This list reflects establishments in the US at the beginning of the twenty-first century – a list from a different time and place would have different types of drinking establishments. For example, an interesting contrast can be made, on the one hand, between the 'golden age at English taverns, with poets, playwrights, composers, and authors making these taverns more like social clubs or even second homes' (Heath 2000: 49) or similar gatherings of intellectuals in the pre-revolutionary cafés of Paris (Brennan 2005), and, on the other hand, the large nightclubs of the contemporary era frequented by thousands of patrons and characterised by slick decors, visible security staff, patrons in expensive often revealing clothes and the central focus on heavily rhythmic music, dancing and seeing and being seen (Hobbs *et al.* 2000; Purcell and Graham 2005; Thornton 1995).

A number of overarching typologies of public drinking establishments have been developed to frame understanding of the variability in drinking establishments and associated behaviours (Clarke 1981; Clinard 1962). Perhaps, the most well-known and frequently used typology is Cavan's (1966) four categories based on the function of the bar: (1) convenience bars (for example, downtown drop-in bars); (2) nightspot bars (venues with entertainment, dancing); (3) marketplace bars (a category that includes 'pick-up' or 'meat-market' bars as well as bars with commercial transactions taking place related to drugs, sex, gambling and stolen goods); and (4) home territory bars (establishments with regular patrons who have characteristics in common such as living in the neighbourhood, sexual orientation, ethnicity).

There is probably no single typology of public drinking establishments that can apply across time and culture. Nevertheless, the different categorisations demonstrate two important points. The first is that there is considerable *variability* in bars in terms of alcohol consumption, clientele, characteristics of the barroom environment (for example, size, activities, décor), and staff roles. The second is that there are also clear *commonalities* among different types of drinking establishments in terms of the core activities of drinking, socialising, and experiencing time out from usual responsibilities.

License to play: the forms and functions of public drinking establishments

The popularity of drinking establishments is understandable because most licensed venues do not just sell alcohol – they also provide a place for games, dancing, socialising, sexual liaisons, partying, behaving outrageously with relative impunity, and, for some, a home away from home. In short, the business of licensed venues is to create a milieu where people can socialise and play in a pleasurable way, mellowed by alcohol, and separated from the roles and responsibilities of both the home and workplace (Roebuck and Frese 1976; Sulkunen, Alasuutari, Kinnunen and Nätkin 1985).

Time out

The first and perhaps most important function of the licensed drinking establishment is to provide time out from the usual roles and responsibilities of life. As described by Byrne (1978: 418):

> ... the individual irregularly takes time out that is bracketed between the past and the future – time in the extended present of the now – for the purpose of pure and immediate enjoyment, sociability, and affirmation of self and his interrelatedness with others.

The time-out emphasis of the public drinking setting, still apparent in the function of the contemporary music-dominated club scene (Malbon 1999), means that many people are willing to engage in behaviours that they would not ordinarily engage in, with the expectation that they will not be held accountable for this behaviour.

Drinking

Alcohol consumption is a key component of living in the moment and casting aside day-to-day worries and responsibilities. Anthropological evidence suggests that the time-out function of drinking occasions is amplified by the effects of alcohol, especially in the context of group drinking. Washburne (1956) observed in his study of drinking cultures how alcohol seemed to make drinkers more focused on the present situation and activities and less aware of internal thought processes and goals, and that this alcohol-induced focus on the present often contributed to positive experiences of the drinking occasion such as increased group solidarity. He noted, however, that the type of behaviour resulting from this reduced awareness of self and focus on present activities was largely determined by cultural and group expectations. That is, if the group and culture saw aggression as a normal part of the drinking occasion, then aggression would likely occur. On the other hand, aggression was rare in cultures where it was not considered acceptable to become aggressive while drinking. Thus, the same effects of alcohol can contribute both to enhanced enjoyment as well as to increased risks of violence (Graham 2003).

Socialising with friends and strangers

The third important function of bars is to provide a setting for socialising with friends and acquaintances and meeting new people, especially potential romantic or sexual partners – as shown in the photo in Figure 2.1 (Forsyth 2006; Malbon 1999; Parks *et al.* 1999; Parks and Scheidt 2000; Purcell and Graham 2005; Roebuck and Spray 1967; Roebuck and Frese 1976; Storm and Cutler 1985). To a large extent, bars and clubs are considered 'open' social spaces where people have the right to initiate social interactions with others as well as some responsibility to accept social overtures from others (Cavan 1966). This open-sociability, however, comes with a price. Specifically, the prolonged socialising and exposure to a variety of strangers provides increased opportunities for conflict, provocation and offence to be given and taken.

Photo by John Dale Purcell

Figure 2.1   Nightclub socialising and meeting prospective sexual/romantic partners

Sharing common interests or culture

A fourth function of many bars is to create a place for people with similar characteristics or interests to come together. This might take the form of a neighbourhood pub that serves as a local meeting place (Oldenburg 1999; Smith 1985), a gay bar that provides a comfortable location for socialising without fear of discrimination or harassment (Cáceres and Cortiñas 1996; Israelstam and Lambert 1984), or a skid row bar where the minimal requirements of respectability provide a haven for marginalised persons (Graham *et al.* 1980). Probably the most common community served by present-day public drinking establishments is comprised of the young and the single (Storm and Cutler 1985), who frequent such establishments to have an exciting night out (Parker and Williams 2003; Tomsen 1997) and to meet sexual and romantic partners (Grazian 2008; Purcell and Graham 2005).

Male-dominated environments

Another characteristic of drinking establishments generally is that they tend to be male-dominated territory (Hey 1986; Pettigrew 2006; Single 1985; Spradley and Mann 1975; Sulkunen *et al.* 1985), although the growth of the night-time economy with the focus on nightclubs and dancing has seen a rapid increase in the participation of women (Grazian 2008; Hadfield 2006). Male domination of public drinking settings is perhaps not surprising given that men are more likely than women to drink and, when they drink, to drink more frequently and in larger quantities (Wilsnack, Vogeltanz, Wilsnack and Harris 2000). In terms of violence, it is well established that young adult men are at higher risk of engaging in violent crime compared with other demographic groups. Therefore, the domination of drinking establishments by young men would serve to increase violence even without other risk factors such as the effects of alcohol and prolonged socialising.

In summary, the social functions of the public drinking establishment and the populations that frequent these establishments make them a high-risk setting for aggression. Thus, although most people who go to public drinking establishments do not engage in aggression, the core functions of such places increase the risk that aggression will occur at least among some individuals. The challenge is to preserve these beneficial functions of drinking establishments while minimising harmful consequences such as violence and injury. As noted by Storm and Cutler (1985: 46) in their discussion of public drinking establishments:

Sociability itself has important social and psychological functions. It strengthens the solidarity of groups, community feeling and the sense of identity of individuals … These social functions of taverns are desirable. Can they be facilitated without increasing the incidence of heavy-drinking occasions and untoward events associated with such occasions? Evidence relevant to these questions should be the goal of researchers. Control agencies should recognize the need for evidence and use it when it is available.

Licence for control: preventing minor trouble from escalating

As we described in the preceding section, licensed drinking establishments are, on the one hand, created expressly as places where people do not feel constrained by the rules and conventions that govern everyday social intercourse. On the other hand, such establishments are formally regulated through agencies of the state; regulation and control of licensed premises has been in existence for hundreds of years, as has legislation holding licensees responsible for the behaviour and harms done by persons to whom they serve alcohol (Brennan 2005; Graham 2005; Kümin 2005). The laws and regulations applying to licensed premises address a range of issues from building standards, local government ordinances, and workplace health and safety rules, to a host of provisions embodied in Liquor or Licensing Acts. Many of the regulations aim to secure the safety of employees and patrons, and some attempt to place limits on their behaviours. For example, many jurisdictions forbid service to intoxicated patrons.

The very title of Cavan's (1966) book – *Liquor License* – involved a play on the double meaning of the word 'licence' (that is, a licence to serve alcohol granted by authorities *vs* licence in the sense of liberty of action or abuse of freedom), highlighting a tension or ambivalence that runs through official, popular and academic discourse on this topic. This tension has been recognised as applying to historical contexts (Kümin 2005) as well as to more contemporary drinking contexts (Parker and Williams 2003). Thus, public drinking establishments are contested environments where 'licence', in the sense of formal but conditional permission to operate a particular kind of business, does battle with 'licence' in the sense of the patron's (and frequently the staff's) expectation of freedom to exceed normal boundaries. The paradox is that rules are used to create environments in which, at least to some extent, rules can be suspended; however, the formal and informal rules about where the boundaries of acceptable behaviour are to be drawn are never quite settled and vary greatly by time and place.

Staff, patrons, the general public, as well as regulators, expect a certain amount of what Cavan termed 'normal trouble' in the licensed venue. This includes quarrels of varying intensity that are often routinely ignored or only casually attended to by staff and other patrons. A variety of social *faux pas*, such as belching, stumbling, falling asleep or falling off bar stools, may also be committed with equanimity in some drinking establishments, while such actions would not be tolerated in others. Similarly, displays of sexual affection, such as openly fondling a partner, are quite acceptable in many establishments (Purcell and Graham 2005), although not in others. Somewhat more controversial are incidents like the one described in Box 2.1 that occurred in a bar patronised by young middle-class people. This was cited by Cavan as 'an extreme example of the social *sang froid* of the public drinking place'.

Box 2.1   'That happens all the time'. San Francisco early 1960s (Cavan 1966: 68)

A young man and a young woman had been sitting together chatting and occasionally dancing for about an hour and a half. Suddenly the man hit the girl in the face, knocking her from the bar stool onto the floor. The general hum of conversation that had been going on among the eight or ten people in the bar stopped for about thirty seconds, during which time the man walked out. No one made any attempt to stop him. One patron quite casually went over to the girl to help her up and the bartender held out a damp towel for her to put to her face. The rest of the patrons went back to their conversations as though nothing had happened. The girl got up, said something to the bartender, and then went to the bathroom. She came out, about ten minutes later, her face back in order, and sat down at the bar, where she remained for about fifteen minutes longer. No one made any further comment on the scene. After she had left, P.C. asked one of the patrons sitting next to him about it and was told, 'They've been living together for months. That happens all the time.'

This incident, observed many years ago in San Francisco, might well elicit a different reaction from staff and patrons if it occurred today, given the seriousness with which both the public and the criminal justice system regard violence against a female partner. However, as we describe in Chapter 4, routine violence, even violence by men against women, still occurs in some types of drinking establishments, such as rough pubs or skid row bars frequented by marginalised populations (Campbell 1991; Clinard 1962; Graham 1980; Macrory 1952).

The fact that the incident of male-to-female violence described by Cavan would not likely be tolerated in most current drinking establishments highlights how boundaries for acceptable behaviour not only differ by type of establishment but can also change over time. Nevertheless, it is still the case that a much greater degree of latitude is accorded to unconventional and aggressive behaviours when they occur in drinking establishments compared with most other settings. Some current-day examples of normal trouble (that is, where staff and other patrons would not be particularly concerned about the behaviour) are described in Box 2.2.

Box 2.2 Normal trouble in Toronto bars and clubs (2000–02) (Graham *et al.* 2000–04)

Two men have an argument. Two intoxicated male friends were standing by the bar arguing. It did not go any further than mild swearing back and forth with finger-pointing by one of the men. Their voices were fairly loud, and the swearing attracted some attention from others, but the incident was short because one man seemed to back down.

Four men pick on a fifth man 'in fun'. Five male friends and an uninvolved female, were sitting together by a pool table. The men were engaged in what appeared to be friendly horseplay, with four of the men taking turns grabbing the fifth man's buttocks, crotch, arms, legs etc. The victim looked uncomfortable but did not retaliate. The female did not pay any attention to them.

Man shoves another man who gets in his way. A male patron grabbed another man's arm to push him out of the way, although there was plenty of room to get by. The second man was knocked a little off balance and glared at the back of the man who had shoved him but did not pursue the matter further.

There would be little need to worry about violence in drinking establishments if the normal trouble that occurred was always as minor as the aggression and provocation apparent in the incidents in Box 2.2. Although the incidents in Box 2.2 were minor, the potential for escalation was apparent. The drunken argument could have escalated if one man had not backed down or an aggressive third party had intervened. Similarly, the victim in the second incident might have become fed up with being pushed around and humiliated by the other men and decided to strike back. The victim in the third incident might have decided to respond to being shoved by the passer-by. In fact, as we describe in Chapter 4, in some drinking establishments frequented by young males, concerns with maintaining male honour actually require a man to respond with aggression to pushing or bumping even when the pushing or bumping was done accidentally (Tuck 1989).

Thus, normal trouble sometimes takes a much more severe, even lethal form. As noted by a number of authors (for example, Tedeschi and Felson 1994; Prus 1978), violence and injury are often the result of a social process where the first steps tend to be minor, but where the interaction of competing viewpoints can result in increasingly violent actions. Thus, the likelihood of escalation is increased if minor incidents of low-level aggressive behaviours are tolerated or even tacitly encouraged, resulting in an atmosphere or set of expectations on the part of some patrons that they are in a drinking establishment where 'anything goes'. An example of a bar activity that encourages minor aggression is 'moshing', a type of dancing that involves pseudo or playful aggression such as bumping others. Moshing was linked to the escalation to more serious aggression in the London, Toronto and Glasgow studies, as in the Glasgow incident described in Box 2.3.

Box 2.3 Moshing leads to dance floor brawl
(Forsyth 2006)

People on the dance floor were drunk and on drugs bumping into each other, moshing and jumping up and down with their arms around each other's shoulders – mostly big groups of young males with a couple of young females. All of a sudden, all the stewards [security staff] except one female steward ran onto the dance floor. There was clearly some kind of fight, and the stewards were separating people with physical force using headlocks and literally dragging them away. It was difficult to see what was going on due to the flurry of fists and jostling about.

The involvement of third parties, including staff (as in the incident in Box 2.3), is an important aspect of drinking in licensed premises that tends to distinguish this setting from many private settings. The involvement of third parties has been recognised as a significant risk factor for escalation of violence, although third parties can also de-escalate violence (Wells and Graham 1999), as shown by the incident observed in Toronto described in Box 2.4.

Box 2.4 Peaceful intervention by friends
(Graham et *al*. 2000–04)

The bar was busy, and the dance floor was packed. Two large men were yelling and exchanging verbal threats, standing close in aggressive stances with chests out and shoulders back, red eyes and glaring at each other. One man seemed to be challenging the other to a fight. A friend moved between them, put his arms around one man and turned him away from the argument, saying something to him. After a few more words from the friend, the two men who had been arguing gave each other a quick hug with one arm, shook hands and smiled at each other. The men then turned to watch the dance floor and the argument seemed to be over.

Several studies (Graham, Bernards et *al*. 2006; Maguire and Nettleton 2003) have found that the more people who are involved in a fight, the greater the severity of violence and the greater the likelihood of people getting hurt. However, whether third parties act to increase or decrease aggression depends on a number of factors, including the norms for behaviour in the establishment. For example, in drinking establishments where aggression is rare, even raised voices will receive disapproving frowns from other patrons, which may preclude any need for intervention by staff. On the other hand, as we describe in later chapters, in highly permissive drinking establishments, it is normative for opportunistic involvement by third parties to escalate violence. The crucial issue about third parties is that they constitute a more important aspect of violence in drinking establishments than in most other settings.

Thus far, we have provided examples of isolated incidents. However, it is not unusual for many incidents to occur on a single night. In Box 2.5, we describe the context in which a series of violent events occurred one night in a busy suburban hotel in Sydney, Australia in the late 1980s. The venue consisted of two bars at the front of the premises and a disco-auditorium at the rear. The hotel was popular with local young people and had a reputation for teenage drinking, drugs (sold in the beer garden), fights and late night rowdiness among disco patrons.

Box 2.5   A 'Big night' at a suburban hotel (description condensed from a narrative by Stephen Tomsen)
(Homel, Tomsen and Thommeny 1992)

We entered the disco just after 11:00 p.m. Three reasonably civil bouncers were around the doorway, and another three were patrolling inside. All were largish and in their 20s, except for one in his late 30s. A female in her late 20s or older took our admission money ($11 each). About 500 or more patrons were present, about 50 per cent male and female, ranging from their late teens (maybe 10 per cent under the legal age of 18) through to 20s and 30s or more. Many appeared to be local young people, arriving with or meeting friends and old acquaintances.

The key feature of the night was the 11 cents drinks. Until about 1:00 a.m. most of the patrons (especially males) were crowded around or near the bar. For an hour or more the bar had lines of people about six deep buying three cheap drinks at a time (the limit), often 'skulling' these quickly and then staying in the queue to buy more. Rates of consumption were very high, and most people were quite drunk, with the small number of patrons (at most twenty) who were not drunk very conspicuous. The bar was extremely busy. However, the one female bar attendant responsible for selling hot food was reading a novel.

The atmosphere was rather rowdy and uncomfortable due to crowding around the bar, a lack of seating (about 50) and the loud but not very entertaining band. But most of the patrons were reasonably friendly and, in the early stages of their drunkenness, many were keen to meet and mix with strangers. Although most were in groups of 3–6 people there was plenty of moving about.

But it was mostly due to the very high levels of drunkenness that violence began to erupt. Oddly this was often without a preceding feeling of aggression, or with very sudden and unpredictable animosity. Patrons appeared to literally lose self-control. The high movement, bumping and sexual competition

27

(several males were seen to approach women who already had partners) were tied to most of the conflicts. But the majority appeared to be unintentional (misread cues), giving them a comical undertone. Fights and brawls were as follows:

1. As we entered the premises, a skinhead male appeared to be arguing with his girlfriend. He pushed people in the crowd aside as he followed her outside. The doorman tried to quieten him, and the man responded by removing his shirt in order to fight the doormen. We could not observe why, but they did not respond. He and his girlfriend made up and returned after.

2. A very drunk male in his 20s who was jumping on and off the stage was removed roughly by three bouncers. He screamed and resisted and was then assaulted by the same three outside. They bashed his head against a steel crate until the older and more professional doorman restrained them. This patron then wandered down the back alley screaming and abusing everyone around. He lay drunk in the alley for about ten minutes before he threatened and then chased a stranger down the street. A conversation with a young female regular revealed that he was a former employee. The bouncers had 'improved' – several had been sacked after having a brawl in the alleyway with a whole soccer team one month previously. It was not clear if they were sacked for brawling or because they had failed to contain and win [the brawl].

3. As the night wore on there were more fights over bumping and crowding. One conflict between two males resulted in a third male defusing things by encouraging them to have an arm wrestle.

4. A male in his 20s re-entered the bar breathing rapidly, covered in dirt and with a black eye, having apparently been in a fight in the alley. He remained in an agitated state for at least 30 minutes, as he told the tale to various mates.

5. A large male (about 6ft 3in, 200 pounds) headbutted a younger and smaller male who had bumped into him. The victim stumbled off – an example of quick and spontaneous violence.

6. A male about 30 who both observers had agreed 'was a fight waiting to happen', in a leather jacket and very drunk, stood and turned about with very aggressive gestures. He created a space around himself and kicked glasses (plastic) along the floor. A much larger male took exception to this behaviour and abused him for it, but he really appeared to be seeking an excuse for a fight with someone smaller and drunker than himself. He totally ignored a girlfriend trying to drag him away. Two of the younger bouncers threw out the leather-jacketed male after pausing and watching the argument. He was cooled out by the older doorman and left the premises.

7. Two short males began to argue, apparently over an approach made on the girlfriend of one of them. The single male who was observed to be curiously either very friendly or hostile to different people in seconds (and probably the most mobile drunk in the place), had the backup of several friends and this probably restrained his more sober opponent. Two bouncers eventually separated the pair.

The big night at the Sydney hotel provides a good introduction to the other chapters in this book. The most striking feature of the night was mass intoxication induced by an $11 cover charge combined with 11cent drinks. The contribution of intoxication to barroom violence is addressed in more detail in Chapter 3. The characteristics of some of the patrons and their willingness to fight are also key components of the sequence of events in Box 2.5, and of bar aggression generally, as we discuss in detail in Chapter 4. Not only was the environment filled with highly intoxicated patrons encouraged by ridiculously low-priced alcohol, but situational factors such as a permissive tone, rowdiness, discomfort, bumping and sexual competition all appeared to increase risk of aggression. Chapter 5 reviews evidence from 13 studies regarding the relationship between the physical and social environment and aggression. Chapter 6 explores a further prominent feature of the Sydney hotel big night, the staff who played an important role in the violence through their total lack of control of the environment and their own assaultive behaviour. The evening at the Sydney hotel also included considerable violence going on outside the establishment, raising the issue of the broader context of violence which we address in Chapter 7. Finally, the events at the Sydney hotel highlight the importance of prevention. Although these observations occurred some time ago, the continuing need for effective prevention is clear from more recent incidents described at the beginning of Chapter 1, as well as from other examples in Chapters 3–7. Accordingly, prevention is the focus of the final two chapters of the book.

The many contributing factors to the big night at the Sydney hotel strongly support an approach to prevention that incorporates both the environmental context and the various roles played by persons who are present, including both patrons and staff. Because the relationship between alcohol consumption and aggression is conditional on cultural, environmental and personality factors (as we describe in Chapter 3), adopting a framework for addressing these conditional variables, as well as the role of alcohol, is critical to prevention. Routine activity theory and situational crime prevention provide a theoretical, research-driven framework for incorporating all of these elements. In the next section, we describe these theories in more detail as a foundation for applying them within the context of each of the individual chapters. We also introduce the use of responsive regulation theory as a vehicle for bringing together prevention strategies.

Putting bar violence and its prevention in a theoretical context

As the narrative in Box 2.5 illustrates, a broad range of issues are relevant to understanding interpersonal aggression and violence in the licensed environment, including the interactional processes involving patrons with staff and other patrons, the effects of alcohol, environmental factors, and the potential for regulatory policies to be introduced to make commercial drinking environments safer. In the following sections, we describe three theoretical perspectives that provide an important backdrop for interpreting and applying knowledge of factors associated with aggression in drinking establishments relating to patron characteristics, environmental risks and staff behaviour: (1) routine activity theory, (2) situational crime prevention theory, and (3) responsive regulation theory. In later chapters, we bring in other theoretical perspectives; we review explanations of how the effects of alcohol heighten the risk of aggressive behaviour (Chapter 3), and introduce the concepts of environmental 'backcloth', 'activity nodes', 'edges', and 'hot spots' for crime or violence from environmental criminology (Brantingham and Brantingham 1993; 1999) to explain violence that occurs in areas around drinking establishments (Chapter 7).

Routine activity theory

Routine activity theory in its original form (Cohen and Felson 1979) proposed that crime is most likely to occur when there is a convergence in time and space of a motivated or likely offender, a suitable target or victim, and a lack of a capable guardian. Routine activity theory was an important conceptual breakthrough because it de-emphasised the offender, who had been the historical focus of criminology, and drew attention to the spatial and temporal configuration of the critical elements in the 'chemistry of crime' (Felson 1993). Using these concepts, Cohen and Felson (1979) showed that the increase in burglary in the United States could be attributed to such changes in lifestyles or 'routine activities' as the proliferation of valuable, highly portable items such as televisions, and the increase in empty houses during the day when both partners worked. The significance of this analysis was that it placed the emphasis on changes in ways of life rather than on an increase in the supply of offenders, and saw crime as a by-product of prosperity and freedom rather than solely an issue of social pathology.

Felson *et al.* (1986) added to the theory by introducing the concept of the 'intimate handler', someone who knows the likely offender well enough to dissuade him or her from crime. Another important contribution was made by Eck and Wiesburd (1995), who proposed adding the role of a 'place manager' (a person who controls the location where a crime might occur) to the other supervisory roles of guardian (for the victim) and handler (for the offender). The idea of place was modified by Felson (1995) to 'amenable place' to emphasise that a place that has no potential for crime does not need a manager. More importantly, Felson distinguished levels of responsibility for supervisors that ranged through 'personal' (for example, one's boyfriend as personal guardian in a bar), 'assigned' (for example, door staff in a nightclub), 'diffuse' (for example, serving staff or other employees who have general responsibilities as staff but no specific responsibilities for control of patrons), and 'general' (for example, other customers in a bar who may act to prevent crime or violence). As we discuss in other chapters, routine activity theory with the added concepts of handlers and place managers provides a very useful framing for understanding both why aggression occurs in drinking establishments and how it can be prevented.

31

Situational crime prevention

Based on the theory that people behave rationally and choose to act in ways that will maximise benefits to themselves and/or to those they care about (Cornish and Clarke 1986), situational crime prevention includes the assumption that, given the right circumstances, a wide range of people might act illegally or in an aggressive or antisocial way, including some who under 'normal' circumstances would never engage in crime or even contemplate illegal or antisocial action. Clarke (1997: 4) has argued that, within this model, prevention should comprise:

> ... opportunity reducing measures that (1) are directed at highly specific forms of crime, (2) involve the management, design or manipulation of the immediate environment in as systematic and permanent way as possible, (3) make crime more difficult and risky, or less rewarding and excusable as judged by a wide range of offenders.

Opportunity reducing measures of this kind include, for example, changes in the physical environment, such as locking doors, and changes in the psychological environment, such as strengthening moral condemnation in order to counteract offenders' moral neutralisation techniques (that is, the excuses people make to themselves and others to justify their actions) (Sykes and Matza 1957).

Clarke and Homel (1997) modified the early emphasis of situational prevention on the physical environment by arguing that the perceived environment was more critical than the actual environment as an explanation of behaviour, because opportunities, risks, and benefits are properties not only of the situation but also of how that situation is viewed and interpreted by potential offenders. They also proposed the inclusion of strategies that increase the likelihood that potential offenders will be deterred from offending to avoid feeling guilty and embarrassed. In these ways, they moved the motivations and interpretations of the actor or potential offender to a more central position in the analysis, and enlarged the situational perspective to include subtle features of the social and psychological environments.

Situational precipitators

Wortley (1997; 2001) suggested a major modification to situational crime prevention theory by introducing the concept of situational 'precipitators'. In contrast to the model proposed by Clark and colleagues, which focused primarily on opportunity and rational decision-making, Wortley (2002: 56) distinguished situational precipitators from situational controls in a two-stage model:

> In the first stage of the model, a range of psychological processes are proposed that may actively induce individuals to engage in conduct that they may not otherwise have performed. The behaviour may be avoided entirely if relevant precipitators are adequately controlled. In the event that behaviour is initiated, then, in the second stage of the model, performance of that behaviour is subject to consideration of the consequences that are likely to follow.

According to Wortley's model, situational precipitators:

(a) prompt or cue the individual to behave antisocially;
(b) exert pressure to misbehave;
(c) reduce self-control and permit individuals to engage in behaviour they would otherwise self-censure; or
(d) produce emotional arousal that provokes a violent reaction.

In his model, he suggests that situational precipitators that prompt antisocial behaviour can be controlled by strategies such as setting positive expectations (for example, cleaning up broken glass and spills to avoid giving patrons the message that rowdy violent behaviour goes on all the time). Pressures to misbehave can be controlled by strategies such as reducing inappropriate conformity (for example, ejecting trouble-makers from the premises rather than allowing them to see themselves as 'heroes' because of their misbehaviour). Situational cues that reduce self-control might be reduced using strategies such as rule setting (for example, not serving highly intoxicated patrons). And situational factors that provoke violence can be controlled by strategies such as reducing frustration (for example, avoiding queues and ensuring that they are managed fairly when queues cannot be avoided). Thus, situational crime prevention explains behaviour in terms of an interaction between an actor and the features of the setting within which an act is performed (Wortley and Smallbone 2006).

Although Wortley (2002) applied this theory to prevention of crime and violence in prisons, the notion of situational precipitators is particularly relevant to drinking establishments because the interactional dynamics of the licensed environment often involve many kinds of precipitators of aggression amplified by intoxication;

moreover, the assumption that intoxicated offenders are 'rational' (as in the original situational crime prevention theory) is often questionable.

In their response to Wortley's (2001; 2002) suggestions for revising situational crime prevention theory to incorporate the two-step process of precipitation and broader control (for example, over opportunities and rewards), Cornish and Clarke (2003: 77) identified five conditions under which precipitators would be most relevant for crime prevention:

1 'When they involve threats to life and limb ...'
2 'When they occur in capsule environments' – that is, situations where noxious stimuli abound, options for their avoidance or control are limited, and repetitive exposure is common.
3 'When they challenge ... the fulfilment of needs or desires' central to 'an individual's lifestyle'.
4 'When they are repeated'.
5 'Or where a single exposure provides the final stimulus that tips an already motivated individual into action'.

Like prisons, drinking establishments often take on the characteristics of a capsule environment and, depending on the occasion, can sometimes meet many of the other conditions proposed by Cornish and Clarke. We show in later chapters how, for example, provocative actions by some patrons occur repeatedly, especially when patrons are under the influence of alcohol. Perhaps most importantly, the effects of alcohol on risk-taking and cognitive functioning described in Chapter 3 may increase the impact of immediate and salient precipitators and lessen the effect or salience of situational controls and regulators of behaviour (proposed by Clarke and colleagues), because these techniques assume a rational person who is seeking to maximise benefits.

The role of situational controls and the rational choice perspective is, however, also important even when participants are affected by alcohol. For example, evidence from interviews with young men who have been involved in bar fights suggests that rewards play a substantial role in their willingness to become involved in aggression in drinking establishments. These rewards include:

> ... feeling righteous about fighting for a worthwhile cause, feelings of group cohesion involved in supporting one's 'buddies' in a fight, getting attention from others (for example,

being pulled away from an incident by friends), feeling like a hero (for example, saving a friend who had been hurt), getting a 'rush' from fighting, increased feelings of power, and showing friends and/or an audience that you are willing to fight, that you can't be intimidated, or that you will not back down. (Graham and Wells 2003: 555)

By contrast, the downsides of fights in drinking establishments appeared to be few from the perspective of many interviewees. Even being injured or arrested could add to one's notoriety and have a net reputational benefit, provided the injuries were not too serious and the penalties not too grievous.

The critical feature of the situational approach is that the emphasis is on the environment, not on modifying the criminal or violent dispositions of offenders. This makes situational theory potentially very useful for understanding and preventing aggression in and around drinking establishments, where so many incidents seem to occur as a result of the mix of environmental permissiveness and precipitators, with willingness to offend and vulnerability to victimisation enhanced by the effects of alcohol.

It needs to be recognised that this brief summary of situational crime prevention theory helps to put bar violence into context but cannot do justice to some of the major controversies in the field. In particular, there is disagreement about how much the perceived, rather than the 'objective', physical environment should be emphasised, whether techniques designed to induce a sense of guilt or shame in potential offenders should be classified as situational (Welsh and Farrington 1999), and the extent to which offenders engage in a process of conscious target selection and decision-making, as opposed to their actions being directly precipitated by provocations or other kinds of immediate environmental contingencies. Thus, our preceding discussion of situational crime prevention introduced some useful concepts for thinking about bar violence and its prevention but could not address in detail the complexities and controversies.

Predatory, opportunistic and provoked offenders

One final aspect of situational crime prevention theory that has relevance to aggression in drinking establishments is the defining of different types of offenders according to their relationship with situational opportunities and precipitators (Cornish and Clarke 2003). These include:

1 the antisocial predator who expends considerable effort to overcome barriers to the achievement of his goals;

2 the mundane or opportunistic offender who has a greater stake in conformity than the predatory offender but who exploits opportunities to engage in occasional, low-level antisocial behaviour;

3 the provoked or situational offender who has no initial intention to offend but reacts to situational frustrations, irritations and social pressures with aggression or some other kind of impulsive act.

Evidence from research into licensed premises suggests that most who are involved in aggression would be classified as provoked or situational offenders (category 3). For example, provoked or situational offenders probably accounted for at least some of the aggressive individuals in fights over bumping and crowding described in point 3 of the 'Big night at a suburban hotel in Sydney' (Box 2.5). However, there is enough evidence for the presence of the two other types in the licensed environment to warrant inclusion in a prevention framework. For example, interview (Graham and Wells 2003), and ethnographic research (Tomsen 1997) with young men in aggressive incidents in drinking establishments identified a category of 'recreational fighters' (Graham and Wells 2003) that is, persons who did not necessarily go to the bar with the intention of fighting but seemed to consider a fight to be part of the night's entertainment. The recreational fighter is probably best viewed as a mundane or opportunistic offender (the second of Cornish and Clarke's categories). There are also examples of predatory offenders in bar settings, evident from the behaviour of the drug dealers in the beating of the two young men in the Sydney hotel and in examples of predatory sexual aggression that are described in Chapter 4.

Responsive regulation theory

Responsive regulation is a theoretical framework developed by Braithwaite and colleagues (1992, 2002) to address a wide range of regulatory problems in a way that takes account of industry history, culture and structure as well as the many potential players in the regulatory process. In contrast to situational and ecological theories, regulatory theories are not explanations of interpersonal aggression and its prevention. Rather, they focus on the routine practices of businesses and provide a framework for analysing how incentives to comply with laws and principles of good practice may be implemented, drawing not only on the formal powers of government regulatory bodies but also on the many kinds of informal pressures that can be applied by community groups, industry associations, and responsible licensees themselves. In the absence of an effective regulatory system that balances formal, legal powers with the informal persuasive powers of industry groups and other bodies, the results of scientific research on what works in preventing aggression and violence may never be applied, and the lessons of situational crime prevention may never be acted upon.

The principles and methods of responsive regulation require a focus on specific industry characteristics. Thus, to be able to regulate in a way that is truly responsive, a great deal of information is required about industry culture and practices – the kind of information that is contained in this book. A clear understanding of the processes involved in aggression and violence, enhanced by an analysis of situational risk factors and by scientific evidence on what works to minimise the effects of these risk factors, can be used to set the agenda for regulators interested in designing policies to address violence related to drinking establishments. We return to a discussion of responsive regulation in Chapter 9, where we incorporate the insights from earlier chapters, especially the evidence on effective interventions, to suggest ways in which knowledge from research might be incorporated into regulatory systems.

In the next chapter, we identify the critical elements of alcohol's effects on aggression, building upon a comprehensive and detailed empirical foundation that goes beyond such imprecise concepts as 'disinhibition' and incorporates interactions between pharmacological, attitudinal, contextual and cultural factors.

Chapter 3

Alcohol: the contribution of intoxication to aggression and violent behaviour

1. *Does every woman in the room look terribly attractive, except your own wife?*
2. *Do you suddenly feel handsome, strong and good-looking?*
3. *Alternatively, do you suddenly feel bleary, bald and blotchy?*
4. *Do you wish to participate in some feat of physical danger or daring?*
5. *Do you suddenly love everyone?*
6. *Do you suddenly hate everyone?*
7. *Do you feel that you, and you alone, have discovered the secret of existence, hitherto denied to the human race?*
8. *Do you feel that life is just wonderful (or alternatively, hideous)?*
9. *Do you feel you could drink all night?*
10. *Do you feel incredibly witty?*

(From Chapter 9, 'On Overdoing It',
The Art of Coarse Drinking, Green 2001: 107)

It is no coincidence that aggressive behaviour is likely to occur in drinking establishments – alcohol has been linked to crime and violence over time and across cultures (Graham and West 2001; MacAndrew and Edgerton 1969; Murdoch *et al.* 1990). Meta-analysis of experimental research (Bushman 1997) suggests that the link is at least partly causal, with the effects of alcohol contributing to, although neither a necessary or sufficient cause of, aggressive behaviour.

Alcohol is particularly likely to be involved in violence that is unplanned and arises out of social interaction and conflict, as is often the case in drinking establishments. In addition, because aggression in drinking establishments is likely to involve more than one person who has been drinking, the effects of alcohol may play multiple roles in aggression by contributing to the behaviour of all persons involved, including the person who initiates aggression, the target and third parties. Thus, prevention policy cannot ignore the important role of the effects of alcohol in aggression in the licensed environment. At the same time, it is clear that there is no inevitable link between alcohol and violence. Most people never become aggressive when they drink, and even those who do become aggressive are not aggressive every time they drink. Moreover, the extent to which people become aggressive when drinking varies greatly across different cultures (MacAndrew and Edgerton 1969). Therefore, it is important to examine more closely how and why alcohol consumption might contribute to aggression and violence in public drinking settings.

The currently accepted understanding of the alcohol-violence link (Graham *et al.* 1997) is that aggression occurs when there is a combination of:

(a)   the pharmacological effects of alcohol;
(b)   a person who is willing to be aggressive when drinking;
(c)   an immediate drinking context conducive to aggression; and
(d)   a broader cultural context that includes tolerance of alcohol-related aggression.

That is, while alcohol alone does not cause aggression, it does contribute to aggression, given the right circumstances. In this chapter, we explore how the effects of alcohol can contribute to aggressive behaviour in and around public drinking establishments. We also address briefly the potential role of drugs other than alcohol in barroom violence.

Linking alcohol effects and bar violence

Experimental research has found that people behave more aggressively when they have been given alcohol than when they have consumed a placebo drink (that is, a drink they have been told contains alcohol but does not actually have any alcohol in it) (Bushman 1997). There is also some experimental evidence suggesting that alcohol increases aggression more for men than for women (Gussler-Burkhardt and Giancola 2005). Alcohol may moreover contribute to the escalation of aggression and, consequently, aggression severity. For example, research on aggression occurring in barroom settings (Graham *et al.* 2006) has found that greater intoxication of participants in aggressive incidents was positively related to greater severity of aggression. Similarly, in a survey of aggression among young adults in Buffalo, New York, Leonard and colleagues (Leonard, Collins and Quigley 2003) found that more severe aggression among male respondents was associated with a higher level of consumption of alcohol at the time of aggression; however, analyses involving female respondents from the same study (Collins *et al.* 2007) did not find the same relationship between severity and intoxication level, although drinking more than usual on a particular occasion was associated with whether aggression occurred.

Alcohol acts both as a stimulant and a sedative (Grupp 1980), producing a variety of effects on the drinker. Because alcohol has many effects, it may contribute to aggression in a number of ways. For example, Pihl, Peterson and Lau (1993) proposed that alcohol increases aggression by making the drinker less anxious about the consequences of his or her actions due to the anxiety-reducing effects of alcohol on the GABA-benzodiazepine receptor complex in the brain (Miczek *et al.* 1997). Other explanations have focused on the effects of alcohol on the prefrontal and temporal lobes of the brain, which are primarily responsible for planning, verbal fluency and memory (Peterson, Rothfleisch, Zelazo and Pihl 1990). According to this theory, aggression becomes more likely when this function of the brain is impaired by alcohol because the drinker is less able to see the other person's perspective and less able to problem-solve in conflict situations (Giancola 2000).

Roughly 50 explanations have been proposed to account for the link between drinking and aggression (Graham, Wells and West 1997; Pernanen 1976), including the effects on anxiety and cognitive ability mentioned above, as well as effects such as increased emotionality, narrowing of the perceptual field and increased concern with personal power described in more detail below. Moreover, it is possible for more than one effect of alcohol to be implicated in aggression. For example, aggression might result from the combined effects of alcohol making the person more emotional, more single-minded, less aware of the other person's perspective, less competent at dealing with conflict and more determined to demonstrate personal power.

In the following sections, we describe in more detail the effects of alcohol considered to be most relevant to barroom aggression, and provide examples of incidents of aggression from observational and interview research that highlight how these effects appear to contribute to aggression in drinking establishments.

The effects of alcohol on risk-taking

Experimental research suggests that when people drink, they are less able to assess risks accurately (Zeichner and Pihl 1979), less likely to give thought to or expect possible negative consequences (Fromme, Katz, and D'Amico 1997), and, even when risks have been accurately assessed; they are more willing to take risks (Pihl and Peterson 1993). Alcohol also appears to reduce impulse control (Fillmore and Weafer 2004). In the incident below (Box 3.1), the respondent noted several effects of alcohol related to risk-taking, including his own misjudgement of risks and his friend's 'liquid courage'.

Box 3.1   Racist comments trigger brawl
(based on interview data from Graham and Wells 2003)

> The respondent who was South Asian described an incident that occurred when he was leaving a bar. A group of men began making racist comments and jokes that, according to the respondent, 'weren't directed towards me but it was, I don't know, they were implied to be directed towards me'. The respondent's friend (who was Caucasian) became angry and confronted the group. One man responded that it was just a joke, but the respondent's friend continued to express his anger. This led to a scuffle resulting in both groups being pushed out of the bar by bar staff. A brawl ensued, and the respondent and his friends suffered a beating from the other group.
>
>   The respondent reported that his friend who started fighting 'had a few ounces of liquid courage.' He also noted that alcohol affected his own judgement: 'rather than assessing the situation, I just jumped in head first without realising that there were more of them than us ... if I had been sober, I probably would have just grabbed my friend and said "Let's just go".'

Other young men interviewed in the same study also noted that alcohol affected their risk-taking in terms of their reduced ability to assess dangers (for example, not realising that the opponent was a lot larger and stronger than they were), increased willingness to take risks (for example, 'you don't think about the consequences or if the guy had a gun or a knife') and increased impulsivity (for example, 'alcohol gives me a licence for my mouth'). Increased risk-taking due to the effects of alcohol has also been noted in observational research, illustrated by the incident in downtown Toronto described at the beginning of Chapter 1 where the brawl involved people being pushed into the path of oncoming traffic. Alcohol-related risk-taking is particularly evident when male patrons taunt and challenge security staff who are obviously larger, stronger and greater in number than they are, as in the incident described in Box 3.2, observed in London, Ontario.

Similar alcohol-related risk-taking was noted in an ethnographic study in the UK (Benson and Archer 2002: 14):

> The link between alcohol and fighting is likely to be complex. Situations become simplified, impulsive behaviour more likely, and judgement is impaired. This, coupled with an exaggerated sense of self-importance and abilities, and reduced sensitivity to pain, easily led to conflict. One example was when two men ran from a restaurant without paying ('it seemed like a laugh at the time') and ended up in a brawl with four waiters who pursued them. In this example, the males seriously overestimated their chance of escape, presumably due to their intoxication.

Focused on the here and now: hyper-emotional effects of alcohol

As we noted in Chapter 2, the time out benefit of drinking is achieved partly by the effects of alcohol increasing the drinker's focus on the present and immediate circumstances and activities, and away from the past, future or day-to-day responsibilities. While this is clearly one of the desired effects that contributes to the pleasures of drinking, it can also increase risk of aggression, in that people who are intoxicated may be both less likely to be able to frame perceived offences within a larger perspective and more likely to respond aggressively, rather than considering the longer term consequences of their actions. As noted by one interviewee in a South African study about the relationship between alcohol and risky sex, 'I learned there is a lack of discipline when you are under the influence. You don't think about tomorrow. You only think about now' (Morojel *et al.* 2006).

Heightened emotionality while drinking tends to co-occur with focusing on the present. Despite the depressant properties of alcohol that may ultimately overtake the drinker, observational research (Graham *et al.* 2000) and interviews (Graham and Wells 2003) have identified alcohol-induced emotionality as often taking the form of

Box 3.2 Smaller man challenges large muscular security staff
(observed incident from Graham, West and Wells 2000)

At about 1:30 a.m., the observers saw three security staff in a
heated discussion with a 21-year old man. The man was allowed
to remain in the bar although he appeared unfocused, did not
walk in a straight line and was obviously drunk. At about 2:20
a.m. (twenty minutes after the establishment stopped serving
alcohol), two of the staff pushed the man toward the back exit.
The man yelled at one of the security staff who was large and
muscular, 'Fuck you! Fuck you!' and tried to punch him. The
staff encouraged the man to go home but he continued to try to
punch them. The man yelled at the larger security staff, 'Come
out and fight!' and tried to hit him again. At this point, the
security staff whom the man had tried to hit reacted by punching
the man in the face. The man fell stumbling backward, and the
owner closed the door.

The man then made his way to the front door. He was no
longer wearing his shirt and his face was bloody. Other patrons
had gathered outside to see what was happening. The man was
very angry and hit the glass on the door with his fists several
times. A security staff member from inside the bar yelled, 'You're
going to jail.' The man replied, 'You think I've never been to
jail?' The four security staff stood at the front door mocking the
man while the man continued to urge the one security staff to
fight him. Yelling and name-calling continued until the police
arrived. The staff member who had punched the patron informed
the police that the bar wanted to lay vagrancy, trespassing and
assault charges against the man. He further told the officer
that he was trying to get the man out of the bar because the
man had tried to start a fight inside. He said that the man had
taken a swing at him and that he had hit him back. The officer
listened to the security staff but did not write anything down at
the time. Later the officer was observed taking statements from
several security staff. The patron allowed the police to put him
in the police car without too much difficulty – denying all the
while that he had done anything.

feeling stimulated or agitated ('hyper', 'hyped-up'), as illustrated by
the following comments from two interviewees in a study of African-
American male violence in bar settings in Utica, New York (Oliver
1993: 256), who note that 'when you drink tempers go quick':

I take a lot of things sober, but it seems when you drink tempers go quick. Especially when we drink heavy.

Well, I feel like after he had more or less verbally attacked me and pissed me off that made me angry. And by drinking that made me twice as angry. Normally if I wasn't drinking I would have just stepped off and just went on.

Research by Steele and colleagues (Josephs and Steele 1990; Steele, Critchlow and Liu 1985; Steele and Josephs 1990; Steele and Southwick 1985) provides a useful model for linking situational and environmental factors with the effects of alcohol on perceptions and emotionality. These authors coined the term 'alcohol myopia' or alcohol near-sightedness to describe 'the short-sighted information processing that is part of alcohol intoxication' (Steele and Josephs 1990: 922). They argued that while this effect will occur every time someone consumes alcohol, the nature of the drinker's behaviour (including whether the person becomes aggressive) depends on the interaction of this alcohol-induced near-sightedness with situational factors. Specifically, alcohol myopia will be most likely to increase aggression in conflict or provocation situations because the near-sighted focus on specific aspects of the present situation means that cues, signals or thoughts that would inhibit or prevent aggressive behaviour are less salient and have less influence on the person's judgment (Giancola 2000, 2002).

In terms of the effect of alcohol on barroom aggression, this near-sightedness could make the person especially responsive to cues in the environment that provoke, trigger or reward aggression, especially if countervailing cues that would serve to discourage aggression are weak or subtle. It is easy to see how this immediate focus, combined with high emotionality, might cause a person to persist in an argument or fight long after he or she would normally have given up the conflict, as might have occurred in the incident in Box 3.2. One impact of this persistence is to increase the likelihood of violence escalating, especially when more than one person in the conflict is experiencing alcohol myopia.

The alcohol myopia or near-sightedness of intoxicated persons and the particular responsiveness to environmental cues that trigger aggression demonstrate how motivation to behave aggressively can depend on the situation, highlighting the potential value of Wortley's (2001) precipitation control strategies to control prompts or reduce provocations. For example, as will be explored further in Chapter 5, reducing crowding with its associated bumping, jostling and other irritants may be especially important in drinking establishments given the emotionality and near-sighted focus on the present circumstances associated with the effects of alcohol.

The intoxicated person's short-sighted emotional focus on winning the immediate conflict also has implications for how staff can best manage the situation. For example, separating groups that are fighting by keeping one group inside for a time while the other group is asked to leave the area of the drinking establishment may be sufficient for both groups to lose interest in the fight, especially if they are distracted by other people or activities.

Effects of alcohol on cognitive functioning

Cognitions and perceptions play an important role in aggressive interactions, and there is no question that alcohol impairs both of these functions. This impairment has been linked to a specific area of the brain, the prefrontal cortex (Pihl, Peterson and Lau 1993), which is responsible for 'executive functioning' – that is the high-level thinking that is needed for problem-solving and understanding complex situations in order to be able to deal with a conflict situation in a non-aggressive manner. Alcohol reduces the ability to appraise the situation (Herzog 1999) and to assess the motives of others, especially with regard to aggressive intent (Zeichner and Pihl 1980). For example, because of intoxication, a person who has been bumped by someone may get angry with the person for being careless, rather than recognising that external factors made the bump unavoidable.

In addition, alcohol has been found to bias perceptions, for example increasing the perception of the aggressiveness of a bogus or hypothetical opponent (Pihl *et al.* 1981; Sayette, Wilson and Elias 1993; Schmutte, Leonard and Taylor 1979). Impaired cognitive functioning also affects problem-solving abilities in conflict situations (Sayette *et al.*1993), making mature and reasoned responses less likely, while increasing the likelihood of immature, irrational and aggressive responses.

Giancola (2000) argued that many of the effects of alcohol that influence aggression reflect impairment of tasks done by the executive functioning part of the brain including:

(a) attending to and appraising the situation;
(b) seeing the perspective of others;
(c) considering the consequences of one's actions; and
(d) defusing a hostile situation.

Thus, a competent person approaching a social situation attends to the situation (that is, pays attention not only to what is being said but also to body language and external and contextual events) and uses information obtained through this appraisal process to judge the motives of the other person, including whether the behaviour of the other person is threatening or intentionally aggressive. In assessing the situation, the competent person not only takes into consideration his or her own desires and perceptions, but also those of others in the situation. For example, the men making racist remarks in the incident in Box 3.1 may have believed that the other men would interpret their remarks as intended to be humourous, when, in fact, the other men found them offensive.

Competent responding also requires planning a few steps ahead to assess the probable consequences of different actions. For example, in the incident described in Box 3.1, the respondent not only misjudged the situation (that is, that he and his friends were outnumbered), but he did not think beyond the immediate consequence of his decision to fight (that is, giving support to his friend) to the ultimate consequence (being beaten up). Finally, effective resolution of a conflict situation usually involves verbal and mental skill in defusing the situation without necessarily giving up one's own desires. All of these skills are impaired by alcohol.

The attentional and emotional effects of alcohol noted in the previous section may intensify cognitive impairment. For example, poor appraisal of the situation and alcohol-induced near-sightedness combined with increased emotionality may make people more likely to attribute blame to others and less likely to see their own role in the escalation of violence (Pernanen 1976; Pihl and Ross 1987). The incident in Box 3.3 below, taken from an ethnographic study of barroom fighting in rural American bars, illustrates not just the focus on the moment and the escalating emotionalism of Y but also considerable cognitive impairment in understanding and resolving the situation peacefully on the part of both Y and X. Specifically, Y took offence at behaviour that X apparently intended as playful. X, for his part, could have reacted by apologising and saying that he was just fooling around – instead, X is described as 'unmoving' and 'iron-eyed'.

Increased concern with personal power and the macho culture of the drinking establishment

A series of studies by McClelland and colleagues (McClelland *et al.* 1972) suggested that consumption of alcohol in larger amounts

Box 3.3 You slapped me!
(Leary 1976: 34)

---

1. Initial situation. Two pool shooters. Both 19–20. Both full of beer. A shot missed. Half playfully, X slaps Y.

2. Exchange of words. Y draws back shoulders, stands upright, red-faced and amazed. Maintains appropriate two seconds' silence, then observes in a bewildered, indignant, low-husky tone 'you slapped me.' X unmoving, iron-eyed. Y repeats the phrase several times, each time raising his voice by decibels, each time expressing increasing amazement. His redundant utterances serve many communicative functions: they burn into his own brain the reality and gravity of the perpetrated offense; they announce to the unfortunate perpetrator three salient facts: (i) *'you* slapped me' – an observation carrying the message: you – white-faced bastard, causer of trouble, two-bit pool player, arrogant fool – are both gutless and stupid; 'you *slapped* me' – idiot, your flat palm whammed against my cheekbones; (iii) 'you slapped *me*' – me, Y, rough 'n' tough but honest guy who only came into this bar to put down beer in the company of my girlfriend and push striped balls into felt holes before facing the cows in the morning.

---

resulted in increased concern about demonstrating personal power among males (although this effect was not found for females – Wilsnack 1974). No experimental research since that time has confirmed this effect; however, similar concerns about demonstrating personal power have been found in interview and ethnographic studies (Benson and Archer 2002; Graham and Wells 2003; Tomsen 1997; Tuck 1989). The following description from an ethnographic study in the UK illustrates that cognitive impairment from alcohol, combined with a macho/power mentality, can result in considerable trouble, with the trouble in this case going beyond the confines of the drinking setting.

Another effect of alcohol is to simplify the appraisal process, to make the individual more sensitive to perceived threats. One 19-year-old man who was interviewed on a number of occasions had clearly misread situations several times, resulting in him getting into fights. He would perceive threats when none was intended and on one occasion challenged another man who was with a large group of friends ('I started on one lad and then his mates laid into me'). Another fight led to his girlfriend breaking off with him. He said: 'I thought this lad was trying it on with her so I hit him.' Unfortunately, she was unimpressed with his behaviour. On most of these occasions, he blamed being drunk for starting the fight. However, even when sober he defended the general principle that 'you've got to stand up for yourself.' (Benson and Archer 2002: 14–15)

As noted at the beginning of this chapter, the relationship between the effects of alcohol and aggression are likely to be multiplied by the number of intoxicated people involved in an incident. Therefore, alcohol might not only increase concern with person power for one of the people involved in a conflict, but if the incident occurs in a drinking establishment where macho power is a central concern, the effects of alcohol are likely to increase power concerns for all of those involved. This combination is demonstrated in the incident described in Box 3.4 below, in which the escalation of aggression seemed to result from the interaction of the effects of alcohol on misjudgement of risk in a generally macho environment, combined with a macho refusal to back down.

The effects of alcohol that are most implicated in aggression in real world settings

Most research testing the effects of alcohol on aggression has been conducted in experimental settings where research subjects are involved in a task in which they set electric shocks for a fictitious opponent. Aggression is measured as the frequency and intensity of shocks delivered by the subject under specific experimentally-determined conditions, such as consumption of alcohol. It is not necessarily the case that alcohol will affect behaviour in a similar manner in real world settings.

To assess the contribution of alcohol to aggression in real-life public drinking settings, 133 incidents of aggression observed in drinking establishments frequented by young adults in London, Ontario, Canada were rated according to the contribution of 13 effects of alcohol (from 1 = this effect was very unlikely to have contributed to the incident – to 5 = this effect was very likely to have contributed to the aggressive behaviour of one or more persons in the incident) (Graham, West and Wells 2000). A slightly different approach to

Box 3.4 'You gotta problem?'
(interview data from Graham and Wells 2003)

R (the respondent) was at a bar with a large group of friends (about 25–30) and was extremely drunk. R's friend was telling R about a scuffle he had been in with a man who was very big. R started pointing jokingly at large men saying 'is that him, is that him?' He pointed at one particularly large man who happened to turn and see him pointing. The man approached R and said 'You gotta problem?' R said he felt very confident because he had so many friends with him, and so he replied 'No. I don't have a problem. Do you have a problem?' The big man pushed R. R pushed back. R's friend grabbed the big guy's arm, saying 'Relax. We don't want any problems' but the big man threw the friend out of the way. R was then hit on the head with a beer bottle by another man. A group of men then pinned R's arms back and started punching and kicking him. The doormen threw R out the door (hitting his head on the door on the way out). R tried to fight with one of the doormen in order to get back into the bar so that he could 'defend his friends.'

Rather than recognising his own provocative behaviour and unnecessarily aggressive response, the respondent attributed the incident to bad luck: 'Basically you know I think it was just bad luck, like a fluke, you know a coincidence. Like I mean what are the chances that this guy just turns around and happens to look at me just when I point at him … He comes over you know to, to see what's going on. It happens to be, to be my birthday, and it happens that I'm very drunk and so instead of being, you know, a logical person and saying listen you know I was just joking with my friend here, it has nothing to do with you, don't worry about it, you know I had to get a little bit lippy. You know, ask him if he's got a problem. So yeah, just a fluke basically, bad luck.'

He also provided a little insight into the context of the incident: 'I pointed at the guy like you know you, you really shouldn't point at people in Toronto – it's not a good idea. It always results in the same thing. Especially at a bar, you know, where a lot of guys are going to, you know, meet girls or, you know, whatever, hang out with buddies. They want to, they want to look tough.'

assessing how the effects of alcohol contribute to aggression was used in a general population survey in Ontario, Canada during the same period (Graham, Wells and Jelley 2002). Respondents were asked about their most recent experience of physical aggression during the past 12 months. Those who reported aggression in which they and/or the other person had been drinking were asked whether the incident happened at least partly because of 12 specific effects of alcohol, such as alcohol making the opponent or the respondent more impulsive or willing to take risks.

Although both studies addressed similar effects of alcohol, these effects could not be measured in exactly the same way in the two studies. In the first study, observers of aggression in drinking establishments did not have first-hand knowledge about the thoughts and intentions of people involved in the aggressive incident or their normal or usual behaviour when they were not drinking. That is, judgments were based solely on observed behaviour, and, therefore, certain kinds of factors, such as whether the person was thinking less clearly due to the effects of alcohol, were more difficult to rate. Despite these limitations, there was an acceptable level of agreement between the two persons rating the role of different effects of alcohol (Graham *et al*. 2000). In the second study, survey respondents had more information (compared with observers) on which to base their ratings of the effects of alcohol on their own thought processes (and sometimes those of the opponent); however the survey format was not conducive to measuring exactly the same effects of alcohol that were rated by observers because of the need to keep survey questions simple and straightforward.

Table 3.1 shows the results from the ratings of the contributing effects of alcohol on aggression for both studies. Because the items from the two studies were slightly different, the wording for both sets of items is provided in the table.

The most important factors from observational research

As shown in Table 3.1, the most frequently observed effect of alcohol judged as contributing to aggression was alcohol making the person focused on the present (and unconcerned about possible future consequences). Other effects rated as contributing to a large proportion of observed incidents included alcohol making the person less anxious about consequences or danger and more emotional. Thus, from the perspective of observers, effects related to focus on the present and hyper-emotionality appeared to make a stronger contribution to aggression than effects related to cognitive impairment due to alcohol. Nevertheless, impaired problem-solving, seeing only one's own perspective and increased concern with demonstrating personal power were also identified as important factors, rated as contributing to over 60 per cent of incidents.

The most important factors from the perspective of participants in aggressive incidents

Several interesting patterns emerged when participants were asked to rate whether specific effects of alcohol contributed to aggressive behaviour committed by themselves or their opponents. First, respondents rated the effects of alcohol as playing a much stronger role for the other person than for themselves, even for incidents in which respondents rated themselves as more intoxicated than their opponent (Graham and Wells 2001a). For example, 81 per cent of survey respondents thought that alcohol made their opponent less likely to see the other person's point of view, while only 23 per cent thought that aggression was at least party due to alcohol having this effect on themselves. This self–other perceptual difference could have important implications for dealing with intoxicated persons in public drinking environments. In particular, people seem to be aware of how alcohol affects other people's ability to handle conflict but may underestimate the extent to which alcohol also affects them – namely, that they too may become more hyper-emotional, less competent in their own thinking and problem-solving, and more likely to take risks.

Secondly, the effects of alcohol implicated in aggression tended to be different when respondents reflected on their own behaviour compared to their opponent's behaviour. For self, the effects tended to relate to taking offence, being more stimulated and emotional, being less likely to think about consequences, being less able to solve problems and being less willing to listen to someone else. While these effects also applied to the opponent, the most frequently endorsed effects of alcohol relating to aggression by the opponent were being less able to see the other's viewpoint, being more brave, tough or powerful, and being less able to think clearly and to consider consequences. Particularly striking was the self–other difference on the assessment of whether aggression was at least partly due to alcohol making the person feel more brave, tough or powerful, with 80 per cent of respondents saying this was a relevant effect for the opponent, but only 16 per cent rating this effect as influencing their own behaviour. Thus, while both observers of barroom aggression and individuals rating aggressive behaviour of their opponents were

Table 3.1. Judgements about the contribution of specific effects of alcohol for observed and experienced aggression

	Ratings of observed incidents	Responses by survey respondents		
Effect of alcohol rated as contributing to aggression for at least one person in the incident	% of incidents rated as involving effect	Aggression judged at least partly due to this effect of alcohol on the opponent/respondent	% of opponents affected	% of respondents affected
Increased risk-taking				
Reduced anxiety or fear regarding social or physical sanctions or danger	73	Less likely to think of the consequences	78	30
Increased impulsiveness	60	More impulsive or willing to take risks	64	29
Increased risk-taking	55			
Reduced ability to assess contingencies	52			
Focused on the here and now: hyperactive-emotional				
Focused on the here and now (increased value of present rewards and reduced subjective penalty of future consequences)	84	Focus on one thing and ignore everything else	66	25
Heightened emotionality	71	More emotional	63	31
Increased psychomotor stimulation	69	More stimulated or hyped up	77	36

Less self-reflective, reduced access to internal values or cues (carried away)	59			
Impaired cognitive functioning				
Impaired problem-solving	64	Less able to solve problems	71	30
Sees only own perspective (not aware of another's perspective)	62	Less able to see another person's viewpoint	81	23
Narrowing of the perceptual field (tunnel vision) – focuses only on part of the situation and not aware of broader context	53	Less able to think clearly	79	26
		Less willing to listen to someone else	78	28
Impaired information processing – less able to process and interpret social situations correctly	31	More likely to misunderstand something another person said or did	67	24
Macho subculture/effects of alcohol on macho concerns				
Increased concern with demonstrating/exercising personal power	65	More brave, tough or powerful	80	16
		More likely to take offence	71	38

able to see how alcohol seemed to make drinkers more macho in their thinking and concerned with issues of personal power, participants in aggressive incidents seemed to be unaware of this effect of alcohol on themselves. This potential lack of awareness regarding one's own macho behaviour has implications for training staff of drinking establishments. As we discuss in Chapter 6, security staff often take challenges to their authority personally. Therefore, training staff to recognise that intoxicated patrons may be unaware of the extent to which they are making macho challenges toward staff could help staff to deal with these situations more effectively.

The effects of drugs other than alcohol on aggression and violence

For most violence in drinking establishments, alcohol is the drug of primary concern (Luke *et al.* 2002). However, the possible contribution of the effects of drugs other than alcohol deserves at least a mention. While there is consistent evidence of a link between alcohol consumption and an increased risk of aggression, the relationship between aggression and illicit drugs is not so clear, and the relationship also varies for different types of drugs (Haggård-Grann, Hallqvist, Långström and Möller 2006).

There is some evidence that the use of tranquillisers such as Valium may increase aggressiveness (see Boles and Miotto 2003; Ben-Porath and Taylor 2002). Amphetamines, phencyclidine (PCP) and cocaine have also been associated with violence, but the extent to which this is a result of drug effects or other aspects of the drug-taking culture is unclear (Boles and Miotto 2003). The evidence with respect to marijuana and hallucinogens is inconsistent (Boles and Miotto 2003; Moore and Stuart 2004).

Reduced violence has been attributed to MDMA ('ecstasy') and increased violence to anabolic-androgenic steroids, but the lack of definitive research on these drugs makes conclusions premature (Hoaken and Stewart 2003). We are unaware of any systematic research on the relationship between drug effects and violence specifically in drinking establishments. Informally, observers from a recent observation study in Toronto, Canada (Graham *et al.* 2004) and interviewees from a study of clubs in Glasgow, Scotland (Forsyth 2006) discerned an association between use of MDMA and lower levels of violence. This is apparent in the following quote from a club-goer who was interviewed in the Glasgow study (Forsyth 2006: 59):

> I think there's a not a trouble there … because people's take drugs very luved up attitude so … you're in a happy mood and you're in love with everyone I think … you're not going to get anyone starting a fight with you. There's less trouble.

With regard to other drugs in drinking establishments, ethnographic research suggests that at least some door staff use steroids (Hobbs *et al.* 2003: 112), but the rate of use and the effects of use on staff violence have not been documented systematically (Monaghan 2003).

In addition to the lack of a consistent relationship between most drugs and aggression, the relationship between drug use and violence may be linked to withdrawal or to long-term use rather than to acute drug effects (Boles and Miotto 2003; Hoaken and Stewart 2003). Aside from the pharmacological effects of drugs, violence may also occur in relation to purchasing or selling drugs. In addition, the association between drug use and aggression in drinking environments may reflect an association between aggression and overall permissiveness rather than the effects of drugs *per se* (Graham *et al.* 1980).

In summary, there is a lack of conclusive information on drug effects generally and a lack of information about the role of drugs in violence in drinking establishments specifically. Moreover, in most licensed premises, as with the rest of society, alcohol is by far the most commonly used substance. Thus, while there is likely to be some impact of other drugs in some barroom environments, the primary focus of this book is on the drug most implicated in bar violence, namely, alcohol.

Minimising the extent that alcohol contributes to aggression

We noted in early parts of this chapter that many of the effects of alcohol that have been linked to aggression are effects that are sought after because they make drinking occasions pleasurable. For example, an intense focus on the present and less acute cognitive awareness can enhance the experience of time out or escapism and promote group fellowship. Increased risk-taking and reduced anxiety about consequences allow people to take social risks that help them to enjoy the company of others more freely than they might if they had not been drinking. Thus, in developing strategies for reducing bar violence, it is important to recognise that people consume alcohol mainly for its positive effects (Baum-Baicker 1987). Therefore, the following suggestions for reducing the relationship between alcohol consumption and aggression take into consideration that drinking is an integral part of positive socialising for most people who go to bars:

1 There is evidence that the balance of positive to negative effects of alcohol decreases as intoxication increases. Observational research in bars has provided consistent evidence of the link between patron intoxication and both the frequency and severity of aggression (Graham *et al.* 1980; Graham, Osgood *et al.* 2006; Homel and Clark 1994). Therefore, the goal of server training and responsible beverage service programs to prevent serving to intoxication is consistent with practices to reduce violence (Wallin, Norstrom and Andréasson 2003).

2 There is consistent evidence that the relationship between alcohol consumption and violence is a conditional one (Wall, McKee and Hinson 2000) – that is, it reflects an interaction of the effects of alcohol and personal, contextual and cultural factors. Therefore, one way of reducing the likelihood that the effects of alcohol consumption will lead to violence is to focus on these interacting factors; that is, to focus on changing situational and environmental factors that moderate the effects of alcohol. For example, reducing environmental irritants may be particularly important in environments where alcohol is consumed, given that for some individuals the effects of alcohol may cause them to be overly focused on these irritants and more likely to respond emotionally and impulsively than if they were faced with the same irritants when sober.

3 Bars are high-risk locations for drinking because of the exposure of patrons and staff to high-risk social interactions. At the same time, however, they are locations with institutionalised guardianship in the form of paid staff (Graham, Bernards *et al.* 2005) whose ostensible function is to ensure the safety of patrons. Bar staff may be the key factor in preventing the link between alcohol's effects and violent behaviour and, as we argue in Chapter 6, the full potential for staff to function as effective guardians of patrons has yet to be realised.

4 Of course, commercial drinking establishments do not exist in a vacuum – they are greatly affected by the cultural, policing and regulatory environment in which they are embedded. As we noted in Chapter 1, it may difficult for bar owners to foster expectations of non-violence if these are not supported by the police and the

licensing system generally. That is, in order to break the link between alcohol consumption and violence, the unacceptability of bar violence needs to be a consistent message given by licensing policies, legislation, enforcement and regulatory practices, as well as by the licensees themselves.

Chapter 4

Patrons: risks for violence associated with who goes out drinking and why

If you cram tens of thousands of individuals together from the age group most prone to criminal behaviour and then fill them with alcohol, does anyone really believe that it won't occasionally 'go off'?
(Hobbs, Hadfield, Lister and Winlow 2003: 11)

In Chapter 2, we discussed the social functions of public drinking establishments and how functions such as prolonged socialising, meeting sexual or romantic partners and a time-out place for behaviour that may be outside the norm of what is usually tolerated are linked to an increased risk of aggression. These functions also shape the characteristics of the type of people who go out drinking, why they go, and the kinds of conflicts and aggression that are likely to occur.

Research across different countries suggests that the demographic characteristics of bar patrons, that is, young, unmarried men who drink more than average (Clark 1966; Single 1985; Lang, Stockwell, Rydon and Gamble 1992; Reilly *et al.* 1998), are also the characteristics of violence-prone populations generally (Felson, Baccaglini and Gmelch 1986). Thus, even without any effects of alcohol or the environment, one might expect an increased risk of aggression solely on the basis of the general characteristics of patrons. In this chapter, we take a closer look at the patron population and the ways in which their characteristics and the social functions that motivate them to go to licensed premises are related to whether aggression occurs and the types of situations that trigger aggression. In the first part of this chapter, we use studies of the relationship between the barroom environment and aggression conducted in Canada, Australia, the UK and the US over the past 30 years to identify patron characteristics that seem to distinguish establishments with more aggression from those with less aggression. In the second part of the chapter, we use narratives of incidents to explore the situations that trigger aggression between patrons, to identify patron characteristics associated with particular types of conflict, and to explore the application of routine activity and situational crime prevention theory to preventing aggression related to patron characteristics.

Studies of the association between the barroom environment and aggression

Thirteen studies (listed in chronological order in Table 4.1) were found that included empirical data regarding the relationship between aggression and the drinking environment. These studies provide the basis for this chapter's review of patron characteristics associated with aggression, as well as the review of environmental risk factors in Chapter 5 and of staff characteristics associated with aggression in Chapter 6. Most of the studies used observational research, although some involved interviews with pub managers, staff or patrons and one used a telephone survey of young adults. All published articles related to each study are listed after the name of the study. The first citation is usually the main source for findings reported in subsequent tables in this chapter and Chapters 5 and 6. These studies also provide many of the case examples used throughout the book. When case examples are drawn from one of these studies, they are referenced simply by the name of the place of the study (for example, the Toronto study, the Sydney quantitative study and so on).

Table 4.2 summarises the results regarding the association between patron characteristics and bar aggression based on the studies listed in Table 4.1. The first column lists the patron characteristic. The second column lists supportive findings (with caveats to these findings shown in italics). The third column lists studies that have examined these variables but not found positive evidence that they are risk factors or have found a negative relationship between the variable and aggression.

Prior to examining the results in Table 4.2, some caveats in interpreting the findings need to be taken into consideration. First, because most studies of aggression in the barroom environment have used observational methods, research has been limited to observable

Table 4.1 A chronological listing of studies of environmental characteristics associated with aggression in licensed premises

Study and authors	Description	Measures of aggression
(1) Vancouver, Canada, Observational Study. (Graham *et al.* 1980; Graham 1985).	Observational research conducted in all licensed premises (except for a small number of late-night venues) in Vancouver in the summer of 1978. Two-hour observational visits were made during days and nights and all days of the week except Sunday (633 hours of observation during 303 visits to 185 premises).	• Number of incidents of physical aggression • Number of incidents of non-physical aggression
(2) Sydney, Australia, Qualitative Study. (Homel, Tomsen and Thommeny 1992; Tomsen, Homel and Thommeny 1991; Homel and Tomsen 1991; Tomsen 1997).	Qualitative study to compare premises known to have been regularly violent with premises noted for their lack of violence in suburban Sydney in 1989 (300 hours of observation in 55 visits to 23 sites (different bars and entertainment areas within the one establishment) in 17 licensed premises).	• Assaults involving some degree of physical violence
(3) England, Interview Study. (Marsh and Kibby 1992).	Summary of findings based on interviews with 300 pub managers in England between 1986 and 1990.	• Qualitative
(4) Sydney, Australia, Quantitative Study. (Homel and Clark 1994).	Observational research conducted after 8:00 p.m. and usually on Thursday, Friday or Saturday nights in Sydney in 1991 in venues frequented by young adults, with over-sampling of high risk premises (294 hours of	• Whether any aggression occurred • Whether physical aggression occurred

	observation in 147 visits to 45 sites in 36 licensed premises).	• Severity of aggressive incidents • Total number of incidents
(5) *Surfers Paradise, Australia, Intervention Study.* (Homel, Hauritz, McIlwain, Wortley and Carvolth 1997; Homel, Hauritz, Wortley, McIlwain, and Carvolth 1997; Carvolth *et al.* 1996).	Observational research conducted on Thursday, Friday and Saturday evenings in 1993 (pre-intervention) and 1994 (post-intervention) (200 hours of observation in 99 visits to 18 nightclubs). Follow-up observational data collected in 1996 and 1999 (Lincoln and Homel 2001) are not included.	• Same measures as Sydney quantitative
(6) *Surfers Paradise, Australia, Study of Nightclub Crowding.* (Macintyre and Homel 1997).	Analyses of incidents and environmental factors observed in 36 visits by a single researcher in three high-risk and three low-risk nightclubs with similar floor areas in Surfers Paradise, Queensland in 1995.	• Number of incidents of low-level aggression • Number of incidents of high-level aggression
(7) *North Queensland, Australia, Intervention Studies.* (Hauritz, Homel *et al.* 1998abc; Homel *et al.* 2004).	Observational research conducted in licensed premises in Mackay, Townsville and Cairns on Thursday, Friday and Saturday evenings in 1994 (pre-intervention) and 1996 (post-intervention) in a replication of the Surfers Paradise Safety Action Intervention (394 hours of observation in 199 visits to 75 licensed premises).	• Same measures as Sydney quantitative

Table 4.1 continues overleaf

Table 4.1 continued

Study and authors	Description	Measures of aggression
(8) *London, Canada, Observational Study.* (Graham and Wells 2001b; Graham, West and Wells 2000; Wells and Graham 1999; Wells, Graham and West 1998).	Observational research conducted on Friday and Saturday nights between 11:30 p.m. and 3:00 a.m. in high risk bars and clubs frequented by young adults in 1996 and 1997 (93 visits of 2–3 hours each to 12 premises)	• Physical and non-physical aggression
(9) *Buffalo, US, Survey.* (Quigley, Leonard and Collins 2003; Leonard, Quigley and Collins 2003; Collins, Quigley and Leonard 2007; Leonard, Collins and Quigley 2003; Leonard, Quigley and Collins 2002).	Two concurrent telephone surveys in Erie County (including city of Buffalo), New York during 1998 to 2000, using a general community sample of 967 adults aged 18 to 30 and a college sample of 433 students. One focus of the study was to compare the characteristics of violent and non-violent bars.	• Bars classified as violent or non-violent • Whether participant was aggressive • Severity of participant's aggression • Whether opponent hurt/ injured
(10) *Toronto, Canada, Safer Bars Evaluation Study.* (Graham *et al.* 2000–04; 2004; 2005a, 2005b; 2006a, 2006b, 2006c; Purcell and	Observational research to evaluate the *Safer Bars* program in which large capacity (>300) bars and clubs in Toronto were visited by male-female teams of observers starting prior to midnight and ending after 2:00 a.m. (closing) on Friday and Saturday nights from November 2000 to	• Whether aggression occurred • Frequency of aggression • Severity of patron aggression

Graham 2005).	June 2001 (pre-test) and from November 2001 to June 2002 (post-test) (1334 visits of 2–3 hours each to 118 premises).	• Severity of staff aggression
(11) Hoboken, US, Observational Study. (Roberts 2002; 2007).	Observational research in bars (79 per cent were considered 'drinking holes' – that is, their primary function was drinking) in Hoboken, New Jersey, from 7:30 p.m. to 10:30 p.m. or 11:00 p.m. to 2:00 a.m. on Thursday, Friday and Saturday nights from February to July 2001 (444 hours during 148 visits to 25 premises).	• Whether any aggression occurred • Number of incidents of non-physical aggression • Number of incidents of physical aggression
(12) Glasgow, Scotland, Observational Pub Study. (Forsyth, Cloonan and Barr 2005).	Observational research using the same data collection procedures as the Toronto study with observations conducted during the summer of 2004 on Friday and Saturday nights between 9:00 p.m. and 1:00 a.m.; follow-up interviews with staff in high- and low-risk pubs (32 visits to eight pubs).	• Incidents of disorderly behaviour (physical and non-physical aggression) • Severity of aggression
(13) Glasgow, Scotland, Observational Club Study. (Forsyth 2006).	Observational research using the same data collection procedures as the Toronto study and Glasgow pub study with observations conducted in city centre nightclubs in March and May of 2006 on Saturday and Sunday mornings (covering the hours from before midnight to after 3:00 a.m.) (96 hours in 32 visits to eight clubs) as well as interviews with 32 club patrons.	• Number of aggressive incidents, • Number of severe incidents (suggested caution because only three premises had severe incidents), • Police call-outs/recorded crime associated with nightclubs – not restricted to clubs or nights in the study.

patron characteristics, such as gender, age, ethnicity and social or economic class. Other characteristics of patrons, such as usual drinking or drug use pattern, personality and mental health, have not been addressed by these studies, with the exception of the Buffalo study where survey methods were used to study barroom aggression.

Secondly, patron characteristics may be correlated with other features of the environment or with alcohol use, and, therefore, significant associations may be due to some third factor that is associated with both the particular patron characteristic and violence (for example, the association found between younger age and violence may actually be a function of high-risk activities such as dancing or pool-playing being more common in drinking establishments frequented by younger adults). Therefore, characteristics found to be significantly related to aggression when other risk variables were controlled in multivariate analyses are marked with an asterisk (*).

Thirdly, patron characteristics may also reflect some stable feature of the drinking establishment that is associated with aggression, such as a 'pick-up' bar where sexual overtures and competition are part of the reason for frequenting the establishment. Thus, an association might be found between younger age of patrons and aggression that is actually an association between aggression and the type of drinking establishment. Only one study (Toronto) used analyses that were able to separate within-bar relationships from between-bar relationships (for example, younger average age of patrons was associated with bars that had more aggression, but no association, or a negative association, was found between patron age and aggression on different visits within a particular bar). Superscripts are used in the table to identify relationships that are significant (a) within but not between bars, (b) between but not within bars and (ab) both within and between bars.

Fourthly, the range and representativeness of findings relating to some patron characteristics were limited because many studies focused on large-capacity drinking establishments, high-risk establishments or establishments frequented mainly by young adults.

Fifthly, these analyses examine the association between the occurrence of violence in the drinking establishments and *aggregate* characteristics of patrons (for example, the proportion of all patrons in the drinking establishment who were male). That is, with the exception of the Buffalo research, the studies do not examine the characteristics of specific individuals and their risk of becoming violent.

Finally, an important criterion for interpretation is consistency in findings across studies. However, each study included a slightly different set of patron characteristics, and even when similar character-istics were measured, these were sometimes defined differently from one study to the next. Therefore, while consistency of findings can be interpreted as supportive of a fairly robust relationship, inconsistent findings do not necessarily imply a lack of relationship, because inconsistent findings may be related to differences in measurement or to differences in the types of establishments included in the study.

Gender and age

Men outnumber women in most drinking establishments, but, except for the findings from the Sydney qualitative study, there appears to be no increased risk of aggression with higher proportions of male patrons. This does not necessarily mean, however, that gender and gender issues are not associated with violence – many studies have found that the majority of incidents of aggression involve men, often only men (Graham and Wells 2001b; Graham *et al.* 2006b; Homel and Clark 1994; Roberts 2007), and, as we describe later in this chapter, aggression is often about male issues such as macho concerns or gender-related issues such as sexual aggression or both.

Although no overall pattern emerged for proportion of men, there was some evidence from the Sydney qualitative study and the Glasgow club study that interactions between *groups of men* who were strangers to each other could lead to violence. However, this finding has not been confirmed by other quantitative research, partly because of difficulties in operationalising this phenomenon as a meaningful quantitative measure.

There is mixed evidence regarding whether younger age of patrons is associated with an increased risk of aggression. Evidence from the Toronto study suggests that this relationship reflects a bar-level relationship (that is, more aggressive bars were frequented by younger patrons) but that there was no relationship between aggression and age of patrons on a particular night within an establishment. (In fact, younger age was negatively related to frequency of aggression in the multivariate model.) In addition, the Buffalo study found that patrons who went to violent bars tended to be younger than patrons who went to non-violent bars, although this difference was no longer significant when bar characteristics were taken into consideration.

Taken together, these findings suggest that the association between younger age and violent bars may be at least partly due to the types of establishments young people frequent and the nature of the activities that they engage in when visiting those establishments, rather than to the age of patrons *per se*. It may also be that the association

Table 4.2 Evidence relating to the association between specific patron characteristics and aggression (based on 13 studies of the barroom environment listed in Table 4.1)

Patron characteristic	Evidence of increased risk	Evidence of no increased risk or reduced risk
Greater proportion of male patrons	*Sydney qualitative.* Greater proportion of males associated with aggression.	*Vancouver, Buffalo, Toronto, Hoboken, Glasgow pub.* Proportion of males not significantly associated with aggression. *Glasgow club.* Greater proportion of females associated with more severe incidents[c] and more police call-outs (in multivariate model only).
Groups of males/ groups of male strangers	*Sydney qualitative.* Presence of males in groups, especially strangers to each other, associated with aggression. *Glasgow club.* More all-male groups associated with more observed aggression* and police call-outs.	*Vancouver, Sydney quantitative, Surfers intervention, North Queensland, Hoboken.* No significant relationships.
Younger age	*England.* Patronage by mostly younger adults identified as contributing to violence. *Sydney quantitative.* Greater percentage of underage females associated with more frequent and more severe aggression. *Buffalo.* Individuals who visited violent bars younger** than individuals who visited non-violent bars; age of patrons generally in violent bars younger than in non-violent bars.	*Sydney quantitative.* Age of patrons overall not significantly related to aggression. *Surfers intervention, North Queensland, Hoboken, Vancouver.* Age not significantly related to aggression. *Glasgow pub.* Older patrons seemed to be at least as likely as younger patrons to be involved in disorder. *Toronto.* Within bars, younger age was negatively

Toronto. More frequent and severe aggression in establishments usually frequented by younger patrons. *Glasgow club.* Younger age associated with more observed aggression and police-call-outs*. related to aggression frequency[a] (significant only in multivariate analyses, not significant in bivariate analyses).

Greater proportion of Aboriginal, First Nations, Pacific Islander patrons

Vancouver. Greater proportion of patrons with First Nations/Aboriginal background associated with more physical and non-physical aggression.
Sydney quantitative. Greater proportion of patrons with Aboriginal background* associated with more frequent and more severe aggression.
Surfers intervention. Greater proportion of patrons with Pacific Islander background associated with physical and non-physical aggression.
North Queensland. Greater proportion of patrons with Pacific Islander background* associated with physical and non-physical aggression; greater proportion of patrons with Aboriginal background associated with non-physical aggression.

Table 4.2 continues overleaf

Table 4.2 continued

Patron characteristic	Evidence of increased risk	Evidence of no increased risk or reduced risk
Greater proportion of unkempt/marginal patrons, social class significantly related to aggression.	*Vancouver.* Greater proportion of unkempt patrons and presence of people talking to themselves associated with aggression, especially non-physical aggression. *England.* Pubs frequented mostly by working-class populations identified as having higher rates of violence. *Sydney quantitative.* Greater proportion of 'marginal' patrons associated with more frequent and more severe aggression; greater proportion of patrons in manual working gear associated with severity but not frequency of aggression. *North Queensland.* Greater proportion of unkempt men associated with more physical and non-physical aggression. *Glasgow club.* More 'working class' clientele associated with more observed incidents and police call-outs.	*Surfers intervention.* Proportion of unkempt men not

| Other patron characteristics, including drinking pattern | *Buffalo.* Compared to respondents who went to non-violent bars, those who went to violent bars were less agreeable and conscientious and more impulsive and angry*+; they drank more, scored higher on alcohol problems*+ and were more likely to believe that alcohol would make them aggressive. |

*Significant in a multivariate analysis; *+significant in multivariate analyses including respondent characteristics but non-significant when bar characteristics in model.

abSignificant within and between bars in Hierarchical Linear Modeling (HLM) analyses; asignificant within but not between bars; bsignificant between but not within bars.

cResults need to be interpreted with caution due to small number (5) of severe incidents.

relates partly to higher intoxication levels found in establishments frequented by underage patrons, as noted in the Glasgow club study (Forsyth 2006).

The lack of association between age and aggression found in some of the studies may also be because many studies focused specifically on young adults, and these studies may have lacked sufficient variability in age of patrons to identify a relationship. Another possible factor that may militate against an overall finding of an effect of patron age is that the type of older adults who go to commercial drinking establishments may not be representative of their age group. That is, while consistent evidence suggests that violence decreases as people age, this pattern may not emerge in drinking establishments if young patrons are generally representative of their age group while older patrons are more aggressive than persons of the same age who do not go to drinking establishments.

Ethnic groups and marginalised populations

The research in Table 4.2 suggests that drinking establishments frequented by socially or economically marginalised persons are more likely than other establishments to be characterised by aggression and violence. The higher risk of barroom aggression for some types of patrons may reflect higher risk generally for aggression among these population subgroups. This general increased risk may also account for the association between manual working gear and aggression in establishments in the Sydney quantitative study and the higher rate of aggression in pubs on housing or council estates and pubs frequented by working class patrons in the England study and the Glasgow club study.

A subculture of aggression and/or marginalisation rather than ethnicity *per se* may also account for associations found between Pacific Island, Aboriginal or First Nations patrons and aggression. Interestingly, the Glasgow club study found that the percentage of patrons from ethnic minorities was *negatively* related to both police call-outs and observed aggression in their multivariate analyses, suggesting that persons from ethnic minorities who go out to Glasgow pubs may be less aggressive than those from the ethnic majority.

Drinking pattern and personality

The survey approach adopted as part of the Buffalo study allowed examination of factors such as heavy drinking, anger and impulsivity which go beyond observable patron characteristics. The association of these traits with violence in drinking establishments is consistent with a large body of criminological literature (for example, Loeber and Farrington 1998), but, interestingly, these traits were no longer significant predictors of bar violence when bar characteristics were included in the multivariate model. This suggests the possibility that the impact of patron characteristics on bar violence may be mediated through their impact on the barroom environment, or that environmental or management factors that characterise the bar as a whole are more important than patron characteristics in predicting bar violence.

In the following sections, we describe common examples of aggression in bars and use these incidents to demonstrate the link between patron characteristics, the function and social milieu of commercial drinking establishments, and the culture and social factors that influence behaviour in drinking establishments.

What are the fights about?

Research to date points to three main issues underlying barroom aggression: (1) macho concerns; (2) sexual or romantic liaisons; and (3) a casual disregard for safety within a subculture of violence in establishments frequented by marginalised persons.

(1) Young men and the macho culture – the single most common source of conflict in many drinking contexts

There is notable consistency, at least across English-speaking countries, in the descriptions of macho concerns leading to violence among men when they are drinking in bars, pubs and clubs (Benson and Archer 2002; Burns 1980; Dyck 1980; Graham and Wells 2003; Oliver 1993; Tomsen 1997, 2005; Tuck 1989). The common theme that emerges is concern about manhood, reputation and the necessity of standing up for oneself and one's mates (even if the mate is in the wrong). Although some authors have attributed this behaviour to class (Tomsen 1997) or racial issues (Oliver 1993), other research (Graham and Wells 2003) indicates that macho concerns are not limited to specific ethnicities or classes, although the extent of such concerns may vary by subculture (Cohen and Nisbett 1994; Cohen et al. 1996) and may change over time (Suggs 2001). In the following discussion of macho aggression in bars, we describe some of the most common triggers, the role of third parties and the issue of macho behaviour by women.

Giving and taking offence/looking for trouble

Often, macho aggression plays out as aggressive reactions to perceived slights or insults (Dyck 1980; Graham and Wells 2003; Tuck 1989), including reacting with anger to an unintentional bump or a spilled drink in a crowded bar. Macho concerns can also be evident in behaviour that intentionally provokes others, for example, intentionally bumping or shoving, as illustrated in the third example of normal trouble in Box 2.2 of Chapter 2 where one man aggressively shoved another man out of his way. Looking for trouble was clearly a precipitating factor in a recent study of violence in drinking establishments among men in Northern England:

> As the night progressed, and more alcohol was consumed, groups of people, primarily men, came into contact with other groups as they moved from pub to pub or pub to club. The groups that were observed generally consisted of four or more young men, usually looking under 21 years. It was evident that some groups enjoyed making remarks to others as they passed. The individuals who made the remarks were apparently doing so to make their companions laugh, and to impress them. According to the guides, this was a fairly common cause of a fight or an assault. Many such remarks were clearly aimed at insulting or abusing others, and were aimed at precipitating conflict. (Benson and Archer 2002: 11–12)

These observations are consistent with findings from several of the environmental studies summarised in Table 4.2 that aggression was more likely when the patron population included groups of males who were strangers to one another.

Data from group interviews with survey respondents who reported having participated in or witnessed pub-related aggression in the UK in the 1980s provide further insight into the 'code' of male honour that determines the giving and taking of offence in drinking establishments:

> The same essential sequence of events was related by everybody. Violence could be triggered by seemingly trivial events. It could be brushing past someone or even just looking at someone. An argument would develop – 'what the f____ are you looking at?' – and escalate verbally to the stage of mild physical involvement – pushing and shoving – and from there it would be but one step to a fight. When groups were involved the 'code' would

necessitate members supporting each other: 'groups can take anyone on.' The key to this pattern is 'machismo', reinforced in this case by the group. If you are the person who is stared at or brushed past you have to make an issue of it, the more so if you had some of your drink spilt. You cannot let it go in front of your friends. Equally, if you are the offender you cannot let any challenge go unanswered, you have to stand up for yourself or lose face ... Finally, nobody claimed to be the instigator of violent action, it was always imposed on them by other forces and they had no choice but to respond. This suggests that participants find it easy to justify their actions as self-defence. There was no doubt however, that a certain amount of 'glory' was involved, people often recounted with relish skirmishes in which they had taken part. (Tuck 1989: 45–46)

Chivalry and loyalty

Macho incidents in bars also occur due to what men perceive to be chivalrous or defensive behaviour. As described by one of Oliver's respondents in his study of bar aggression among Black men in Utica, New York:

I don't disrespect women. That's probably my biggest problem. That's why I get into so many fights. Most of the time I get into a fight, it has been about a woman. I am always sticking up for them or defending them. Other than that, I don't have any trouble. (Oliver 1993: 263)

When the person does not need or want defending, chivalry may be an excuse rather than a reason for violence, as illustrated by the incident described in Box 4.1 from an interview study conducted in London, Ontario. This incident is interesting because of the way in which alcohol was consciously used to 'hype up' the group and facilitate the commission of the assault through a process of disinhibition that the respondent recognised as somewhat artificial. The assault was premeditated, motivated by a desire to affirm male honour through the physical defence of his sister's right to be treated non-aggressively, and so, unlike much violence in bars, could not be regarded as having been precipitated by situational factors. Nevertheless, the fact that the men planned to attack the perceived offender at a bar (rather than some other location), and that they expected to get away with it, implies something about bar culture generally and the drinking establishment where the incident occurred, in particular.

Box 4.1 Don't push my sister!
(based on interview data from Graham and Wells 2003)

A week before the incident, the man who became the victim had asked the respondent's (R) sister out and had apparently sworn at her and pushed her when she refused. R heard about what had happened although not from his sister (who, according to R, didn't tell him because she knew he would 'go after' the guy). The night of the incident, R and his friends spent a couple of hours drinking at one of their homes talking about how they were going to find this man at a local bar where he was likely to be on a Friday night and beat him up. They went to the bar, and R confronted the man. According to R, the man reacted 'kind of like macho sort of none of your business, sort of don't worry about it or something like that.' R's reaction was '... it's my sister. Of course, it's my business ...' The man put his hand on R's shoulder and R 'just flipped ... sort of totally enraged' and hit the guy until he was down, at which point, R and two of his friends stood around the man and kicked him.

The interviewer asked whether the drinking was just for fun or part of getting ready 'to go confront the man'. R said it was part of getting ready – 'Of course, there's an inhibition, so the more we drink the less we'll be inhibited ... We even like verbally said it ... It's got to be done. So even if it takes getting a little drunk to do it, then we'll do it.' R also described the group as being very hyped when they walked into the bar. However, later in the interview, R said alcohol was not a factor, that he would have done it anyway.

Afterwards, he reported that they felt good and 'celebrated.' Looking back on it, how do you feel? 'Oh, just fine. Nothing else was appropriate so ...' Although R was later charged with assault, he was not convicted – apparently because the other man had touched him first by putting a hand on his shoulder.

As with defence of women, loyalty to friends or family is another important aspect of the male code of behaviour in drinking establishments. As noted by one of Oliver's respondents in Utica, New York, with regard to loyalty and the responsibility to defend friends and family, 'Right or wrong, I am always in their corner. I always feel one way and that is, they are right.'

Aggressive third parties

Incidents between males over macho concerns are especially likely to involve aggressive third parties. Forsyth (2006) described how loyal friends often serve as 'seconds', joining a fight on the side of their friend. Graham and Wells (2003) identified two major reasons for third-party escalation of aggression based on interviews with young men involved in bar violence: (1) perceived loyalty to a friend, and (2) fighting for fun. An example of third-party escalation due to loyalty was illustrated by the incident described in Box 3.1 in Chapter 3, in which the respondent's friend became embroiled in a fight with a group of men because the men had made a racial slur directed toward the respondent. The respondent also joined the fight because he, in turn, had to be loyal to his friend who was defending him.

Several studies suggest that men also get into fights in bars because they find it fun. A particularly colourful description of third parties fighting for fun was provided by Tomsen (1997: 98) in the qualitative study of bar violence conducted in Sydney with Homel and Thommeny in 1989:

[After watching some street brawling for about 15 minutes] … I [the researcher] delivered one of my standard conversation starters to a young man standing next to me by asking, 'What's this all about?' He told me that as he had just left the club he had no idea about this fight or who the people involved were. He stood silently next to me and watched for a few minutes more. Then unexpectedly and without uttering a word, he rushed forward to throw a body punch at one of the passengers who had got out of the car, and became fully involved in the remainder of the conflict. A big crowd of more than one hundred patrons had gathered and watched intensely. One girl snapped 'who cares, pissoff' to my questions about the reason for the conflict, and continued to stare straight at the fight. Two males, who were not among the original combatants, drifted across the street and punched each other repeatedly …

Male security staff and the macho culture

As we discuss in more detail in Chapter 6, there is no question that the culture of security staff is enmeshed in the macho culture of the commercial drinking establishment. Moreover, recent studies suggest that the culture of door staff at licensed premises, in itself, is one of heightened masculinity, threat and violence (Hobbs *et al.* 2002, 2003,

2007; Lister *et al.* 2000; Monoghan 2002; Winlow 2001; Winlow, Hobbs, Lister and Hadfield 2001). As described by Winlow (2001: 541):

> Being a bouncer allows a demonstrative cultivation of hyper-masculine persona: from body language to the cut of their clothes to the way they smoke their cigarettes, these men present their behaviour for display and their bodies become tools of 'impression management' (Goffman 1969). Their bodies, bearing, expressions and scar tissue are passing on easily decoded messages to bar and club patrons: do as we tell you and do it quickly.

Thus, as described in other parts of this book, the macho behaviour of bar patrons is often increased by the presence of male security staff who amplify the 'machoness' of the environment with their demeanour and behaviour.

Macho females

While a consistent pattern of male macho violence is found across studies from a number of countries, the pattern with regard to the frequency, intensity and precipitating factors for female violence is less clear. Most research on licensed premises has found aggression by females to be relatively rare (Benson and Archer 2002; Graham *et al.* 2006b; Graham and Wells 2001b; Homel and Clark 1994; Leonard *et al.* 2002; Roberts 2002) outside of skid row environments (Graham *et al.* 1980), although at least some violence by women was observed in all studies. For example, in the Buffalo study, 12 per cent of female respondents in both the community and college samples reported experiencing aggression inside or outside a bar compared with 25 per cent of men in the community sample and 17 per cent in the college sample. In the Toronto study, the gender difference in aggression was even larger with 709 (71.8 per cent) of the 987 incidents of patron aggression involving aggression by male patrons only, 150 (15.2 per cent) involving aggression by females only, and 128 (13.0 per cent) involving aggression by both male and female patrons. Moreover, in this study, even when female patrons were aggressive, they used less severe forms of aggression (for example, pushing rather than punching) compared with male patrons (Graham, Tremblay *et al.* 2006). Women were also less likely than men to engage in macho-type behaviours such as threats and challenges or glaring at or intimidating someone (Graham, Tremblay *et al.* 2006), although a few such incidents were observed as illustrated by the incident described in Box 4.2.

Box 4.2   Fuck you bitch!
(Toronto)

> Two women who appeared intoxicated (glassy eyed, loud, boisterous) inadvertently bumped into each other while dancing with their boyfriends. One woman said, 'Sorry!' to the other woman. Apparently irritated, the other woman replied calmly, 'Fuck you.' This clearly agitated the first woman (possibly because they had mutually bumped into each other due to crowding, and it was no one's fault). And so, in a raised voice, she countered with, 'No! Fuck you!' The second woman looked the first in the eye and with a sarcastic smile on her face said, 'Fuck you bitch!' The two men looked at each other and nodded knowingly. They got their girlfriends attention, held them closely, and continued dancing while moving the couples away from each other.

Although most studies of aggression in drinking establishments have found less frequent and less severe aggression and less macho behaviour among women compared to men, the Glasgow club study identified substantial severe violence by female patrons, with the process of female-to-female aggression appearing to be more dangerous and unpredictable than the more ritualised fighting by men:

> Male conflicts tended to first involve two men 'squaring-up'. They may be 'assisted' by 'seconds', who would either encourage or hold back the two combatants. If a fight did start then these two men would trade punches standing up, perhaps trying to get each other onto the floor by using headlocks. When a male combatant was floored the other male would then kick him when he was down. At this point 'seconds' may help the floored man to his feet ... By contrast female fights were described by observers as being more difficult to spot when trouble was 'brewing' as, unlike the fixed 'choreography' of male disputes, these could suddenly 'kick off' from what had previously only appeared to be a (perhaps heated) conversation. This tended to involve hair-pulling, which usually resulted in the combatants falling to the floor and punching each other in the face or hitting each other on the head with an object at close range. Any other female who tried to break it up risked being pulled into the fight herself (that is, by the hair) resulting in several women becoming entangled in a melee, leaving the stewards

with a much more difficult situation to resolve. (Forsyth 2006: 41–42)

One explanation for the greater frequency of female aggression in the Glasgow club study (although still less frequent than aggression by men) compared to the low frequency observed in other studies was that the majority of patrons were female in the clubs included in the Glasgow study. This contrasts with the Toronto study where females accounted for about 40 per cent of patrons (Graham, Tremblay *et al.* 2006) and were in the minority in almost all types of establishments (Purcell and Graham 2005).

Alcohol consumption and binge drinking by young women has increased in recent years in many countries, as has drinking by women in licensed premises (Plant and Plant 2001; Plant, Miller and Plant 2005). This phenomenon has given rise in the UK to the term 'ladette' to describe young women who increasingly resemble the stereotype of the hard-drinking male ('lad') in their drinking patterns and other behaviours, such as macho concerns and fighting. A recent qualitative study of 'women who drink and fight' (Day, Gough and McFadden 2003) found that threats to their reputation (similar to lack of respect described in the previous section for males) were cited as key triggers for aggression, at least among working-class women. The macho, ready-to-fight attitude was also apparent among some of the female doorstaff interviewed as part of an ethnographic study in the UK (Hobbs, O'Brien and Westmarland 2007).

However, the aggressive behaviour by women in Glasgow clubs and the aggressiveness of female security staff may not necessarily reflect behaviour in the UK generally. For example, data from the TASC project in Cardiff, Wales (Maguire and Nettleton 2003) found that men accounted for 88 per cent of persons arrested for city centre disorder or violence in which over half of the incidents were associated with licensed premises. In summary, while it is clear that some females engage in what appears to be macho aggression, the extent to which aggression is associated with female macho attitudes may depend on the type of establishment, the type of women who are attracted to the establishment and the culture or region in which the drinking establishment is located. As described in the following section on the second main reason for aggression, females appear to be much more likely to be involved in conflict over sexual overtures than they are in fights over macho concerns.

(2) Aggression related to sexual/romantic overtures

Sexual aggression is one of the most common forms of aggression observed in many drinking establishments, especially dance clubs, nightclubs or discos and other places where many patrons go for the explicit purpose of meeting sexual and romantic partners (Forsyth 2006; Grazian 2008; Parks and Scheidt 2000; Purcell and Graham 2005). These establishments are sometimes called 'meat-markets' and the process of searching for sexual partners referred to by various local expressions such as 'scoping' in Toronto (Purcell and Graham 2005), 'pulling' in Glasgow (Forsyth 2006) and 'hooking up' in Philadelphia (Grazian 2008).

The process of making and receiving sexual overtures is full of risk and ambiguity and, not surprisingly, aggression can occur due to misperceptions, inappropriate behaviour and other social errors. For example, in some premises, highly sexualised body contact may take place among strangers on the dance floor and be clearly acceptable (Purcell and Graham 2005). However, as is discussed in more detail in Chapter 5, in these environments, the boundaries for acceptable overtures may be unclear, leading to situations where one person believes that his or her overture is appropriate within the context while the target finds the overture highly offensive. In addition, social overtures relating to meeting a sexual or romantic partner are vulnerable to misunderstandings and problems because they typically involve a sensitive process (Cloyd 1976; Snow, Robinson and McCall 1991) that is affected by a number of social mechanisms, including expectations of both parties, how the target responds, how the initiator perceives this response, and the presence of an audience (Berk 1977).

There are also gender differences in the kinds of actions that are perceived as appropriate (Garlick 1994; Rotundo, Nguyen and Sackett 2001), and men and women may have different expectations regarding obligations to accept overtures (Ferris 1997; Grazian 2008; Parks and Miller 1997; Parks and Scheidt 2000; Russell and Trigg 2004) or have different standards for judging behaviours that communicate refusal (Wade and Critelli 1998). The process of meeting sexual romantic partners in drinking establishments is so fraught with difficulty that Grazian (2008: 140) refers to it as 'the myth of the pickup'.

The ambiguity of the situation for some individuals may also be increased by style of dress and other behaviours of the potential target. For example, despite public education programmes describing women's moral and legal right to say 'no', potential male offenders may view women as suitable targets of sexual harassment and aggression because of the way they dress. This was illustrated by comments about women's appearance and its role in sexual aggression made in a focus group study of male bar goers aged 18 to 50 years in Buffalo, New York:

> When asked what puts a woman at risk for aggression in a bar, one man explained: 'The way she's dressed. Some girls whose boobs are hanging out, skirts up to here, no underwear on, you know something's going to happen.' (Parks and Scheidt 2000: 936)

Enhanced risk of sexual aggression is readily apparent when the previous comment by a male bar goer is considered within the context of highly sexual styles of dress by women when they go out 'clubbing' (Grazian 2008) and the sexualised style of dancing that typically occurs in contemporary clubs (Forsyth 2006; Purcell and Graham 2005). Parks and Schedit (2000: 936) noted other kinds of behaviours which men saw as putting women at risk:

> They also felt that moving from male to male in a bar, while letting them buy drinks could put a woman at risk by increasing male expectations. These expectations could then influence the likelihood that a male might become angry and thus, physically or sexually aggressive …

Thus, the fact that patrons, especially female patrons, are dressing and behaving in ways that signal that they are interested in meeting sexual or romantic partners appears to lead to the erroneous interpretation on the part of some male patrons that these women are required to accept sexual overtures from whomever cares to make them. However, the solution is probably not as simple as educating men that 'no means no'. For example, the ambiguity regarding appropriate overtures is apparent in the incident in Box 4.3 where the positive reaction from the second woman served to reward the man for his somewhat invasive style of making sexual/romantic overtures and his persistence in not taking no for an answer.

Intentional sexual harassment and assault
While the man described in Box 4.3 was actually looking to meet women, it is clear that exploitive and aggressive behaviour that has nothing to do with courtship or sexual/romantic invitations

Box 4.3 'I can't believe it didn't work! It usually works when I tell them they are beautiful'
(Toronto)

As a woman was walking by a man he grabbed her wrist and tried to interlock his fingers with hers. She avoided interlocking their fingers, but his hand remained around her wrist. With an angry scowl and look of disgust on her face, she tried to pull her hand away from his grip, but he held on, saying something to her as he moved his face very close to hers. She leaned away, pulled her arm a little harder, made a disgusted face and shook her head slightly. He then released her wrist and let her continue walking through the crowd. When the man saw that the observers had witnessed the interaction, he commented to them in a rambling and slurring manner, 'It didn't work. I can't believe that didn't work. It usually works when I tell them they are beautiful'.

The man then approached another woman, this time leaning quite close to her ear before taking her hand. This new target seemed much more receptive. At one point, the man was heard to say to her, 'I'll marry you! That's sincerity. I'll marry you!' The woman was dancing with two friends while looking over her shoulder at him suggestively and giving him a dance show. The man stood about three feet away from her, looking her up and down and smiling broadly. He repeatedly looked over at one of his friends and back to the woman saying, 'Oh my God! Oh my God! I'll marry you!' This pick up continued for several minutes, as the man put a lot of effort into talking with the woman, holding her hand, and watching her dance. After a few minutes, and lots of loud cheering from one of her friends, the woman gave the man a phone number and asked for his. The couple was still standing together at the end of the night. The observers noted that the interaction between the man and the second woman could probably have been removed from the incident description, except that the man's interaction with the second woman suggested that his motivation (even with the first woman) was actually to meet/pick-up women rather than to assault them, as might have been concluded if the encounter with the first woman were viewed out of context.

also occurs. This was apparent in both the London and Toronto studies where men were observed grabbing women's breasts and then disappearing into the crowd. An interview study with young female pub goers in South Australia (de Crespigny, Vincent and Ask 2000: 451) also found that respondents expressed concerns about 'the discomfort and perceived risks from male sexual harassment and violence'. Other examples of predatory behaviour were documented by Parks and colleagues in studies of female bar goers in Buffalo, New York:

> You'll be standing at the bar and you'll be talking and all of a sudden you feel this presence behind you. And a voice over your ear is going, 'I'm going to f— you brains out!'…You turn around and they're gone. Now you get scared, because you don't know who did it and you're afraid to walk out of the bar. (Parks *et al.* 1998: 709)

Or as stated by another woman:

> They [men] just assume that because you're there [in a bar], you're there to sleep with them, screw them right on the dance floor, let them feel you up all over, mess your hair up, whack your face. I don't like that. (Parks and Miller 1997: 519)

An incident from the Toronto study in Box 4.4 illustrates in more detail behaviour that seems to go beyond acceptable boundaries of sexual invitation and playfulness into the arena of predatory aggression.

Aggression arising as part of the sexual/romantic overture process

Even when the initial overture is non-aggressive, there are a number of ways that the sexual overture process can result in aggression. For example, the target of overtures may react with aggression as in the incident described in Box 4.5.

The social overture process can still turn aggressive even when both the initial overture and the target's response are non-aggressive. For example, the person making the overture may become aggressive in a later stage of the process if he or she is made to feel embarrassed or rejected by a blunt refusal (Berk 1977), especially if other people witness the rejection or the rejection is seen as unfair (Felson 1978). On the other hand, if the refusal of the sexual overture is too subtle,

Box 4.4   Unwanted 'Dirty Dancing'
(Toronto)

A woman was stumbling around on the dance floor looking for her friends. A man who was dancing with some other people intentionally hit her with his butt as she attempted to get past. She went flying, landing on a couch and looking surprised. The man then 'dirty-danced' with his butt shaking in front of her face. She was laughing and very drunk but also appeared shocked by his behaviour. The man then took the woman by her hands and continued to dance with her on the dance floor, holding her close to him. She started screaming, not very loud, but loud enough to indicate that she was not enjoying it. He then turned around and pretended to thrust into her with his groin, this time facing her and 'dry-humping' her. He then held her up and grabbed her and made her dance with him by restraining her arms to the side and moving her around. The man followed the woman as she rejoined her group of friends (five women and one man). He danced with one of the other women, rubbing against her and then squatting down in a simulated oral sex position. The woman did not try to stop him but her facial expression suggested that she did not like what he was doing. The man eventually left when the woman did not respond to him.

the initiator may not perceive it as a refusal and may, as a result, behave aggressively by persisting in the hope that the target will ultimately submit (as appeared to be the case in the incident in Box 4.3 where the man held the first woman against her will). In addition, not only can incidents involve aggression by the initiator and the target, sexual overtures can lead to conflict with third parties related to issues such as jealousy or possessiveness (Forsyth 2006; Graham, West and Wells 2000). For example, the serious brawl that started in a Toronto club described at the beginning of Chapter 1 began with aggression by a man in response to a sexual overture made toward his girlfriend.

Aggressive sexual overtures by women toward men and between
same-sex patrons
Although sexual aggression by women toward men is much less frequent that the converse (Graham, Tremblay *et al.* 2006), aggressive

Box 4.5 Persistent man gets punched in the face (Toronto)

A woman who was somewhat intoxicated (swaying, glassy eyes) was dancing seductively by herself off the regular dance floor. A man who was intoxicated and staggering a bit began dancing in front of her, trying to dance with her. The woman's body language made it obvious she did not welcome his approach. She looked annoyed and turned her back to him and continued dancing. He moved away a bit but then approached her again and began to dance with her from behind, rubbing his body up against hers. She became even more angry and annoyed and said something to him. He took a step away and was still watching her but then began to look away, continuing to drink. The woman went over to her female friends and whispered something to them. They said something back to her, looking in the direction of the man. The woman returned to her dancing, and the man went up to her and put his arms around her, with a drink still in one hand. She whirled around, pushed him away and took a swing at him with her left hand. Her punch grazed his cheek. Then a second man intervened. The man who had persisted with his overtures backed away and raised his arms in a gesture of non-violence. He touched his cheek where the woman had hit him but did not reciprocate with aggression and finally moved away.

---

and predatory overtures by females also occur, as argued by some male respondents in the study by Parks and Scheidt (2000: 936):

> Another participant expressed frustration with sexually aggressive behaviour that some women direct toward men, which would not be acceptable from a man toward a woman: 'And women are a lot more [sexually] aggressive now too. They might look at you and I mean, I didn't ask you to touch my butt! They put their hands on me and I know that wouldn't be acceptable for me to do it. Or grab between your crotch!'

Nor is sexual aggression restricted to heterosexual encounters. Aggression related to sexual overtures was observed in gay and lesbian bars in the Toronto study, with these incidents reflecting similar processes and ambiguities to those between heterosexual couples.

(3) Aggression related to a subculture of violence

The third main aspect of bar violence that can be connected to characteristics of patrons and the function of the drinking establishment is the violence that occurs among persons from a violent, often marginalised, subculture. Aggression has been associated with establishments frequented by patrons from marginalised groups, including the poor, aboriginal or indigenous populations, those engaged in illicit trades, and skid row patrons (Graham *et al.* 1980; Pernanen 1991). Skid row establishments, in particular, tend to have at least some patrons who are evidently damaged from chronic alcohol abuse and/or suffering from psychiatric problems (Graham *et al.* 1980). Many of these establishments function as 'home territory' bars in Cavan's typology (Cavan 1966); that is, as places where these marginalised subgroups feel at home and accepted in ways that they would not be in mainstream establishments. At the same time, such establishments are often also, in Cavan's terms, 'marketplace' bars where illicit commerce is conducted, including the selling of drugs, sex and stolen goods. Thus, the atmosphere has a risky and volatile edge, and many patrons appear to have almost total disregard for their own safety and well-being.

There is less research documenting aggression associated with patrons from marginalised subpopulations than there is for the types of aggression associated with drinking establishments frequented by young adults. However, incidents documented in the Vancouver study and from one of the establishments in the Toronto study suggest that patrons at these locations may be at especially high risk of severe violence and injury. The casual violence in drinking establishments frequented by marginalised groups appears to be a consequence of the 'life is cheap' culture, characterised by cold-blooded acceptance of aggression and violence and disregard for one's own safety.

The incidents also appear to be about different issues from those that trigger aggression in mainstream bars and clubs. As is described in more detail in Chapter 5, these environments often seem to have an ongoing hostile atmosphere that occasionally flares into a major incident, in contrast to the generally friendly social atmosphere of more mainstream establishments where incidents tend to arise due to macho posturing and sexual overtures gone wrong. As is evident from the sequence of events described in Box 4.6, aggression regarding commercial transactions, drug deals or money owed by one person to another may be more likely to trigger violence in skid row establishments than concerns over manhood or sexual overtures.

Box 4.6   Slapped, kicked and ejected
(Toronto)

Two females were squaring off angrily. Suddenly, one slapped the other's face twice hard enough to knock her head back. The slaps were heard across the room. Both women shouted at each other and both made the same threatening gesture (a finger across the throat combined with pointing) to emphasize this. A third woman started shaking the slapped woman who looked shocked and afraid and did not resist or fight back. It is possible that her intoxicated state (likely not only from beer but also possibly from crack) made it difficult for her to fight back. The third woman then slapped the head and body of the woman who had already been slapped – it was an angry, forceful slap and appeared painful – punched/pushed her to the floor (backwards out of her chair), then kicked her in the head (hard enough that her head moved), paused for a second to change her relative angle and kicked her head as hard again. This happened one more time – the pause, adjustment of position, and kick in the head. The pauses are significant because they made it very obvious that the other patrons in the bar, as well as the one staff member on duty, were not going to step in terribly quickly.

At this point, the staff member approached, sent the kicker back to her chair and helped the victim up. While he was doing this though, he was picking up empty beer glasses from another table. His behaviour indicated a certain casualness about the incident. The woman who had done the kicking started walking toward the other woman with a steel-legged chair over her head as if to use it as a weapon. The staff member turned, directed the woman to put the chair down and go sit down, which she did at the table with the woman who had done the initial slapping, and they continued drinking their beer. The staff member talked to the victim some more and then went about his work. The victim re-took her original chair and began verbally taunting the woman who had slapped her from her seat about ten feet from the other woman. Eventually, they both got up and moved closer to each other – each shouting insults at the other. The woman who had done the slapping started shaking the other woman. Just as they both started fighting – both were locked in struggle, grabbing each other with their hands on their arms – a male patron moved over to break them up, joined by the staff member. The staff member convinced the woman who had been the victim of the slapping and kicking to leave.

Later that night, the staff member sat next to the observers and offered his opinion that the fight resulted over the one woman (the victim) having drank all the money to be used by the other women to buy crack.

The applications of situational crime prevention and routine activity theories to risks associated with patron characteristics

Understanding the influence of patron characteristics on aggression means understanding why certain kinds of people come to bars and clubs, how they interact when they are there, and how an environment that is sexualised, exploitative, permissive, macho, rough or skid row helps set the scene. On the whole, the quantitative evidence is that specific patron characteristics such as age and sex are not as important in themselves as how young men and women interact and how those interactions are influenced by environmental factors.

The incidents related to macho issues and encounters are consistent with many aspects of situational and routine activity theory presented in Chapter 2. First, these environments often seem to involve the routine activities triad of (1) likely or willing offenders, (2) suitable targets (who may at times also be willing offenders) and (3) ineffective guardians (that is, staff or other patrons) who are also at times themselves willing offenders. Consistent with situational crime prevention theory, offenders not only feel that their violent behaviour is excusable but often believe that it is necessary, for example, in reacting to perceived insults or defending a friend (Tuck 1989). In addition, situational precipitators (Wortley 2001), such as rough horseplay, competitive games and pressure from peers to behave aggressively, are endemic to the macho culture and activities. A good example of the normative and fully acceptable nature of male-to-male violence in bars was provided in Leary's (1976) ethnographic study of fighting in rural Indiana. As noted in Box 3.3 in Chapter 3, the incident began with two men playing pool where one took offence at a playful slap from the other man. The excerpt from Leary in Box 3.3 described the initiation of the fight. From there, the bartender pushed the two opponents into the street where they had a brief fight. Leary described the resolution of the fights as follows:

> The two, impressed by each other's strength and exhausted, shake hands and go back inside to drink beer. Their girlfriends comfort them, their boyfriends slap them on the back, and everybody talks about the fight. (1976: 35)

This romantic view of bar fights ignores the fact that people are sometimes injured or even killed and illustrates the general acceptance of male-to-male bar violence that appears to persist to the current day (Benson and Archer 2003; Graham and Wells 2003; Tomsen 1997).

The examples of aggression related to sexual overtures and sexual behaviour illustrate how these kinds of overtures can result in aggression. These problems are, of course, by no means restricted to drinking establishments, but clubs and bars do have the distinctive feature that they are, by social convention, open social spaces in which overtures from strangers and appropriate responses are expected. Moreover, the risks of harassment, aggression and violence are exacerbated by intoxication of the initiator of the overture, the target or both.

As with macho violence, the function of the bar or club as a place for men and women seeking sexual or romantic partners provides some of the key components for a routine activity theory explanation of sexual aggression – namely, the presence of willing offenders and suitable targets. As noted by Parks and Scheidt (2000), the vulnerability of targets may be emphasised by the type of clothing worn and other behaviours – at least from the perspective of the potential offender. The lack of guardianship, the third component of routine activities, is also evident in these environments. Specifically, observational research suggests that staff ignore most incidents of sexual aggression, even outright sexual assault. In some environments, sexual aggression even appears to be encouraged, as we describe in Chapter 5.

In terms of environmental controls over offending (Clarke 1997), signals of permissiveness and a lack of situational controls over sexual aggression include employing scantily dressed female servers and the playing of sexually explicit music with violent overtones. In addition, the whole process and atmosphere of sexual overtures includes enormous potential for situational precipitators (Wortley 2001), such as provocation through rejection, humiliation, dominance and other factors at play in this complex process. The role of the sexualised environment and its effect on behaviour is explored further in Chapter 5.

Although the casual disregard for safety and a subculture of violence was central to much of the aggression observed in the

Vancouver study, the study also found considerable variation in how this atmosphere was managed, with the less aggressive establishments notable for keeping some control on aggression through the employment of staff who related well to patrons and by the presence of other patrons who were in turn helpful at quashing trouble. Thus, it may be that the best way to reduce the risk of severe violence in these settings is to increase the effectiveness of guardianship.

Much of the analysis in this chapter points to features of patrons that are hard to change, such as being young and male or being part of a socially marginalised group where it is normative to use violence or abuse to solve problems. These populations and their issues help construct commercial drinking establishments as risky settings. With the exception of the possibility of banning particular individuals who are predatory or repeatedly aggressive, it is through environmental controls and improvements in staff behaviour that the violence in these settings can be reduced. In subsequent chapters, we explore in depth the relationship between aggression and the environment, staff behaviour and regulatory policies and practices.

Chapter 5

Environment: understanding why some drinking establishments are high risk for aggression

To understand the causes of violence in pubs, we should stop being so concerned about alcohol consumption and drinkers' personal characteristics (age, sex, ethnicity, etc.) and instead probe more deeply into their social relationships and the norms of appropriate behavior that guide them.

(Graves, Graves, Semu and Sam 1981: 114)

Most human beings are exquisitely sensitive to environmental controls on behaviour – we dress and behave one way at work and another way at the beach, party or nightclub. Moreover, research has shown that the associations between aggression and the environmental factors in drinking establishments are strong and predictable (Graham *et al.* 1980; Graham, Bernards *et al.* 2006; Homel and Clark 1994). In Chapter 4, we described how aggression that occurs in drinking establishments is often related to macho concerns, sexual/romantic overtures or a subculture of marginalisation and violence. These issues link the functions of drinking establishments for patrons with environmental factors that discourage or precipitate aggression. For example, the men who beat up a man for pushing one of the men's sister (Box 4.1) selected a bar as the location for the attack, presumably because they believed there would be no serious adverse consequences for behaving violently in this location. The incidents of sexual assault and harassment took place in full view of other patrons (and probably staff), yet no one chose to intervene. Thus, one reason that these forms of aggression occur in drinking establishments is because some drinking establishments are environments where aggression is known to be tolerated. In this chapter, we review how specific aspects of the environment of drinking establishments are related to an increased risk of aggression, explore possible explanations for these relationships and identify some environmentally-based strategies for prevention.

To set the scene with respect to environmental influences, we begin by contrasting two distinct drinking environments alluded to in the previous chapter, skid row establishments and contemporary dance clubs, in order to identify some commonalities in risk factors, despite differences between the two settings in terms of social and physical environmental characteristics and the age and wealth of patrons.

A tale of two settings

Skid row

In 1978, the typical skid row beer parlour in Vancouver, Canada had a number of distinctive characteristics:

> A fairly large proportion of the clientele of this type of bar are people without regular work (unemployed, disabled, retired) or people with illegal work (prostitutes, drug dealers). The bar is frequented by at least one minority group (American Indian, Black, homosexual). Patrons tend to be in and out of the bar all day and use the bar as a 'home base' for social and other activities. For many of the patrons, this bar is one of a circuit of bars they visit during the day. The older people talking to themselves (sometimes shouting and fighting with fictitious opponents), the disoriented conversations, the highly intoxicated patrons and the 'business' dealings going on in the bar give the place a bizarre atmosphere. There is almost total tolerance of these types of behaviour. Unusual behaviour is accepted and often the source of gentle (or not so gentle) amusement; for example, one man came into the bar and said sociably to another, 'Still talking to yourself, Iffy?' Similarly, extreme drunkenness is common and usually acceptable. The only reason for refusal of service seems to be that the person is unconscious – and some instances were seen in which a person was awakened to be served another drink. Patrons were seen 'helping out' for free drinks and, in one case, trading a watch for a drink.

In summary, the aggressive bar (at least the Skid Row variety) tends to be a haven for those who are not accepted elsewhere. There are few limits on acceptable behaviour and little pressure for patrons to behave 'normally.' This accepting attitude seems to be combined with suspicion and hostility ('tense atmosphere'), possibly because of the deals going on. Most of the barworkers are not friendly and avoid interactions with patrons as much as possible. Finally, the bar tends to be physically unattractive with a shabby, run-down décor, tables close together in rows and poor ventilation. (Graham *et al*. 1980: 289–290)

Within this generally high-risk environment, however, there was considerable variability in the level of aggressiveness, largely governed by the attitude and behaviour of staff and the general ambience that had developed over time. Thus, while the same patrons might be observed frequenting a number of skid row bars, even within these similar environments, they would modify their behaviour to suit the social climate. In some skid row bars, kind staff were seen jollying patrons out of an argument, facilitating social interaction among solitary patrons and generally attempting to maximise a safe and pleasant environment for patrons, despite the overall context of a rough culture that has low disregard for safety or even life.

The twenty-first century club scene

According to Bellis, Hughes and Lowey (2002: 1027): 'The nightclub at its most basic is a building that provides loud music, often with a repetitive beat, a dance area that usually has low background light and intermittent bright lighting effects, and a licensed bar.' Macintyre and Homel (1997: 92) provide an expanded description of the nightclub based on their observations in Surfers Paradise:

On entering, one typically finds a Surfers Paradise nightclub dominated by the dance floor and its lighting. Coloured and strobe lights flash in time with the beat of the music, while video screens display complementary images, often highlighting footage of sports or depicting scantily clad women and men. The music usually ranges from painfully loud to deafening. Away from the dance floor the general lighting varies from dim to dark. Movement is extremely restricted, and it can often take many minutes to travel only a few meters. Moving from a location to a bar, getting service, then returning to the original location with a drink order intact is a very time-consuming, difficult and draining experience. The tobacco-laden atmosphere can become very hot and humid as a result of the crowd size, density, and movement, and the whole experience may be tinged with the menace of an unpredictable and potentially nasty reaction should one be imprudent enough to bump a drunken patron or (worst of all) spill his or her drink.

Purcell and Graham (2005: 133), using qualitative data from the Toronto study, described the larger context of clubs and bars as follows:

More than 30,000 people can be in this area during peak times, frequenting more than 100 clubs, bars, and restaurants, some with licensed capacities of 2,500 customers or more. These clubs are noted for their slick and stylized décor, with elaborate light shows, provocatively dressed go-go dancers and bar staff, strong security presence, and popular DJs. This proliferation of nightclubs within the central core of the city is similar to the pattern observed by Chatterton and Hollands (2003) in several cities across England.

Types and locations of premises that are high risk for aggression

The skid row bar, although of historical interest, may be less relevant as a focus for prevention than it was in previous years. While there is no question of the frequency and severity of aggression in these bars (Graham *et al.* 1980; Homel *et al.* 1992), due to gentrification and the high cost of property in the core areas of many cities, drinking and drug-taking appear to have moved out of licensed premises and into alleys, public parks and other areas. Ironically, although these were violent establishments compared to other pubs and bars at the time, they were probably safer places than the streets for marginalised persons because of the potential for oversight and guardianship by staff.

Although skid row or 'rough' drinking establishments that continue to operate should still be a focus of prevention, the decline of the skid row bar along with the growth of the club scene (see for example, http://www.signonsandiego.com/uniontrib/20061111/news_1n11bars.html) suggests that violence and disorder related to the many thousands of young adults who patronise nightclubs should be a higher priority for prevention in the twenty-first century. As we noted in Chapter 1, the night-time economy, with chaotic and sometimes dangerous entertainment areas and the proliferation, upsizing and consumer targeting of clubs is a big business that has been emerging in many cities around the world. Hobbs and his colleagues (2000: 707) described the growing night-time economy in the UK in the following terms:

> The night-time economy is based upon consumption, primarily of alcohol, and the breakdown of old rules and protocols has been hastened by marketing strategies of entrepreneurs who put together special offers and packages aimed at both attracting customers to their premises and keeping them there. Scantily clad bar staff, striptease artistes, organized drinking games, hen nights, stag nights, and special nights for nurses are laid on, as well as fifty pence a pint nights, and the inevitable three shots of whatever's not selling well for a pound.

Variants of nightclubs have been identified as high risk in quantitative research on barroom aggression, including late closing and discotheque establishments in Sydney, Australia (Homel and Clark 1994) and band bars, sports bars, dance clubs and hybrid bars in Hoboken, New Jersey, US (Roberts 2002)

Given the notoriety of entertainment districts as hot spots for problems, a surprising finding of the study of large capacity drinking establishments in Toronto was the increased risk of serious aggression associated with suburban premises when assessed within the multivariate analyses, controlling for other environmental risk factors such as crowding and permissiveness (Graham, Bernards *et al.* 2006). One reason for the higher risk of aggression in suburban establishments may have been that staff in suburban bars and clubs were not as well trained as staff in downtown establishments (Graham, Jelley and Purcell 2005). Regardless of the reason, the high risk for suburban bars and clubs suggests that, while the downtown or high street club scene is an important focus for prevention, it should not be the only focus.

The physical environments of the skid row bars and contemporary clubs are radically different, yet they share the overriding characteristic of freedom from restraint with few limits on acceptable behaviour. However, even within their respective categories, individual drinking establishments can vary greatly in the risk of violence, depending on the way staff interact with patrons and the social rules and expectations that have been established. Moreover, even within particular establishments, risk factors and aggression can vary from one night to the next (Graham, Bernards *et al*. 2006). In the following sections, we review environmental factors that have been found to be related to variability in aggression between and within venues, identify the probable mechanisms by which these factors contribute to risk, and describe some approaches for changing the environment to reduce risk of aggression.

The relationship between aggression and the environment of the drinking establishment

In Chapter 4, we drew on 13 studies conducted in various English-speaking countries over the past 30 years (Table 4.1) to examine the relationship between patron characteristics and aggression (Table 4.2). In this chapter, we use these same 13 studies to examine the extent and consistency of evidence for associations between environmental factors and aggression. As with the findings reported in Table 4.2, research on environmental factors has some limitations and features that need to be considered in interpretation.

First, the data are correlational and do not necessarily imply causation. For example, the Vancouver study found that aggression was more likely in drinking establishments where there were rows of tables (compared to other types of furnishings). It is quite possible that this relationship was due to the kinds of establishments that had tables in rows, rather than any effect of the rows of tables *per se*. That is, in most of the studies, the environmental characteristic being measured may have been confounded with other stable aspects of the establishment, such as type of patrons. As noted in Chapter 4, the Toronto study used hierarchical linear modelling to distinguish associations that varied from one night to the next within establishments from environmental factors that were associated with differences between bars. Superscripts are used in the table to identify relationships that are significant (a) within but not between bars, (b) between but not within bars and (ab) both within and between bars.

Secondly, many environmental variables associated with aggression are correlated with one another. Therefore, it is often difficult to distinguish between variables that have a direct impact on aggression, those that are indirectly related to aggression, and those that have no actual impact on aggression but are correlated with aggression because they are correlated with other variables that do have an impact on aggression. Some studies have included multivariate analyses in order to identify significant environmental factors, while controlling for others. The problem with this approach is that it cannot rule out indirect or mediated effects. For example, most aspects of the physical environment became non-significant in the multivariate analyses in the Toronto study. It cannot be concluded, however, that there is no relationship between aggression and the physical environment. For instance, it could be that some aspects of the physical environment (for example, being unclean, shabby) indirectly contribute to aggression through their effects on more powerful direct environmental factors such as an atmosphere of permissiveness. In other cases, variables emerged as significant *only* in multivariate analyses – meaning the variable only assumes importance when other variables are controlled. A good example of this related to suburban location in the Toronto study, as noted above. Suburban location was significantly related to severity of aggression in the multivariate analyses but not in the bivariate analyses. This suggests that all other things being equal (for example, equally intoxicated patrons, equally permissive environment, equal level of crowding, etc.), aggression would be more severe in suburban drinking establishments than in establishments in the downtown area. However, possibly because suburban and downtown establishments were not equal on some risk factors (including possible rural/urban differences in hospitality practices (Daly *et al.* 2002)), suburban and downtown establishments were not significantly different on any of the aggression variables in the bivariate analyses. In summary, care needs to be exercised in interpreting results from multivariate analyses. Nevertheless, such analyses are useful in identifying factors that are likely to be of particular importance. Variables in Tables 5.1 and 5.2 are marked with an asterisk (*) when there is evidence that they were significant predictors of aggression, controlling for other variables in a multivariate analysis.

Factors of key importance are also identifiable by replication of findings across studies. Because each study used a different set of variables, however, multivariate analyses are not necessarily comparable across different studies. Therefore, in Tables 5.1 and 5.2, we describe all environmental variables that have been found to be significantly associated with aggression in bivariate or multivariate analyses, specifying where possible whether these variables were related to physical or non-physical aggression and to frequency or severity. When evidence was mixed from a particular study (for example, the variable was related to physical but not non-physical aggression), the study is included in the 'evidence for' column with the non-supporting finding italicised.

The physical environment

Table 5.1 focuses on those aspects of the physical environment that have been found to be related to aggression, while Table 5.2 (next section) summarises risky aspects of the social environment. In the discussion of the findings in these tables, we link the findings with potential causal mechanisms drawing on routine activity and situational crime prevention theories described in Chapter 2.

Goings-on outside

The link between the aggression and the presence of queues or line-ups found in several studies may be due to a direct impact of queues on violence through environmental precipitators such as frustration and provocation caused by long waits, queue jumping, guest passes and bribes, as well as by officious, arbitrary or confrontational behaviour by door staff (analysed in detail in Chapter 6). However, the queue may also have a broader impact on behaviour within the premises in at least two ways. First, frustration, provocation and perceived unfairness in the line may affect the patron's mood and willingness to behave appropriately within the establishment; secondly, tolerance of rowdiness or aggression by people in the line may suggest that aggression and other problem behaviour will be tolerated or even rewarded within the establishment.

The strong link between the number of people hanging around after closing and the frequency and severity of aggression found in the Toronto study reflects the importance of better management of the area in which drinking establishments are concentrated (discussed further in Chapter 7). Although availability of transportation has been identified as an important factor in clearing patrons from core areas (Marsh and Kibby 1992; Responsible Hospitality Institute 2006), as shown in Table 5.1, the evidence from systematic research is mixed with regard to the association between transportation availability and aggression.

Size of establishment, décor, seating arrangements, upkeep, lighting

The bulk of evidence described in Table 5.1 suggests that the presence of a greater number of patrons is associated with an increased risk of aggression overall; however, number of people did not appear to be associated with increased risk of physical or severe aggression, and the association was not found in all studies. The

Table 5.1 Evidence relating to the association between physical aspects of the drinking environment and aggression (based on 13 studies of the drinking environment listed in Table 4.1)

Environmental variable	Evidence of increased risk	Evidence of no increased risk or reduced risk
Queues/line-ups to enter	*London, Ontario.* Queue was frequent location for aggression. *Toronto.* Presence of queue[a] associated with aggression frequency and severity.*	
Patrons hanging around outside at closing	*Toronto.* Higher number of people hanging around after closing[ab]* associated with more frequent and severe aggression.	
Queues for public transport	*North Queensland.* Availability of public transport associated with reduction in physical aggression in multivariate analysis, *although not significant in bivariate correlations.*	*Sydney quantitative, Surfers intervention.* Availability of public transport not significantly related to aggression.
Larger capacity or greater number of patrons	*Sydney quantitative.* Higher number of patrons in view associated with more frequent non-physical aggression *but not significant for physical aggression.* *Surfers intervention.* Higher number of patrons whose conversations could be overheard by the observers associated with more physical and non-physical aggression; higher average minimum and maximum number of patrons associated with more physical aggression.	*Vancouver.* Seating capacity, maximum number of people at any one time, and total number of people present not significantly related to aggression.

North Queensland. Number of patrons in view, higher average, minimum and maximum number of patrons associated with physical and non-physical aggression.
Toronto. Number of people[a] in the bar at peak crowding associated with aggression frequency.
Hoboken. Approximate number of customers positively associated with aggression; *bar capacity was not significantly related to aggression.*
Glasgow club. Number of patrons* associated with police call-outs but not observed aggression; being rated full to capacity* associated with severe incidents[c] *but not total observed incidents or police call-outs.*

Sydney quantitative, Surfers intervention. Shabby décor and lack of theme not significantly related to aggression.

Shabby or unpleasant décor/lack of theme/low expenditure and maintenance

Vancouver. Shabby décor, lack of theme, low expenditure and maintenance associated with greater risk of physical and non-physical aggression. Pleasantness of physical surroundings was negatively associated with physical and non-physical aggression.
North Queensland. Shabby appearance (*but not theme*) associated with physical aggression.
Hoboken. Attractiveness was associated with aggression.
Glasgow pub. 'Style bars' had less disorder than 'dirty or clutter' pubs.

Table 5.1 continues overleaf

Table 5.1 continued

Environmental variable	Evidence of increased risk	Evidence of no increased risk or reduced risk
Seating style of tables in rows	*Vancouver.* Tables in rows positively associated with non-physical and physical aggression. *Surfers intervention.* Tables in rows associated with physical aggression.	*North Queensland.* Seating style not significantly related to aggression.
Low level of lighting	*Sydney quantitative.* Lower level of lighting associated with more frequent and severe aggression. *North Queensland.* Better lit premises had fewer incidents of physical and non-physical aggression ($p < .10$). *Buffalo.* Violent bars were rated as significantly darker than non-violent bars.	*Vancouver, Hoboken.* Lighting level not significantly related to aggression.
Extent to which premises were unclean and messy	*Vancouver.* Dirtiness associated with more physical and non-physical aggression. *Sydney quantitative.* Dirtiness associated with more frequency and severe aggression. *Surfers intervention.* Dirtiness associated with more physical aggression. *North Queensland.* Dirtiness associated with more physical and non-physical aggression. *Buffalo.* Violent bars dirtier than non-violent bars. *Toronto.* Extent that premises were unclean or messy[a][b] associated with more frequent and severe aggression.	

	Hoboken. Unclean premises and rarely cleared tables, ledges and bar surfaces associated with aggression. *Glasgow pub.* Dirtiness scale used as one dimension to identify high risk pubs.[d] *Glasgow club.* Dirtiness scale positively associated with observed aggression,* severe aggression[c] and police call-outs.	
Greater crowding	*Sydney quantitative.* Crowding associated with aggression frequency and severity. *Surfers crowding.* High aggression clubs had higher levels of crowding indicators (for example, bumping)* than low aggression clubs, controlling for density (persons per square metre). *North Queensland.* Overall crowding and crowding around the bar associated with more physical and non-physical aggression. *Hoboken.* High crowding/difficulty moving associated with higher risk of aggression. *Buffalo.* Violent bars more crowded than non-violent bars.	*Vancouver.* Crowding was not significantly related to aggression. *Glasgow pub.* No clear relationship between crowding and crime/disorder.
More patron movement	*Vancouver.* Lots of table-hopping was positively associated with both physical and non-physical aggression *but high turnover was negatively associated with physical aggression.*	

Table 5.1 continues overleaf

Table 5.1 continued

Environmental variable	Evidence of increased risk	Evidence of no increased risk or reduced risk
	Surfers intervention. Movement/wandering about positively associated with non-physical *but not physical* aggression. *North Queensland.* Movement/wandering about positively associated with non-physical aggression.	*Hoboken.* Non-significant trend for aggression to be more likely in noisier bars.
Higher noise level	*Vancouver.* Higher noise level associated with more physical aggression. *Surfers intervention.* Loud voice levels *but not loud music* positively associated with physical and non-physical aggression. *North Queensland.* Loud music *but not loud voice level* positively associated with physical and non-physical aggression. *Buffalo.* Violent bars noisier* than non-violent bars.	
Crowding/movement/ noise level	*Toronto.* Noise level, crowding and amount of movement were highly correlated and combined into one scale. Scale[a] significantly related to frequency *but not severity* of patron aggression.	
Smokiness/poor ventilation/warm temperature	*Vancouver.* Poor ventilation associated with more physical and non-physical aggression. *Sydney quantitative.* Smokiness and poor ventilation were positively associated with aggression frequency and severity.	

Surfers intervention. Poor ventilation (which included warm temperature) and smoke level positively associated with non-physical and physical aggression. *North Queensland.* Poor ventilation (including warm temperature) *but not smoke level* positively associated with non-physical and physical aggression. *Buffalo.* Violent bars smokier, more poorly ventilated* and warmer* than non-violent bars. *Toronto.* Smokiness/poor ventilation[ab] associated with more frequent *but not more severe* aggression. Bars that were usually smoky/poorly ventilated tended to have more severe staff aggression[b]. *Hoboken.* Smokiness and hot room temperature associated with aggression.

Low comfort/ inadequate seating

Sydney qualitative. Aspects of the environment that reduced comfort including crowding, poor ventilation and inadequate seating associated with higher risk of aggression. *Sydney quantitative.* Inadequate seating associated with more frequent and severe aggression. *North Queensland.* Lower comfort associated with physical and non-physical aggression; improvement in overall comfort associated with reduced physical aggression and increased number of comfortable chairs with reduced non-physical aggression, controlling for other variables.

Table 5.1 continues overleaf

Table 5.1 continued

Environmental variable	Evidence of increased risk	Evidence of no increased risk or reduced risk
	Hoboken. Lower comfortableness associated with higher risk of aggression. **Surfers intervention.** Measures of comfort not significantly related to aggression.	
Inconvenient bar access	**Surfers intervention.** Inconvenient bar access associated with non-physical *but not physical* aggression.	**North Queensland.** Inconvenient bar access not significantly related to aggression.
Aversive stimuli scale/ ambience scale	**Hoboken.** Aversive stimuli scale* consisting of appearance of bar, comfort of bar, temperature, smokiness, crowding, ease of movement, clearing of tables, clearing of bar surfaces and cleanliness of bar associated with aggression. **Glasgow pub.** Ambience scale consisting of smokiness, ventilation, noise, movement, crowdedness used as one dimension to identify high risk pubs.[d]	**Glasgow club.** Unhealthy ambience scale not significantly related to observed or severe aggression or police call-outs in bivariate analyses, but related to police call-outs in multivariate analyses.

*Significant in a multivariate analysis.

[ab]Significant within and between bars in Hierarchical Linear Modeling (HLM) analyses; [a]significant within but not between bars; [b]significant between but not within bars.

[c]Results need to be interpreted with caution due to small number (5) of severe incidents.

[d]Pubs identified as high risk based on environmental risk factors were found to have more crimes documented by police and generally more severe observed incidents.

association could be due to increased numbers of potential targets available to motivated offenders and less capable guardianship due to the venue size (consistent with routine activity theory). However, the association could be partly artifactual, with more aggression occurring simply because there are more people present. That is, on a *per capita* basis, larger bars may not harbour more aggression than smaller establishments. Another potential explanation, consistent with the multivariate findings from the Toronto study, is that establishment size is indirectly associated with aggression through its impact on other factors, such as crowding and noise level, that may, in turn, increase the likelihood of provocation and irritants in the environment. Bar size/capacity has also been found to be associated with patrons being more intoxicated (Graham 1985), suggesting that size of establishment may have an indirect influence on aggression through reduced opportunities for servers to prevent patrons from becoming intoxicated.

Aspects of physical appearance, such as shabbiness, seating style and lighting, have been associated with aggression in some studies but not in others. The mixed findings suggest that these associations may be more related to the types of bars that have these characteristics and to the patrons who frequent them than to any specific effect of the characteristics themselves. The associations between seating layout and level of lighting may be particularly sensitive to time and place. For example, in the Vancouver study, nicer bars had lower level lighting while skid row bars were brightly (sometimes unpleasantly) lit. In other contexts (for example, Buffalo, Sydney), lower lighting levels may have concealed flaws in the establishment's upkeep while shielding a range of nefarious behaviours including drug dealing and violence. Two general conclusions might be drawn from these findings. First, the overall décor, maintenance and structural arrangements *do* contain messages about behavioural expectations, although these messages may, to some extent, be culturally specific. The second conclusion is that the social environment (permissiveness, intoxication) and staff and management practices may override lesser effects of décor and upkeep.

Unclean premises
The relationship between unclean premises and both physical and non-physical aggression was surprisingly consistent across the different studies. Because it is unlikely that a lack of cleanliness is a direct cause of aggression, one explanation for the relationship might be that aggressive individuals are more likely to patronise unclean/

messy establishments, as suggested by Roberts (1998). However, the Toronto study found a visit-level (that is, within bar) relationship between unclean/messy premises and aggression, suggesting that the relationship was unlikely to be due solely to the characteristics of the usual clientele. A second explanation is that unclean/messy premises are associated with other factors that more directly influence aggression, such as how busy the bar is. Again, however, the Toronto study demonstrated that unclean/messy premises were still associated with frequency of aggression both within and across bars even when crowding and number of people in the bar were controlled.

Therefore, a third, and probably the most likely explanation, is that unclean/messy environments are associated with generally permissive and poorly controlled environments. This is supported by multivariate analyses of both the Sydney and Toronto data in which the relationship between aggression and the extent to which premises were unclean and messy was no longer significant when permissiveness, intoxication and other factors in the social environment were controlled. Although the association between unclean premises and aggression may be purely an artifact of its relationship with social environmental factors related to aggression, it is also possible that cleanliness has an indirect influence on aggression. Specifically, cleanliness is one of the most visible signs of the behavioural expectations and level of permissiveness in an establishment – if the establishment is run down, spills are not cleaned up, empty bottles and ashtrays are not cleared away, toilets are filthy and other signs of sloppy care are evident; patrons are likely to feel that aggression will be tolerated, and this perception may influence how they react to provocation. A well-maintained environment, on the other hand, suggests a well-managed environment where misbehaviour is less likely to be tolerated.

This indirect relationship (mediated by expectations) between unclean premises and aggression is consistent with a study of expectations by Leather and Lawrence (1995), in which they examined the extent to which environmental cues influenced expectations about how likely aggression was to occur, how safe the environment was, and how effective the staff would be at handling disputes. In their experiment, participants were shown photographs of drinking establishments and given a brief vignette describing either physical or non-physical intervention by the manager in an incident of aggression. The photographs varied as to whether the interior environment was clean and orderly or dirty and messy, and whether the exterior environment had three door staff or no door staff. The study found that aggression was expected to occur more frequently when the interior environment was messy, when the photo showed the presence of door staff, and when landlords were described as using a physical intervention. There was also an interaction between the interior conditions (messy/orderly) and the intervention strategy of the landlord (physical *vs* non-physical). Pub environment and safety were rated most highly when an orderly environment was combined with non-physical intervention by the landlord, while non-physical intervention did not result in positive ratings if the establishment was messy.

High level of crowding, patron movement and noise
Overall, the results shown in Table 5.1 suggest a higher risk of aggression occurring in crowded, noisy establishments with lots of movement among patrons, although there were a few negative findings in specific studies, and some evidence that these factors are less important for severe aggression than for aggression generally. Crowding and patron movement probably affect aggression by increasing environmental precipitators in the form of provocation, frustration and irritants through associated bumping and shoving. This interpretation of crowding was supported by research comparing the effect of patron density (defined as the total number of patrons per square metre) versus crowding (defined as the rate of unintended low-level physical contacts between patrons) in three high-violence and three low-violence nightclubs with similar floor areas (Macintyre and Homel 1997) (drawn from the 18 clubs included in the Surfers Paradise intervention study). The results suggested that, for any given level of patron density, some venues exhibited higher levels of crowding than others, and the more crowded venues (as opposed to the more densely populated) tended to be the more violent. Moreover, as shown in Figure 5.1, violent incidents increased more rapidly with crowding in high-risk venues than they did in low-risk venues.

The Surfers Paradise crowding study found that crowding appeared to arise partly from inappropriate pedestrian flow patterns caused by poor location of entry and exit doors, dance floors, bars, and toilets. Figure 5.2 displays the main pedestrian vectors for each nightclub. It is clear that, overall, the low-risk clubs had fewer design-induced cross-flows – and hence fewer potential collision points – than the high-risk clubs. For example, Nightclub 1 (low-risk) had three major pedestrian cross-flows, whereas Nightclubs 15 and 16 (high-risk) had six.

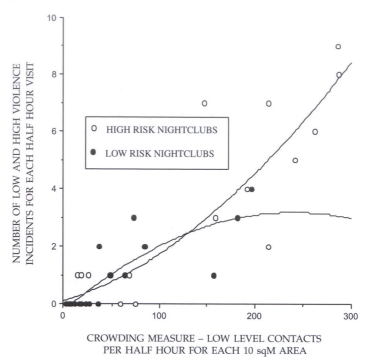

From Macintyre and Homel (1997: 108).
Reproduced with permission.

Figure 5.1 Relationship between violence and crowding in low- and high-risk venues

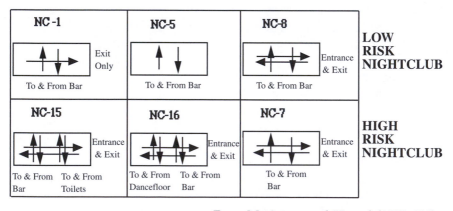

From Macintyre and Homel (1997: 104).
Reproduced with permission.

Figure 5.2 Main pedestrian vectors for each nightclub

The relationship between traffic flow and aggression is also illustrated in Figure 5.3, in which the Xs marked on the floor plan show the location of incidents of aggression observed across a number of different visits to one establishment in the Toronto study. As shown in this figure, incidents were concentrated around the pool tables, the dance floor and passageways – that is, high-risk areas were those where there was considerable movement and greater opportunities for precipitating events.

With regard to noise level, the association with aggression in drinking establishments is consistent with evidence from other sources showing a link between an adversely loud environment and aggression (for example, Donnerstein and Wilson 1976; Glass and Singer 1972; Konecni 1975) and may reflect the irritation effect of loud noise. However, inter-correlations among variables suggest that some of the relationship between high noise level and aggression may be due to noise level being correlated with other risk factors in the environment, such as crowding and patron movement, rather than an effect of noise *per se*.

Smokiness, poor ventilation, warm temperature

As with cleanliness, there is fairly consistent evidence that aggression is more likely in smoky, poorly ventilated premises. The two most plausible explanations for this relationship are (1) that poor ventilation along with a lack of cleanliness signals a poorly cared for and managed environment signalling a high level of permissiveness, or (2) that poor ventilation and uncomfortable temperature along with high noise level serve as irritants and make patrons more likely to respond aggressively.

Low comfort, inadequate seating and inconvenient bar access

Low comfort level was associated with aggression in several of the Australian studies and the Hoboken, New Jersey study, and improvements in comfort level were associated with reduced aggression in the North Queensland study. It is difficult to assess, however, whether the relationship with comfort relates to reduced irritation or possibly to the overall ambience of the establishment. Similarly, the relationship between aggression and inconvenient bar access could reflect discomfort in the form of precipitators such as frustration and bumping, but could also be spurious, reflecting the relationship between aggression and crowding.

Roberts' qualitative study of barroom aggression (1998: 104) aptly captures the synergies of poor physical design, crowding, lack of

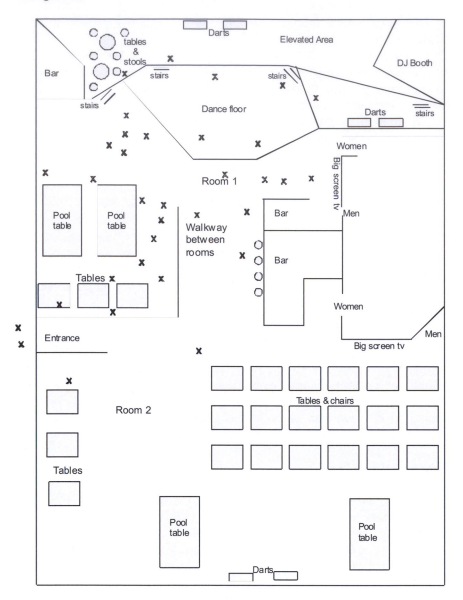

Figure 5.3 The floor plan of one drinking establishment in the Toronto study showing the location (marked with an X) of each incident observed over a number of visits to that establishment

comfort, dim lighting, heat and smoke in his description of New Jersey bars:

> The level of comfort within aggressive bars is low due to a number of factors. For one, these establishments have poor interior designs, with bathrooms, bar stations, and entrance/exits positioned so that areas of congestion emerge. The poor interior design of these bars also contributes to conflicting flows of traffic, which lead to confrontations among customers. These establishments generally have too many chairs, stools, and tables. These items are often positioned in areas where they come into contact with areas of congestion, such as dance floors. The overall lighting in these establishments is dimmer than average and strobe lights are used on the dance floor and stage as special effects. Aggressive bars are also smokier and hotter than most. The presence of lit cigarettes in areas of congestion is common. High temperatures in aggressive bars are directly related to overcrowding and congestion.

Roberts also noted the disorienting experience and difficulty judging distance from other patrons due to different coloured strobe lights flashing on and off repeatedly during the band's performance in two establishments. Significantly, he observed at least one incident of violence on each of these dance floors. He noted, in addition, that dance floors tended to be hotter than other parts of the bar, especially as the night wore on and overall temperatures increased, and he linked this rise in temperature to aggression. In the words of a male bartender:

> It may just be a coincidence, but the hottest area of the bar is on the dance floor and that's where most of the problems occur. I'm sure there's other factors that contribute to violence on the dance floor but when people are hot and sweaty they don't like to be mauled by other people, especially strangers. (Roberts 1998: 74)

In summary, aspects of the external features of a bar and its internal physical environment can be related in a variety of direct and indirect ways to an increased risk of aggression and violence. However, multivariate analyses completed in several studies suggest that many of these factors became non-significant when more powerful social environment variables are included in the models. In the next section, we describe evidence linking the social environment to aggression.

The social environment

Table 5.2 contains a summary of the findings relating to the social environment from the 13 studies that examined the association between the barroom environment and aggression. In the discussion of these findings, we again draw upon situational crime prevention theory and other theoretical approaches to help identify probable mechanisms for the associations.

Intoxication level of patrons, round buying, cheap drinks, drink specials

As shown in Table 5.2, overall level of intoxication of patrons was significantly related to both frequency and severity of aggression by patrons across all studies, and was associated with escalation of aggression in the Glasgow study. Moreover, a reduction in male intoxication in the North Queensland study was associated with a reduction in physical aggression in a multivariate analysis. Not only was intoxication consistently related to aggression across studies, variables likely to be associated with patrons becoming intoxicated (fast rate of drinking, round buying, cheap drinks, drink specials) were also significant. As described in Chapter 3, there are a number of ways that the effects of alcohol may increase the risk of aggression. That is, greater intoxication may be associated with increased aggression due to the effects of alcohol on people's thinking, emotions, and so on. In addition, patron intoxication may be characteristic of a highly permissive environment (for example, people being loud, raucous and staggering about due to intoxication). These results are consistent with other studies suggesting that both level of consumption by the individual drinker, as well as being in a licensed environment where intoxicated persons are served alcohol, independently contribute to aggression and harm (Graham, Osgood *et al.* 2006; Stockwell, Lang and Rydon 1993).

Permissiveness, rowdiness, swearing

Although intoxication is clearly an important predictor of aggression, the results from some of the studies in Table 5.2 suggest that permissive behavioural expectations, including tolerance for rowdiness and swearing, predict aggression even more strongly. This association is consistent with situational crime prevention theory, in that the situational message in highly permissive and rowdy environments is that bad behaviour, including aggression, will not be punished, will

Table 5.2 Evidence relating to the association between social aspects of the drinking environment and aggression (based on 13 studies of the drinking environment listed in Table 4.1)

Social environmental variable	Evidence of increased risk	Evidence of no increased risk or reduced risk
Greater intoxication/ round buying/cheap drinks	*Vancouver.* Higher level of intoxication and rate of drinking associated with more physical and non-physical aggression. *Sydney qualitative.* High level of intoxication of patrons characterised many violent occasions. Cheap drinks/drink specials were more frequent in aggressive establishments. *Sydney quantitative.* Faster drinking rate, buying rounds (males)* and level of drunkenness (males* and females) positively associated with aggression frequency and severity. *Surfers intervention.* Faster drinking rate, buying rounds and level of drunkenness positively associated with physical and non-physical aggression. *North Queensland.* Drunkenness *but not drinking rates* positively associated with physical and non-physical aggression. Buying rounds associated with greater risk of non-physical *but not physical* aggression. A reduction in male intoxication* associated with a reduction in physical aggression in multivariate analyses.	*Toronto.* Greater intoxication[a]* associated with <u>less</u> severe aggression by staff when other variables controlled.

Table 5.2 continues overleaf

Table 5.2 continued

Social environmental variable	Evidence of increased risk	Evidence of no increased risk or reduced risk
	Buffalo study. Violent bars had lower cost drinks than non-violent bars.	
	Hoboken. Drinking in rounds and drink specials associated with aggression.	
	Toronto. Higher level of intoxication[ab] associated with more frequent and severe patron aggression, but significant only at bar level* in multivariate analyses.	
	Glasgow pub. Greater intoxication associated with escalation of aggression.	
	Glasgow club. A higher percentage of drunk patrons associated with more observed* and severe[c] aggression and police call-outs.	
Higher level of permissiveness/ rowdiness/swearing	*Vancouver.* Overall decorum and swearing associated with more physical and non-physical aggression.	
	Sydney quantitative. Rowdiness by males (*but not females*) and swearing positively associated with aggression frequency and severity.	
	Surfers intervention. Lower decorum expectations positively associated with non-physical aggression. Greater rowdiness and swearing positively associated with non-physical and physical aggression.	

Surfers nightclub crowding study. Greater rowdiness positively associated with physical aggression.

North Queensland. Lower decorum expectations positively associated with physical (*but not non-physical*) aggression. Greater rowdiness and swearing positively associated with physical and non-physical aggression. Reduction in male swearing* associated with a reduction in non-physical aggression in multivariate analysis.

Toronto. Combined measure of permissive behavioural expectations (for example, presence of swearing, open sexual contact, etc.) and rowdiness (shouting, horseplay) associated with more frequent[ab]* and severe[a]* aggression by both patrons and staff.

Sexual activity or contact/sexual competition

Vancouver. Sexual contact associated with more physical and non-physical aggression.

Sydney quantitative. Sexual activity and discreet necking (by males* *but not females*) and sexual competition positively associated with aggression frequency and severity.

Surfers intervention. Heavy necking/touching positively associated with physical aggression, overt fondling and sexual competition associated with non-physical and physical aggression.

Table 5.2 continues overleaf

Table 5.2 continued

Social environmental variable	Evidence of increased risk	Evidence of no increased risk or reduced risk
	North Queensland. Heavy necking/touching and overt fondling* positively associated with non-physical and physical aggression. *Extent of sexual competition not associated with aggression.* *Toronto*. Combined variable including sexual activity, sexual contact and sexual competition associated with more frequent[a]* and severe[a] aggression. *Glasgow pub*. Sexual tension scale ('pulling', sexual activity, female harassment) used as one dimension to identify high risk pubs.[d] *Glasgow club*. Higher scores on sexual tension scale associated with more observed aggression and police call-outs.	
Illegal activities/drugs being used or sold/ prostitution	*Vancouver*. Drugs being used or sold associated positively with physical aggression. Solicitation for prostitution positively associated with physical and non-physical aggression. *Sydney quantitative*. Drug dealing positively associated with aggression frequency and severity. *North Queensland*. Marijuana use positively associated with non-physical aggression, *but drug dealing on the premises not associated with aggression.*	*Glasgow club*. Percentage of patrons on drugs not significant for observed aggression or police call-outs in bivariate analyses, <u>negatively associated</u> with observed aggression in multivariate analyses.

Hostile vs. friendly atmosphere	*Buffalo.* Violent bars significantly more likely to have illegal activities* than non-violent bars.
	Vancouver. Tense/hostile atmosphere and hostile talk positively associated with physical and non-physical aggression. *Openness to strangers positively associated with non-physical aggression.*
	Sydney quantitative. The presence of hostile males (*but not females*) positively associated with aggression frequency and severity.
	Surfers intervention, North Queensland. Patron hostility positively associated with physical and non-physical aggression.
	Surfers crowding. Patron hostility positively associated with physical aggression.
	Surfers intervention, North Queensland. Cheerfulness, friendliness and boredom not significantly related to aggression.
Bored patrons	*Sydney qualitative.* Aggression positively associated with bored patrons and poor quality entertainment.
	Sydney quantitative. Patron boredom positively associated with aggression frequency and severity.
	Surfers intervention. Boredom not significantly related to aggression.
Aggravation scale	*Glasgow pub.* 'Aggravation scale' of rowdiness, drunkenness, pub decorum, hostility used as one dimension to identify high-risk pubs.[d]
	Glasgow club. Higher scores on aggravation scale associated with more observed and severe[e]* incidents and police call-outs.*

Table 5.2 continues overleaf

Table 5.2 continued

Social environmental variable	Evidence of increased risk	Evidence of no increased risk or reduced risk
Pool playing/billiards/ other activities/games	*Vancouver.* Pool playing positively associated with non-physical aggression but *not significant for physical aggression.* *England.* 20 per cent of violent incidents described by pub managers identified as related to pool tables. *Buffalo.* Violent bars more likely than non-violent bars to have billiards.* *Toronto.* Pool tables in use positively associated with occurrence of aggression *but not to aggression frequency or severity.*	*Sydney quantitative, Surfers and North Queensland intervention studies.* No aspects of entertainment, games, activities or types of music were significantly related to aggression. *Hoboken.* Pool tables/playing, sports programs, non-sports programs, dart boards, card machines, video machines, other entertainment not significantly related to aggression.
Dancing	*Vancouver.* Dancing positively associated with physical aggression but *not significant for non-physical aggression.* *Buffalo.* Violent bars more likely than non-violent bars to have dancing. *Toronto.* Dancing positively associated with. aggression frequency *but not severity; not significant in multivariate.* *Hoboken.* Dancing associated with aggression.	*Sydney quantitative, Surfers and North Queensland intervention studies.* Dancing not significantly related to aggression.

| Availability of meals/snacks | *Sydney qualitative.* Premises known for violence had limited food available; non-violent premises had full meals available.

Sydney quantitative. Lack of food available positively associated with aggression frequency and severity. | *Vancouver, Surfers intervention.* Availability of food not significantly related to aggression.

North Queensland. The absence of full meals associated with non-physical aggression but may be Type I error since 30 food-related correlations were tested.

Hoboken. Availability of food generally, free nibbles, small snacks to buy, appetizers, full menu, tap water, bottled water or sports drinks not significantly related to aggression. |

*Significant in a multivariate analysis.

[ab]Significant within and between bars in Hierarchical Linear Modeling (HLM) analyses; [a]significant within but not between bars; [b]significant between but not within bars.

[c]Results need to be interpreted with caution due to small number (5) of severe incidents.

[d]Pubs identified as high risk based on environmental risk factors were found to have more crimes documented by police and generally more severe observed incidents.

probably be excused, and may even be rewarded. The permissive environment also incorporates many of the precipitators identified by Wortley (2001: 66), including provocations, social pressures, triggers to offend, and high acceptability of aggressive and harmful behaviours. As well as setting up behavioural norms, cues and expectations for patrons generally, rowdy behaviour may also increase the risk of aggression through direct provocation. For example, rowdiness and rough-housing may reflect low-level aggression and, even if not originally intended as aggression, can serve to provoke aggression from others (Hadfield 2006; Roberts 1998). The importance of these factors as precipitators is strongly suggested by their relationship in a number of studies not only with frequency of aggression but also with severity of aggression (Forsyth *et al.* 2005; Graham *et al.* 1980; Graham, Bernards *et al.* 2006; Homel and Clark 1994) where possible confounding with low-level aggression is ruled out.

Sexual activity, sexual competition

As we have described in previous chapters, making sexual overtures involves ambiguity and risk; therefore, it is not surprising that sexual activity and sexual competition are consistently correlated with frequency of aggression, as is evident in Table 5.2. A highly sexualised atmosphere has implications for aggression toward staff as well as patrons. In previous years, sexual harassment, primarily of female staff by male patrons, was considered part of the job (Spradley and Mann 1975). This atmosphere of sexism persists in many contemporary drinking establishments (Grazian 2008) despite greater awareness of sexual harassment and violence against women and greater equality for women in society at large. A sexist atmosphere can be encouraged by such practices as the employment of 'shooter girls' wearing skimpy outfits – that is, female servers who circulate selling 'shooters' (straight shots, often of some sweet liquor) from a tray (similar to 'cigarette girls' in bygone days). The incident in Box 5.1 provides an example of blatant harassment involving unwanted physical contact (touching and holding a female member of staff), thereby creating an environment suggesting that sexual harassment and aggression will be tolerated and excused, especially if the perpetrator is drunk.

Illegal activities, drug use and dealing, prostitution

The story of Danny and Mark who were beaten in a Sydney hotel (presented at the beginning of Chapter 1) reinforces the popular perception of an association between violence and drug dealing in

Box 5.1 Physical harassment of shooter girl
(Toronto)

> Just after closing, a 'shooter girl' walked between two male
> patrons. One of the men who was clearly intoxicated (staggering,
> droopy eyes) put his hand affectionately on her stomach. The
> shooter girl kept walking to the bar computer and began typing
> in her order. The man followed her, keeping his hands on her,
> touching her stomach and back (which were exposed as she
> was wearing a small revealing shirt). She pushed him away
> appearing mildly annoyed. The bartender who was nearby did
> not react at all. The second man tried to get his friend to leave
> but the man continued to pester the shooter girl, asking her for a
> hug. Eventually she gave him a patronizing one-armed hug and
> rolled her eyes. She had a smile on her face but looked annoyed
> and made it obvious to onlookers that she was annoyed.

licensed premises. This perception was substantiated by most of the
observational research described in Table 5.2. Violence and illegal
activities in drinking establishments might be linked for a number
of reasons:

1 The types of patrons who frequent premises where illegal
  activities take place may be more willing than others to engage in
  violence.
2 Violence may arise out of the actual commercial transactions
  related to drugs or other illegal trade.
3 Illegal activities on the premises may contribute to a permissive
  environment.
4 There may be an association between drug dealing and control of
  the premises by organised crime (as found by Hobbs, Hadfield,
  Lister and Winlow 2003).

It is impossible to know which of these possibilities accounts for the
association between drug use and aggression based on correlational
data alone. Nevertheless, the presence of illegal activities, as with
general permissiveness, is minimally a signal of lax controls on
behaviour and possibly an indicator of the presence of organised and
violent criminal elements.

  The evidence for drug taking, *per se*, as a risk factor for aggression
is less clear. Forsyth (2006) found that the proportion of patrons who
were on drugs was *negatively* associated with observed aggression

when other variables were controlled in multivariate analyses. This may mean that drug use is less important than other more powerful predictive factors. However, another interpretation relates to the nature of drugs used in some types of contemporary clubs. As noted in Chapter 3, anecdotal evidence from the Toronto study suggested that clubs where patrons were primarily using ecstasy were less violent than other clubs; however, this hypothesis could not be adequately tested in quantitative analyses due to the small number of visits to ecstasy clubs. Interviewees in the Glasgow club study also expressed the view that ecstasy users were less likely to be violent than were alcohol users. Thus, the importance of drug use and drug dealing in the occurrence of aggression may depend on the type of drug, the type of patrons and the general context.

Hostile vs. friendly atmosphere, bored patrons
It is clear from the results in Table 5.2 that aggression is positively associated with the level of hostility of patrons and negatively with a friendly relaxed atmosphere. The following comments by one of the observers in the Glasgow club study (Forsyth 2006: 30) about one of the most violent clubs nicely captures the impact of the hostile environment (combined with a high level of permissiveness and intoxication):

> People were rough and would have kicked your head in if you looked at them the wrong way. Like being back at school disco. Lots of random snogging, rave dancing, people passed out, gurning, chants of 'here we here we here we fuckin' go'. Lots of pushing, horseplay, spilled drinks. Very tense atmosphere. Lots of stewards [security staff], people constantly being asked to leave. Dancefloor dangerous with brawls, fights and moshing. (Female Observer Team A)

The extent to which observed findings reflect the predispositions of patrons as opposed to controllable aspects of the environment cannot be determined from existing correlational data. While certainly there are establishments patronised by highly aggressive people or subcultures, the Vancouver study also found that frequency and severity of aggression varied among different establishments frequented by the *same* skid row patrons. Other factors relating to patron demeanour such as patron mood and boredom showed no consistent pattern, possibly because these are difficult constructs to measure in many settings.

Activities and entertainment

Pool playing and dancing were associated with an increased risk of aggression in some but not all studies. While fights related to pool playing (for example, aggressive interactions between players such as in the argument described in Box 3.3, arguments about whose turn it is to have the pool table, passers-by bumping pool players) may account for this relationship when it does occur, other explanations are needed to account for the inconsistency in findings across studies. For example, in some countries, pool tables may attract patrons who are more willing to become aggressive, while this may not be the case in other countries.

Dancing has been found to be associated with aggression across a number of studies in the US and Canada but not in Australia. There are several plausible mechanisms for the link between dancing and aggression, including specific irritants such as unintentional bumping on the dance floor or excessive heat. The association of aggression with dancing could also be related to a style of dancing involving *intentional* bumping (that is, moshing), which was identified as a trigger for aggression in the London, Ontario study as well as in the Glasgow club study (an incident where moshing led to a brawl in a Glasgow club was described in Box 2.3 in Chapter 2). Alternatively, as discussed in Chapter 4, at least some of the relationship between dancing and aggression might be due to the sexual overtures and competition that arise on the dance floor. However, these explanations account for the relationship between dancing and aggression when it is found, but do not explain why the relationship is found in some countries but not others.

Generally, no consistent relationships were found between aggression and other types of entertainment, games, activities or music. However, quantitative methods may not be very effective in capturing the subtle aspects of the influence of entertainment. For example, in a qualitative study of New Jersey bars, Roberts (1998: 82) concluded that entertainment could have quite marked effects on levels of violence, as described by one lead singer:

> We could definitely contribute to violence in the bar. For example, years ago, when many of these bars would allow moshing (that is, aggressive dancing, pushing, shoving) to occur, I used to group songs together that I knew would incite fights and incidents of aggression. Now, I have to play a couple of mellow songs between heavier songs so that people don't get so riled up … Two weeks ago we played up in North Jersey at a

real dive. The place was really packed. Right before we started the second set I turned to one of the guys in the band and said, 'Watch this, I'm going to bring these people over the edge'. We had to stop playing for ten minutes while the bouncing staff tried to clear people who were fighting out of the bar. (Male Lead Singer, Band X)

DJs interviewed by Roberts (1998) were just as frank as this band member in describing how they could manipulate the mood to influence level of aggression, consistent with the impact of DJs described in ethnographic research by Hadfield (2006: 99) in the UK. Other types of entertainment may also incite or encourage aggression (Forsyth 2008), and, in some settings, the entertainment itself involves aggression. For example, in the incident described in Box 5.2, the drag queen engaged in sexual aggression presumably for the purpose of entertaining the crowd and raising the level of excitement and edginess. What is most revealing about this incident is that, because a club employee perpetrated it, the incident reflects both sanctioned sexual aggression against women as well as exactly the sort of behaviour that fosters a highly permissive atmosphere.

Box 5.2   Assault by a drag queen
(Toronto)

During the show, one of the drag dancers grabbed the hand of a woman in the audience and stuck it up his dress against his crotch. The drag dancer moved the woman's hand up and down for about 30 seconds while the woman looked traumatized and kept trying to pull away. After the drag dancer moved away, the woman looked upset by the clearly unwanted action. Later, the same drag dancer stopped in front of another woman and stared at her. The drag dancer got the woman to dance seductively with him. He then grabbed the woman by the neck and forced her down onto her knees by pushing on her neck and shoulders. He held her in place for a while and then grabbed her by the ears and shoved her face into his crotch. This went on for 10 seconds, with the woman resisting but unable to leave his grip. When the dancer finally let her go, her face was red. Although it appeared that she did not like the treatment, she continued to watch the show. The observers noted that this sort of behaviour seemed to be a normal part of the show, and that patrons might expect to be abused by the performers.

In summary, entertainment and recreational activities in drinking establishments are complex and diverse phenomena, and a greater understanding of their contribution to both situational encouragement and situational precipitators of aggression is needed. Some clues for better understanding the link between activities and aggression within any individual setting might be obtained by mapping if possible the precise locations within the establishment of incidents of aggression and tracking the triggers, using charts like that depicted in Figure 5.3 as a starting point.

Availability of meals
Availability of food could potentially reduce risk of aggression by defining the establishment as being about food as well as drinking, and by encouraging consumption of food to slow the rate of absorption of alcohol into the blood and decrease the risk of intoxication. However, the evidence is mixed regarding whether the availability of food is associated with a reduced risk of aggression. One possible explanation for the lack of consistent findings is that availability of food does not necessarily mean that people are consuming full meals. Indeed, in the account of a big night at a suburban hotel in Sydney in Box 2.5, it was noted that 'the one female bar attendant responsible for selling hot food was reading a novel ...'. Most research in drinking establishments has found that food consumption (especially meals) is rare even when fully available. Thus, the availability of food may not be a promising direction for reducing bar violence if patrons are generally uninterested in eating during the highest risk periods.

Applying knowledge of environmental risk to prevention

The results in Tables 5.1 and 5.2 show considerable consistency of environmental risk factors based on systematic objective research across English-speaking countries. Thus, they provide a template for comprehensive and systematic approaches to risk reduction that are firmly grounded in a thorough examination of empirical realities.

Situational crime prevention and routine activity theories, described in Chapter 2, are particularly relevant in the interpretation of the relationship between environmental factors and aggression in drinking establishments. Accordingly, for almost every environmental risk factor, it was possible to hypothesise the mechanism for the link and draw on situational regulators (for example, tacit rewards for aggression), situational precipitators (for example, frustration, provocation, cues or triggers) or routine activity theory (for example, opportunities for guardianship). As we describe in Chapter 6, these same theories are also highly relevant to the role of bar and security staff – who comprise one of the key aspects of the bar environment.

In terms of prevention related to the physical environment, the outside of the building, signage, other aspects of the exterior décor, and the experience of patrons as they enter the establishment signal the kind of customers that the establishment hopes to attract and the kinds of behaviour expected. For example, the presence of cues related to aggression, such as broken glass and aggressive door staff, not only communicates expected behaviour but may also attract patrons who are actively seeking aggressive environments. Changes to the exterior can incorporate situational crime prevention strategies to increase perceptions by potential aggressors that aggression will not be tolerated, excused or rewarded and reduce situational precipitators such as visual cues for aggression. Thus, addressing the external environment could be useful in reducing patronage by motivated offenders and setting standards of behaviour that reduce the likelihood of aggression.

Queues were associated with aggression in several studies, indicating a need for this aspect of the bar setting to be managed fairly and non-aggressively by staff, including preventing entry into the establishment of persons who cause problems in the line. The presence of people hanging around outside after closing was strongly associated with aggression. Solutions to these kinds of problems may involve strategies such as increasing the responsibility for staff to manage the area surrounding the establishment, regulation of movement between bars, appropriate transportation, police presence, and possibly better lighting and the introduction of closed circuit television cameras. People hanging around at closing tends to be mainly a problem in areas where establishments are clustered, such as entertainment districts in the city core. The finding from the Toronto study of higher risk for aggression in suburban drinking establishments, however, is an important reminder that prevention and regulatory policies need to focus on all licensed premises and not just on those bunched together in entertainment districts. These findings also suggest that the high visibility of entertainment areas as problem locations may be partly related to the concentration of large venues in those areas, rather than to specific risks of the establishments themselves (an issue discussed further in Chapter 7).

There is some evidence that there is an increased risk of aggression in larger drinking establishments. However, multivariate analyses (Graham, Bernards *et al.* 2006) of environmental risk factors suggest that the relationship between size of establishment and aggression are likely to be reduced or eliminated by increasing guardianship, introducing serving practices that do not allow mass intoxication, instituting management practices that promote the message that aggression will not be tolerated or excused, and modifying the establishment's physical design to alter traffic flow, activities and entertainment in ways that reduce frustration and provocation.

Findings related to the link between aggression and décor and other stylistic aspects appeared to be somewhat idiosyncratic, related to time and place of the particular establishment. However, there is a clear and consistent relationship between aggression and other aspects of the environment such as cleanliness, ventilation and temperature. Operating a clean, well-maintained and orderly establishment is likely to set high expectations for behaviour among patrons. Because there is consistent evidence from criminological research of the role of temperature as a factor in its own right contributing to violence and crime (for example, Anderson 1989; Fields 1992), it is reasonable to conclude that improving temperature and air quality might independently contribute to lowering the risk of aggression beyond the role of these factors in influencing expectations. In terms of the greatest impact on prevention, cleanliness, temperature and air quality could be addressed not only at the level of the individual establishment but also through health and safety regulations, in the same way that smoking bans were introduced.

The overall conclusion from the research is that crowding and movement are likely to result in irritants and provocation (bumping, spilled drinks) that could lead to aggression, even though not all studies found that crowding was significantly associated with aggression. Therefore, using the layout of the establishment to ensure easy traffic flow is an important strategy for reducing environmental precipitators of aggression, and increasing the monitoring of high congestion areas may also be useful for decreasing the risk of escalation from low-level bumping.

The research summarised in Table 5.2 identified key aspects of the social environment associated with aggression. Intoxication of patrons was shown to be an important risk factor and, as we describe in Chapter 8, controlling intoxication has long been the target of interventions in licensed premises. Responsible beverage service training programs to teach staff how to recognise intoxication and refuse service to intoxicated persons are widely available but have shown only modest and inconsistent effectiveness, with at least some research suggesting that training needs to be backed by laws and enforcement in order to have a sustained effect on reducing serving to intoxication (see Graham 2000).

There are at least three considerations that may limit measures to reduce intoxication: (1) becoming at least mildly intoxicated is part of the reason for drinking among some patrons; (2) owners and staff may have concerns that refusing service will be inhospitable and may reduce profits; (3) increasingly, people are 'pre-drinking' or 'pre-gaming' before going out to drinking establishments, especially nightclubs (Forsyth 2006; Grazian 2008; Hughes *et al.* 2007). Consequently, it is unlikely that intoxication will be fully eliminated from drinking establishments; however, as discussed in Chapter 8, a combination of training, enforcement, legal liability and other strategies may be able to eliminate the worst instances of this (for example, the mass intoxication associated with 11c drinks at the suburban Sydney hotel described in Box 2.5).

Not only is it unlikely that intoxication will be eliminated from drinking establishments, it is also unlikely that eliminating intoxication will eliminate all bar violence. Therefore, a realistic approach to preventing bar violence would not focus solely on serving practices. As described in other chapters in this book, there are multiple contributing factors to violence in drinking establishments, including the social functions of drinking establishments, the characteristics and lifestyles of patrons, the physical and social environment and the skills and behaviour of staff. Nevertheless, preventing *mass* intoxication and managing intoxicated individuals remains one of the key aspects of preventing violence in drinking establishments. In addition, implementation of situational crime prevention strategies, such as not allowing intoxication as an excuse for bad behaviour, may help to diminish the contribution of intoxication to aggression even when intoxication occurs.

As with intoxication, a permissive environment is one of the attractions of drinking establishments. Thus, it is necessary to balance the pleasures of the time-out experience with setting boundaries sufficient to prevent aggression. Changing the balance by reducing permissiveness can also be a good business decision, in that many of the really violent establishments identified across several research studies were neither popular nor necessarily profitable. The same balance of boundaries and permissiveness can be applied to sexual activities, games and entertainment and other social aspects of the drinking establishment. That the time-out experience sought by patrons of licensed drinking establishments occurs in a regulated environment with staff who can serve as guardians of safety is actually an advantage of licensed premises over other drinking settings such as the home or street.

Some considerations for environmental approaches to prevention

It needs to be recognised that sometimes strategies can backfire despite strong theoretical justification. The availability of breathalysers for self-testing level of intoxication is an example of an environmental change that backfired. Although intended to help patrons avoid intoxication, the presence of breathalysers actually seemed to produce the opposite effect on intoxication and ultimately on aggression – that is, the availability of breathalysers for self-testing was associated with an *increased* risk of physical and non-physical aggression in the Sydney quantitative study and the North Queensland study. This suggests that the opportunity of self-testing one's blood-alcohol level was more likely to serve as an incentive to obtain higher levels of intoxication (for example, demonstrating who in a group can get the drunkest) than as an aide to self-control, as was presumably intended when the machines were made available. In recent years, however, some Australian establishments have tried to avoid this unwanted outcome by capping the reading that self-testing devices can give at 0.10, a high enough limit to warn serious patrons that they are well over the limit for driving, but not high enough to encourage drinking competitions.

In his research on prisons, Wortley (2003) described the concepts of hard and soft prevention, with soft prevention designed to 'normalise' prisons and hard prevention involving strict security and a highly restricted lifestyle. He noted the need to balance hard and soft prevention and suggested that failures of control, such as prison riots, have occurred both because rules are too strict and because they are too lax. Thus, it is possible that 'hard' procedures such as machine and hand searches for weapons at the entrance to a bar (depicted in Figure 5.4) will actually increase rather than reduce the risk of violence, by increasing expectations of violence, by frustrating patrons, or by setting a challenge to overcome, as occurred with breathalysers.

Given these and other concerns about how best to apply environmental techniques to preventing aggression in drinking establishments, some methodological issues with regard to the current state of knowledge and directions for research in this area are

Photo by John Dale Purcell

Figure 5.4 Entry checks for weapons in a Toronto club

worth considering. For example, the Buffalo research found gender differences in environmental risk factors. As noted in Table 4.1, the Buffalo research data were collected using different procedures from most of the other studies. Specifically, survey respondents were asked to rate various characteristics of establishments where they had either observed or experienced aggression. This method allowed assessment of the relationship between aggression and both person and bar characteristics. Those who reported being aggressive in a bar were asked to rate the severity of the most serious act that he or she had perpetuated. The Buffalo research found that the severity of male respondents' aggression was positively related to higher ratings on risk factors in the physical environment (smokiness, ventilation, crowdedness, cleanliness, lighting, noise, temperature) (Leonard, Collins and Quigley 2003), but the opposite was true for female respondents (Collins *et al.* 2007: 310). That is, 'bars that were darker, warmer, dirtier, and more crowded were associated with less severe physical aggression by the [female] respondent.' It is difficult to know how to interpret this anomalous finding, but it has some implications for future research. Specifically, research needs to pay greater attention both to the type and severity of aggression, including the characteristics and behaviour of those involved in the aggressive incident. If some of the risks for severe female aggression are different from those for severe male aggression, this not only tells us that there are limits on the generalisability of risk factors but it may also help to further identify probable causal mechanisms for environmental influences and prevention techniques.

Although the cross-national validation of many risk factors suggests that relationships are reliable across time and several cultures, a problem with existing research is that all of the risk factors were identified using correlational rather than causal designs. Nevertheless, some of the studies were better able than others to isolate specific environmental factors and provide stronger evidence regarding their contributing role to aggression. For example, the Surfers Paradise nightclub crowding study (Macintyre and Homel 1997) was able to discriminate between the relationships of aggression to density of patron per square metre versus its relationship with crowding as a subjective experience. The North Queensland study, on the basis of a multivariate analysis of factors pre- and post-intervention, identified a small number of environmental factors that appeared to be related to a *reduction* in aggression over time, as opposed to level of aggression. These findings provide useful directions for future research that can manipulate these variables using an experimental design.

The Toronto study included several important innovations in methodology that pointed to specific mechanisms while ruling out others. First, using hierarchical modelling allowed separation of within-bar relationships from between-bar relationships. Thus, the finding that aggression was more frequent and more severe on nights when the atmosphere was more permissive (controlling for bar-level associations between aggression and permissiveness) meant that the association could not be attributed to some stable bar characteristics, such as the type of patrons who usually frequented the establishment. A second innovation was the careful systematic documentation of aggressive incidents. This refinement in measurement made it possible to distinguish environmental factors associated with frequency of aggression from those associated with severity of patron aggression and severity of staff aggression.

The qualitative research (Graham and Wells 2003) done in conjunction with the London, Ontario study led to a better understanding of the rationale for certain behaviours among young males. Similarly, Forsyth's Glasgow club study supplemented observations with patron interviews that provided important data for interpreting and clarifying findings from the observational research.

Although it may be difficult to conduct controlled experimental studies of environmental influences of aggression in drinking establishments to provide conclusive evidence of the causal role of environmental factors, the use of innovative techniques and designs, the combination of different methodologies and cross-national validation has led to a firm foundation of knowledge in this area, despite the relatively small number of studies. Strategic research and evaluation studies are needed now to test empirically the impact on aggression of *specific types of changes* in the environment.

Chapter 6

Staff: redefining their role as guardians, not guards or enforcers

Our study of prison life began, then, with an average group of healthy, intelligent, middle-class males. These boys were arbitrarily divided into two groups by a flip of the coin. Half were randomly assigned to be guards, the other to be prisoners. It is important to remember that at the beginning of our experiment there were no differences between boys assigned to be a prisoner and boys assigned to be a guard....

There were three types of guards. First, there were tough but fair guards who followed prison rules. Second, there were 'good guys' who did little favors for the prisoners and never punished them. And finally, about a third of the guards were hostile, arbitrary, and inventive in their forms of prisoner humiliation. These guards appeared to thoroughly enjoy the power they wielded, yet none of our preliminary personality tests were able to predict this behavior....

I ended the study prematurely for two reasons. First, we had learned through videotapes that the guards were escalating their abuse of prisoners in the middle of the night when they thought no researchers were watching and the experiment was 'off'. Their boredom had driven them to ever more pornographic and degrading abuse of the prisoners.

Second, Christina Maslach, a recent Stanford Ph.D. brought in to conduct interviews with the guards and prisoners, strongly objected when she saw our prisoners being marched on a toilet run, bags over their heads, legs chained together, hands on each other's shoulders. Filled with outrage, she said, 'It's terrible what you are doing to these boys!' Out of 50 or more outsiders who had seen our prison, she was the only one who ever questioned its morality. Once she countered the

> *power of the situation, however, it became clear that the study should*
> *be ended.*
>
> *And so, after only six days, our planned two-week prison simulation*
> *was called off.*
>
> (quoted from: http://www.prisonexp.org/; see also *The Lucifer*
> *Effect. Understanding How Good People Turn Evil*, Random House,
> 2007)

In 1971, Phillip Zimbardo, a Professor at Stanford, conducted
an experiment that showed the immense power of situational
determinants and group processes on behaviour. As described above,
the situation turned some ordinary young men into cowed prisoners
and cruel prison guards, and the study had to be ended prematurely
due to its profound negative effects. The point of the quote as an
introduction to the chapter on bar staff is not to compare bar staff to
prison guards, although for some security staff the comparison is apt.
Rather, the point is to draw attention to the importance of situational
demands on behaviour. That is, much of behaviour has to do with
how the situation is structured and defined, which is one reason why
we draw on the principles of situational crime prevention throughout
this book. Situational structures have important implications for how
staff behave and for preventing bar violence.

In previous chapters, we have described how the drinking
environment and the characteristics of those who go out drinking,
along with the effects of alcohol, contribute to an increased risk of
aggression. In the present chapter, we focus on the role of staff and
how their behaviour is both determined by the environment and
affects the environment. Our analysis is not limited to security staff
(also called door staff, crowd controllers, stewards and bouncers),
but this role is the major focus of this chapter given the increasing
importance of security staff in many contemporary drinking
establishments.

The relationship between staff practices and violence and the move toward club empires with highly specialised and gendered staff roles

The role of bar staff in the occurrence of aggression and violence
has received increasing attention in recent years, primarily from
researchers in the UK (Hobbs *et al.* 2002, 2003, 2007; Lister *et al.* 2000,
2001; Monaghan 2002, 2003, 2004; Winlow 2001; Winlow *et al.* 2001)

but also in other parts of the world (Graham *et al.* 2004; Homel and Tomsen 1991; Rigakos 2004; Tomsen 2005; Wells *et al.* 1998). However, most early research on bars, clubs and pubs did not address the role of staff in bar violence or included this topic only in passing. Even research that included discussion of violence, such as Cavan's (1966) research identifying 'normal trouble' (discussed in Chapter 2) and Dyck's (1980) study of barroom violence in Canada (1980), paid very little attention to the role of bar staff in preventing, managing or even causing violence. Although there has been some research focused specifically on staff of drinking establishments (for example, Spradley and Mann's 1975 anthropological study of the cocktail waitress), the emphasis of this research has been on social roles, especially gender roles, among staff and between staff and customers. Thus, even research specifically about bar staff has provided few insights into the role of staff in preventing or managing problem behaviour, other than noting that part of the job of female staff was to tolerate or even encourage sexual harassment by both male customers and staff (Reobuck and Frese 1976; Spradley and Mann 1975). We have found only one early reference to bar staff and violence in Clark's (1981) review, in which he quoted a 1939 study of London pubs (Ardizzone and Gorham 1939: 440) describing 'dominating barmaids who could quell a riot with a look'. Clark also noted that one role of staff at an after-hours club (Roebuck and Frese 1976) was to screen customers to keep out troublemakers.

By the 1980s and 1990s, however, research began to focus more on the role of staff in bar violence (Felson *et al.* 1986; Graves *et al.* 1981), including violence *by* staff (Graham *et al.* 1980; Homel and Tomsen 1991; Homel, Tomsen and Thommeny 1992; Marsh and Kibby 1992; Wells, Graham and West 1998). For example, as noted by Marsh and Kibby (1992: 54), while managers and security staff maintained that they used non-violent approaches – 'We try to stop all the trouble at the door. Fighting is not our method of making people leave … If any door staff are reported to do anything wrong they are sacked immediately …' – a different picture emerged in interviews with customers from the same area:

The video cameras are in the wrong position to show the doormen taking people out of the back door and kicking shit out of them. I won't go back to the P__ P __. OK, I was drunk and deserved to be thrown out, but I wasn't being violent or anything – I just couldn't stand up very well. I was sick on the steps and it went over the bouncer's shoe. I just couldn't help it. He banged me all around the face and then dislocated three of my fingers by bending them backwards. (Marsh and Kibby 1992: 54)

As the potential for gratuitous violence among door staff became recognised, various jurisdictions made attempts to license and regulate this job (for example, Sabic *et al.* 2005; Prenzler and Hayes 1998; Stockwell 1994). However, as we describe in more detail in other parts of this chapter, violence seems to be intrinsic to the role, especially to the way security is operationalised in twenty-first century club settings (Tomsen 2005). For example, Rigakos (2004) interviewed 52 security staff and 189 police officers in Halifax, Canada, and found that security staff were significantly more likely than police officers to report experiencing physical violence in the year prior to the survey:

There is routine violence in a nightclub. We witnessed this throughout the research. Bouncers are violent because this is their prescribed role. They have this to sell. They are experienced pugilists and are trained in talking down and taking down aggressive patrons. (Rigarkos 2004: 59)

Similarly, Maguire and Nettleton (2003), in their intervention study of violence in licensed premises in Cardiff, Wales, found that staff were involved in 34 per cent of violent incidents taking place inside pubs or clubs, and, of these, 70 per cent involved allegations of assaults by door staff.

In addition to recognition of bar staff as agents of violence and not just as referees in customer conflicts, recent research has focused on the changing nature of drinking establishments and the increasing specialisation of staff roles. In much of the English-speaking world, drinking establishments have changed from the small family-run pubs operating out of part of the family's home in the early modern times of Europe (Kümin 2005), to the neighbourhood tavern, pub or 'local', to larger beer halls (or 'beer parlours' as they were known in Canada) and cocktail lounges of the mid twentieth century (Clark 1981), to the discos of the 1980s and 90s, and, finally, in the latter part of the twentieth century to the present time, to the huge clubs that are often part of corporate chains or empires (Hadfield 2006).

With the emergence of the club scene, staff roles have become highly specialised and gendered. In his qualitative study of clubs in Hoboken, New Jersey, Roberts identified the following specific job roles of modern large establishments: doormen, bouncers, bartenders, waitresses, shot-girls (also called shooter girls: females in revealing clothes who circulate with trays of shots, often served in test-tubes to be downed in one go), tub girls (females who sell beer from ice buckets filled with bottles of beer), bar backs (persons, usually male, who keep the bar stocked during the night), and bottle-boys (also called busboys or bussers whose job it is to pick up empty bottles and glasses, empty ashtrays, and so on). Roberts described how these roles were interconnected and mutually dependent:

> Throughout the course of any given night, staff members must rely on each other to perform certain tasks so that everyone is able to do their job effectively. For example, bartenders and bouncers rely on doormen to meet and greet customers so that they tip well and do not act out upon entering the bar. Doormen are also relied upon by bartenders and bouncers to not admit already drunken patrons. These individuals can be a liability to every worker inside the bar. Bartenders rely on bouncers to break up fights and remove trouble patrons from their bars. Bouncers, in turn, rely on bartenders not to overserve their customers in hopes of preventing acts of aggression from occurring in the first place. They also rely on bottle-boys to remove broken bottles (that is, possible weapons in fights), and on disc jockeys to play music that will not make the crowd too aggressive. Doormen, especially those collecting a cover charge, may rely on bouncers for protection against potential offenders. As you can see, each position within the barroom environment is interconnected, and each employee must rely on one another in order to effectively perform his or her job. (Roberts 1998: 86–87)

The specialisation of staff roles and the move toward mega-sized establishments has had a considerable impact on the ways that staff both prevent and manage problem behaviour and aggression. The narrowing of rigid and often gender-based roles is very different from the blended roles of drinking establishments in the pre-disco age, in which one employee might do table service, bartending and eject patrons when necessary.

The specialised roles of staff in contemporary large clubs is also different from the way in which staff interacted in bars and pubs, especially establishments frequented by 'regulars' – that is, patrons who went to the same establishment often enough to develop relationships with staff and one another (Cavan 1966; Hadfield 2006). In the new mega clubs, patrons move about the establishment, obtaining drinks from bartenders, shooter girls, tub girls and anyone else floating around selling drinks. In this type of context, there is usually no personal relationship established between staff and patrons and no way to monitor consumption or identify and intercede in incipient conflict. This contrasts with the old-style establishments where customers sat at tables and obtained their drinks from the same server over the course of the evening, or sat or stood at the bar, drinking under the watchful eye of the bartender. With patrons seated at tables or serving bars, the server or bartender was able to establish a relationship, monitor consumption and keep the table and surroundings clear of bottles, glasses, and general detritus. A good example of how this approach can be used to maintain an orderly and cooperative environment while still ensuring a good time by customers, thereby maintaining a viable commercial enterprise, is provided by Hadfield (2006: 109–110). He quotes the licensee of a regulars' pub on how he would typically establish rapport and keep control of a group of men who arrive as part of a stag party:

> The way I do it is, it's quite simple. I get them at the early stages, just say: 'Who's the unlucky boy then, getting married? What y'a drinking?' Get them a beer or whatever they want, something just to try an' get friendly with 'em and they're less likely to kick off because you're providing the groom with a free drink, see? Then, if you have to say 'calm it down a bit lad, you're upsetting other customers', they take it on board.

In many contemporary clubs where people purchase drinks from a variety of personnel, this kind of rapport cannot be established and maintained. In fact, it is the security staff who control who enters the establishment, and who have primary responsibility for how customers behave while inside and for ejecting any customers who misbehave. Moreover, the door-screening role is often carried out in an impersonal way rather than as a way of 'meeting and greeting' customers (Hobbs *et al.* 2003: 114).

Not only do the security staff have primary responsibility for controlling customer behaviour and dealing with problems when they occur, role specialisation has sometimes resulted in their having *sole* responsibility – that is, in some establishments, dealing with problem customers is assigned exclusively to security staff, even though serving staff may be well-positioned and capable of dealing with minor problem behaviour. For example, Hadfield (2006: 105) noted that because of the high turnover and young age of many staff in large clubs, 'bar, floor and promotional staff were often encouraged *not* to deal with clients' complaints or other forms of "trouble", but rather to refer such matters to their supervisor, or a member of the management team, lest they react in a manner which might exacerbate the situation'.

The following section of this chapter summarises the evidence on the relationship between aggression and staff variables based on the studies of the barroom environment listed in Table 4.1 in Chapter 4. We then focus in more detail on the ways that staff in drinking establishments handle, and sometimes even create, problem behaviour and violence. For the most part, these descriptions refer to security staff, because most available recent data are from large drinking establishments where incidents of problems and violence are dealt with mainly by security staff. However, in the concluding section of the chapter, we discuss various issues related to the role of staff in preventing violent behaviour, including the need for all staff to be involved.

Staffing characteristics and staff practices associated with aggression and violence

Table 6.1 lists the findings from the 13 studies in Table 4.1 on the relationship between aggression and environmental measures related to staffing and staff practices. It should be noted that staff environmental variables are complex and less easily defined and measured than such relatively simple factors as size of premises or cleanliness. Therefore, inconsistencies in findings across studies may be as much a reflection of measurement problems as evidence for real differences over time or between places. And, as with similar results reported in Chapters 4 and 5, it needs to be recognised that these findings are correlational and do not necessarily imply causal relationships.

Staff to patron ratio

While it might be expected that having a larger number of staff to manage patrons would allow greater preventive behaviours and control by staff and thereby reduce aggression among patrons, as shown in Table 6.1, a higher staff to patron ratio was found to be protective only in the Sydney study, while the Toronto study found that having more staff was associated with more, not less, severe staff aggression. One interpretation of the Toronto finding is that a past

Table 6.1 Evidence relating to the association between staffing characteristics, behaviours and practices and aggression (based on 13 studies of the drinking environment listed in Table 4.1)

Staff variable	Evidence of increased risk	Evidence of no increased risk or reduced risk
Low staff to patron ratio	*Sydney quantitative.* Low staff–patron ratio associated with aggression frequency and severity.	*Surfers intervention, North Queensland.* Staff–patron ratio not significantly related to aggression. *Toronto.* Number of staff[a] (controlling for number of patrons) positively associated with aggression frequency and severity of staff aggression.*
Male staff	*Vancouver.* All male staff associated with more aggression and all female with less. *Buffalo.* Higher proportion of male* than female staff in violent *vs* non-violent bars.	*Sydney quantitative, Surfers intervention, North Queensland, Toronto.* Staff-gender ratio not significantly related to aggression.
Presence of security staff	*Sydney quantitative.* Presence of bouncers, especially Pacific Islander bouncers,* positively associated with aggression frequency and severity. *Surfers intervention, North Queensland.* Number of bouncers positively associated with physical aggression (Surfers) and non-physical and physical aggression (North Queensland).	*Hoboken.* Lack of security staff* positively associated with increased risk of aggression compared to visits when security staff were present and not drinking. *Sydney quantitative, Surfers' intervention, North Queensland.* Security firms at the entrance, in car parks (parking lots) or in other places outside not significantly related to aggression.

	Buffalo. Violent bars more likely than non-violent bars* to employ bouncers. *Toronto.* Presence of security staff positively associated with aggression frequency and severity of staff aggression ($p < .10$). *Hoboken.* Presence of security staff who had been drinking* associated with increased risk of aggression (lowest risk was when security staff were present who had not been drinking).
Young security staff	*Surfers intervention.* Presence of bouncers who were mostly under 30 positively associated with non-physical aggression.
Small sized security staff	*North Queensland.* Mostly small or medium (compared to mostly medium or large) bouncers positively associated with non-physical and physical aggression.
Staff hostility *vs* friendliness	*North Queensland.* Hostile or rude and unfriendly bouncers positively associated with physical aggression. *Vancouver.* Staff friendliness not significantly related to aggression. *Sydney quantitative.* Bouncer friendliness not significantly related to aggression. *Surfers intervention.* Bar staff friendliness or hostility, bouncer friendliness not significantly related to aggression.

Table 6.1 continues overleaf

Table 6.1 continued

Staff variable	Evidence of increased risk	Evidence of no increased risk or reduced risk
		North Queensland. Bar staff friendliness or hostility not significantly related to aggression. *Hoboken.* Staff friendliness not significantly related to aggression.
Drinking by staff	*Hoboken.* Drinking* by bartenders, servers and non-servers associated with aggression.	
Monitoring, coordination, communication, teamwork	*Surfers intervention.* Stationary patrol style [rather than moving around monitoring] positively associated with physical aggression. *North Queensland.* Haphazard ID checks (rather than selective or rigorous) and stationary patrol style positively associated with non-physical aggression. *Glasgow club.* Lack of staff alertness positively associated with severity of aggression* *but not related to observed aggression generally or police call-outs.* *Toronto.* Lack of monitoring[a]* by staff associated with severity of patron aggression.	*Sydney quantitative.* ID check method and patrol style not significantly related to aggression. *Hoboken.* Several measures of staff communication not significantly related to aggression. *Toronto.* Better staff coordination[a] not significantly related to aggression for patron aggression and positively associated with severity of staff aggression.

Ability of bar workers to control/defuse situations	*Vancouver.* Poor control by staff positively associated with physical and non-physical aggression. *England.* Management skills, style and experience identified as key factors in preventing and managing aggression. *Sydney quantitative.* Permissiveness by staff positively associated with aggression frequency and severity. *Surfers intervention, North Queensland.* Staff inability to defuse aggression associated with physical and non-physical aggression. Permissiveness positively associated with physical aggression in North Queensland but *not significant in Surfers.*
Lack of professionalism or professional boundaries	*Toronto.* Lack of professional boundaries by security staff was associated with more frequent[a] aggression and more severe aggression by staff[a] (p < .10 in multivariate). *Toronto.* Lack of professional boundaries by serving staff not significantly related to aggression. *Glasgow club.* Staff socialising not significant in bivariate analyses for observed or severe[c] aggression or police call-outs but negatively associated with police call-outs in a multivariate model.

Table 6.1 continues overleaf

Table 6.1 continued

Staff variable	Evidence of increased risk	Evidence of no increased risk or reduced risk
Lack of responsible beverage service practices	*Sydney quantitative.* Lack of responsible serving practices* positively associated with aggression frequency and severity. *Surfers intervention.* Lack of responsible serving practices positively associated with physical and non-physical aggression. Use of drinks promotions and gimmicks positively associated with non-physical aggression. *North Queensland.* Topping up drinks and lack of a house policy notice clearly displayed and positively associated with non-physical aggression. Drinks promotions associated with physical aggression. *Toronto.* The presence of people with two or more drinks at closing associated with more frequent[ab]* aggression. *Hoboken.* Number of bartenders and other servers of alcohol, frequency of serving to intoxication and indicators of irresponsible serving practices (drink specials, jello shot cups, shots in test tubes) associated with aggression. *Glasgow pub.* Pubs whose staff had received external server training including social responsibility components tended to have less crime and observed disorder.	

Lack of refusal of service to intoxicated patrons	*Surfers intervention.* Failure to intervene with highly intoxicated patrons positively associated with non-physical aggression.	*Sydney quantitative.* Interventions with and refusal of service to intoxicated patrons* positively associated with aggression frequency and severity. *North Queensland.* The need to call management (post-intervention)* to deal with intoxicated and ordering patrons positively associated with non-physical aggression.
Combined measure of poor staff practices	*Glasgow pub.* Scale consisting of poor teamwork, monitoring, serving practices, servers and security socialising, server and security hostility, and poor exit management used as one dimension to identify high-risk pubs (pubs identified as high risk had more crimes documented by police and more severe observed incidents). In this study, security practices were found to both prevent and cause disorder.	

*Significant in a multivariate analysis.
[a,b]Significant within and between bars in Hierarchical Linear Modeling (HLM) analyses; [a]significant within but not between bars; [b]significant between but not within bars.
[c]Results need to be interpreted with caution due to small number (5) of severe incidents.

history of an aggressive clientele leads to establishments hiring more staff. However, the association between number of staff and greater severity of staff aggression was significant as a visit-level relationship – that is, staff aggression was generally more severe on nights when there were more staff even within the same establishment. Thus, overall, the results suggest that it may not be staff numbers, *per se*, that provide greater control of patrons and prevent aggressive patron behaviour, but rather how staff behave. Another possibility is that there may be a non-linear relationship between the staff-to-patron ratio and aggression, with both too few and too many staff increasing the risk of violence. One observer in the Glasgow club study noted the problem of too few staff as follows:

> It's not really the stewards' fault that they were so slow. When the first steward got there he grabbed two of the boys but there was no back up, so what could he do? It is not their technique of dealing with the trouble that's the issue: it's the fact that there are not enough stewards monitoring the club. If something does kick off it will take a while for the stewards to notice, and further time to get back up if needed.

In contrast to the problem of too few staff, staff were quite numerous in relation to patron numbers at the suburban Sydney drinking establishment described below in Box 6.1, but a tense atmosphere prevailed and low-level incidents seemed to be the result of petty, unfriendly, and dictatorial staff practices. As noted by the observers, the overall atmosphere of the disco was that of a school dance patrolled by officious prefects or monitors.

Staff gender

No consistent pattern was found relating to staff gender, although findings from specific studies were significant, suggesting that gender of staff may be important but only in certain contexts. For example, a higher proportion of male staff may reflect a more macho environment compared to establishments where there is a more even staff gender distribution. On the other hand, a more even gender distribution may not necessarily result in reduced macho concerns and aggression if rigid gender roles remain, such as large muscular men assigned to maintain order while women in skimpy outfits serve drinks.

Box 6.1 'School dance' disco, Sydney
(Sydney qualitative study) (narrative by Steve Tomsen – abridged)

The staff and patrons were civil, but not friendly. There were three doorstaff at the front, who were somewhat rude. In order to stamp my hand, one of the doorstaff grabbed my arm without speaking to me and in a way that would have justified abusing him. There were about 600 people present, and at least 800 or 900 had arrived by 1.00 a.m. Despite the numbers, crowding was not high and there was plenty of ventilation. The staff numbers were quite high, totalling about 30. Between two and three of these stayed on the door, while the others literally patrolled the whole auditorium area throughout the night.

A highly paternal and often petty manner with patrons was shown by the floor staff, treatment that an older group of people would probably not tolerate. Under the command of a hard-faced woman (about 40) with an almost manic manner, they patrolled all areas like a school m'am and her prefects seeking out miscreants. Such grave offences as having a loosely hanging shirt or resting feet on orange vinyl chairs, were watched for and caused offenders to be spoken to. One girl was spoken to for resting herself on the stage area in front of the dance floor – and at least two prefects were put on guard all night to watch for other such troublemakers. Spontaneity could mean trouble here – staff gathered at one point around a group of young people who seemed too rowdy and jovial. At one point, a drunken male was removed in a very unprofessional manner. One staff member attacked this man about the face and had to be restrained by others in what seemed almost like a personal fight. This patron was cornered by about six staff in the front corridor who demanded that he 'get out' while completely blocking his exit. He was eventually led from the club, while the bouncer he had been fighting followed him closely seeking a rematch.

Presence of security staff

Employment of security staff was the most consistent predictor of aggression across studies, although these data cannot address the causal direction of the relationship – that is, it is unknown whether security staff are employed because aggressive patrons tend to frequent the establishment or whether the presence of security staff actually increases the risk of aggression. Even the Toronto study was unable to disentangle the relationship, because if bars and clubs employed security staff at all, they were usually present on all visits to the establishment; therefore, it was not possible to separate visit-level associations from bar-level ones. Certainly, expectations may play a role as suggested by the study by Leather and Lawrence (1995), who found that that the pub atmosphere was rated as more unfriendly, tense, threatening and unwelcoming by persons shown a pub picture with three doormen in the photo, compared to ratings of the same picture with no doormen present.

Hostility, friendliness and professionalism

The construct of staff friendliness and professionalism has been measured differently in each study with no apparent consistency in findings across studies. Although the events at the disco dance described in Box 6.1 suggest that staff demeanour plays an important role in aggression, this role has been difficult to quantify in ways that permit meaningful comparisons across studies.

Monitoring, coordination, ability to control or defuse situations

Staff behaviours reflecting people management skills, communication skills or ability of staff to work as a team have also been included in some studies, but again it is difficult to compare across studies because of a lack of consistency in measurement. Overall, there appears to be some evidence that more systematic and conscientious oversight by staff may prevent aggression and possibly the escalation of aggression, although the evidence for a causal relationship is weak. In addition, there were some contrary findings. For example, the Toronto study found that better coordination by staff was not significantly associated with patron aggression, but was actually positively associated with more severe staff aggression. As with the relationship between aggression and the staff-to-patron ratio, this latter finding probably reflects situations of well-coordinated but highly officious staff, as described in Box 6.1.

Drinking by staff

Logic suggests that staff drinking would greatly impair their ability to enforce rules and resolve patron conflict, but quantitative support, other than from one study, has been difficult to obtain. Unless staff drinking (for example, holding a beer bottle) or intoxication is overt, whether staff are or have been drinking tends to be difficult for observers to assess; however, the Hoboken study found that this was a key predictor of aggression even when other variables were controlled in multivariate analyses.

Lack of responsible beverage service and refusal of service
There was evidence from several studies indicating that overserving (for example, topping up drinks in North Queensland, serving to intoxication in Hoboken, the presence of patrons with two or more drinks at closing in Toronto) and other poor serving practices are linked to aggression. Probably the strongest evidence linking serving practices to aggression was reported in Chapter 5 in which intoxication level of patrons was shown to be linked consistently to aggression. This suggests an indirect link – that is, serving practices lead to intoxication which contributes to aggression. Moreover, refusal of service to intoxicated patrons (a key component of responsible serving) is unlikely to be a successful strategy if poor serving practices led to the intoxication in the first place. This would account for findings from some studies that refusal of service was associated with greater likelihood of aggression.

A survey study of drinking patterns and aggression (Stockwell, Lang and Rydon 1993) found that both the intoxication level of the individual and establishments having the practice of serving intoxicated persons independently predicted aggression in licensed premises, suggesting that there may be other links between serving practices and aggression that are not mediated entirely through intoxication (for example, poor serving practices may communicate a high level of permissiveness). Consistent with this, the Toronto study found that the presence of people with two or more drinks at closing was associated with more frequent aggression, a relationship that remained significant in multivariate models controlling for other factors such as intoxication level. As we discuss in later chapters, closing time is a particularly risky time for aggression, and over-serving at this time can increase the risk of aggression, both by forcing people to drink quickly before they leave (increasing intoxication) or by provoking anger and resentment when people are not allowed time to finish drinks they have purchased.

In summary, the results in Table 6.1 provide some insight into the relationship between aggression and staff behaviour, particularly staff factors such as the presence of security staff and their professionalism and skills, as well as serving practices that lead to high patron intoxication levels and provocative situations such as refusal of service and ejections. Other critical aspects of staff behaviour have been difficult to quantify. In the following section, we use qualitative analyses of staff interactions to further identify and clarify the relationships between staff behaviour and aggression for the two main functions relating to managing patron behaviour: rule enforcement and intervention in patron conflict.

Rule enforcement versus intervention in patron conflict

The rule enforcement function involves enforcing rules and policies pertaining to such things as who is allowed to enter, appropriate behaviour within the establishment, when a patron is required to leave, and behaviour in the vicinity around the establishment, particularly after closing. Intervention in patron conflicts, on the other hand, includes preventing conflicts from escalating to physical aggression and stopping aggression when it does occur. These functions, although quite different, overlap somewhat – for example, staff might intervene with patrons who are yelling and swearing at one another, both to prevent the conflict from escalating and because such behaviour is not allowed in the establishment. The critical feature of this distinction, however, is that aggression that arises from rule enforcement is between patrons and staff, while interventions in patron conflicts involve aggression between patrons with staff intervening as third parties. It is important to distinguish these two distinct functions because they require different skills and strategies, and staff in one establishment may be good at one of the functions but poor at the other.

The extent to which aggression is associated with enforcement versus intervention between patrons will vary depending on the type of establishment. In the Toronto study, which included late-night, weekend visits to large capacity clubs and bars, 806 security and serving staff (most were security staff) were involved in 416 incidents of aggression. Of these, 505 staff (92 per cent of whom were male) had an active role in the incident, 207 (88 per cent male) were involved in the form of monitoring or providing back-up but had no active role, and 94 (54 per cent male) had other roles (for example, arguments or fights between staff). Of the 505 *actively* involved in aggressive incidents, 277 (55 per cent) were in aggressive incidents related to their enforcement function while 228 (45 per cent) intervened as third parties in aggression between patrons. Thus, during late-night weekend hours in Toronto's large capacity bars and clubs, staff were slightly more likely to be involved in incidents related to enforcement than to intervention.

Staff were also rated on whether their behaviour was aggressive. For behaviour to be rated as aggressive, the behaviour had to be intentional (that is, not accidental) and had to use more verbal or physical force than necessary for defence of self or another person (Graham, Tremblay *et al.* 2006). Thus, pushing and shoving by staff to separate fighters, or the use of necessary force to eject someone from the establishment, would not be counted as aggression if the force and aggression used was clearly the minimum needed to accomplish the goal. Of the 277 staff involved in aggression related to the rule enforcement function, 35 per cent were rated as aggressive (with 57 per cent of staff in these incidents considered to be the initial aggressor), while a slightly smaller proportion (29 per cent) of staff who intervened in aggression between patrons were judged as being aggressive. In the following sections, we describe in more detail good and bad practices related to the functions of enforcement and intervention.

Rule enforcement

Rule enforcement involves three main controls over patron behaviour: (1) controlling who enters; (2) enforcing rules within the establishment, including refusal of service, setting standards for behaviour, and ejecting patrons who break rules; and (3) making sure that patrons leave the premises in a timely way at closing. In the following examples, we show both effective and ineffective or aggressive strategies employed by staff as they fulfil the rule enforcement role.

(1) Controlling who enters

One of the main functions usually performed by security staff (or doormen or doorstaff) is to control who enters the establishment. Licensing restrictions in most jurisdictions require that staff refuse entry to intoxicated persons and to those who do not have proof that they are of legal drinking age. Staff are also required to ensure that the number of people entering does not exceed the legal capacity for the premises. In addition, they may implement house policies regarding such factors as dress code and entry fees, and prohibit people from entering if they feel the patron might cause trouble. Large clubs in the contemporary era also tend to have a range of other official or de facto entry controls, such as VIP passes that allow some patrons to enter ahead of others and policies that allow women to go to the front of the line. Sometimes, club practices lead patrons to believe that staff at the door must be bribed in order to avoid a long wait.

Refusal of entry often causes problems because the patron is thwarted from doing what he or she wants to do, namely enter that particular establishment. Sometimes, excluded patrons react with anger and aggressive words and actions, consistent with the finding shown in Table 5.1 where queues were found to be associated with an increased risk of aggression. The situation is, of course, aggravated if people have waited in line for a long time (especially during unpleasant weather conditions) only to be refused entry when they finally make it to the door, or if the refusal is done officiously or disrespectfully, or if patrons feel they are being treated unfairly (for example, refusal of entry apparently related to ethnicity or skin colour). In his ethnographic study, Monaghan (2002) described the arbitrary and inconsistent decisions made with regard to who was allowed to enter a club based on the doorman's perceptions of people they considered 'rubbish' or unworthy. Certain kinds of policies or practices, such as maintaining a line solely to make the establishment look busy, can also increase the risk of aggression by people waiting to enter an establishment, as in the incident described in Box 6.2.

Box 6.2 Line-ups are 'club policy'
(Toronto)

Patrons had been waiting in line for approximately 50 minutes in very cold conditions (about minus 18 Celsius made worse by wind chill). Although many people were leaving the club, few were being let in. A large group of approximately 10 people got out of cabs in front of the club. They walked directly to the front of the line and were allowed to enter after a brief conversation with the security staff. A man in line became angry and agitated, yelling: 'What the fuck is that?' One man in the group bypassing the line laughed, saying: 'We're celebrities'. The man in line and his friend yelled obscenities at the group. Security staff made no comment and ignored them. The men and their friends finally left the line-up, refusing to wait longer. On a later visit to this club, someone in line asked why they had to wait so long and was told by the doorman: 'It's club policy'.

(2) Enforcing rules within the establishment
Much of rule enforcement that has been observed in drinking establishments seems to involve patrons behaving like 'bratty' children while staff assume the role of exasperated parents, as in the incident in Box 6.3. In this incident, the exemplary behaviour by staff involved

tactics similar to 'positive parenting techniques' (Sanders *et al.* 2000): they refused to accept the persistently disrespectful behaviour of the patrons (thus the limits were clear); they maintained their good humour and acted firmly but fairly; and they intervened effectively without physical contact.

Box 6.3   Calm in the face of repeated defiance
(Toronto)

Three very intoxicated men were near the serving bar when a Celtic song with lyrics about drinking came on the speakers ('Home for a Rest' by Spirit of the West). The men began shouting the lyrics in unison and dancing recklessly arm-in-arm, kicking their legs 'Rockettes-style'. They became increasingly loud, almost screaming the lyrics, bumping into and spraying drinks on others. After a minute, one of the security staff firmly but good-naturedly told them to behave themselves. The men settled down for a few seconds but soon resumed their dance even more defiantly this time. At this point, two staff members intervened with one man telling the men in a friendly way that they would have to leave. The men went willingly with staff following them close behind. There was no touching. The men were led to the exit while continuing to do their Can-Can dance. At the stairs, two staff assisted in bringing the customers down the stairs without touching them. The staff were laughing at the men as they led them out to the street. All staff were calm and composed throughout the incident.

Refusal of service is a key aspect of rule enforcement in drinking establishments. As with regulations regarding entry into the establishments, it is against the law in most jurisdictions for staff to serve patrons to intoxication. If this requirement is to be met, staff must refuse service to patrons who show evidence of intoxication. However, refusing further service to intoxicated patrons can be one source of staff–patron conflict. For example, an interview study of bartenders and owners in bars in New York and Ireland (Felson, Baccaglini and Gmelch 1986) identified refusal of service as the trigger for about one-quarter of aggressive incidents.

In the older style establishments with patrons seated at bars or tables, refusal of service to intoxicated patrons is an important rule enforcement function for serving staff, and the patron who is 'cut off' from alcohol will often be allowed to remain in the establishment provided that he or she does not drink alcohol. However, in large contemporary clubs where most people are standing or milling about and able to obtain alcohol from a variety of sources (serving bars, shooter girls, etc.), including having friends purchase alcohol for them, the only practical way to ensure that an intoxicated person does not consume alcohol is to force the person to leave. Therefore, the function of refusing service in these settings has been assumed mostly by security staff who are responsible for ejecting patrons. Although observations in drinking establishments have found that some ejections involve non-aggressive staff operating in a well-organised way, at other times ejections are done with undue officiousness, force or aggression. Observations in drinking establishments also suggest that aggressiveness of staff is likely to escalate in the process of ejecting a patron, especially in response to resistance. For example, Wells, Graham and West (1998) identified from both interviews and observations in the London, Ontario study the practice of a 'wrecking crew', whereby four or more staff eject a patron by holding the person by the arms and legs and bashing his or her head into the exit door in order to push it open.

Ejections occur for a number of reasons, in addition to refusal of further service of alcohol. For example, patrons are ejected because they persistently disobey house rules or requests by staff (as in Box 6.3) or are identified as having caused trouble previously. Regardless of the reason for the ejection, the same principles of coordination among staff and respect for the patron apply, as we discuss later in this chapter.

(3) Managing patrons leaving the establishment

In addition to controlling entry into the establishment and behaviour while inside, staff are responsible for controlling exiting patrons, both at closing time and when patrons are made to leave prior to closing. When patrons are forced to leave before closing time, ejected patrons often provoke and bait staff. Observations in drinking establishments suggest that staff often show considerable restraint in the face of extreme provocation. However, sometimes staff become aggressive out of frustration and anger with patrons, as in the incident described in Box 3.2 in Chapter 3 where the staff member finally punched the man who was provoking him.

As has been noted in a number of studies (Graham, Bernards et al. 2006; Hadfield 2006; Marsh and Kibby 1992), closing time is particularly high risk for aggression. Patrons are generally at their most intoxicated; often, they are reluctant to leave; and crowding and other hassles related to exiting can also cause problems. For example, in cold weather climates, the coat check can be a place where rule enforcement leads to conflict pertaining to issues such as losing the ticket or tag for retrieving the coat. In addition, aggression may arise in the coat check queue at closing, related to jostling and people being impatient to leave. The incident in Box 6.4 from the Glasgow club study shows abuse being directed towards a female coat attendant by a female patron, providing some insight into the nature of problems around closing time.

Box 6.4 'Listen here you bitch. I've had enough shit tonight' (Glasgow club study)

A female customer shouted at the female cloakroom attendant, 'Where's my coat?' The attendant replied that the customer hadn't given her a ticket. The customer said: 'Yeah, I did, and there were three coats on it'. The attendant replied: 'No. The lady in front gave me her ticket but you didn't give me one'. The customer leaned toward the attendant and shouted, 'Listen here you bitch. I've had enough shit tonight you fucking me about'. The woman shouted to a nearby male patron: 'They've lost our fucking coats' and walked over to him shouting to everyone how 'fucking unbelievable' it all was. By this time, more customers had congregated and it was getting quite crowded so the security moved the observers away from the incident and down the stairs to the exit.

Staff interventions in conflicts between patrons

In the analyses of staff behaviour in the Toronto study, 29 per cent of those intervening in conflicts between patrons were judged as using an unnecessary level of force or aggression. While this suggests that the large majority did not use excessive force, it identifies considerable aggression by staff, consistent with findings from other observational and ethnographic research (Forsyth 2005; Graham *et al.* 1980; Graves *et al.* 1981; Hobbs *et al.* 2003; Homel *et al.* 1992). Moreover, even if staff did not use undue force to break up a conflict, this does not necessarily mean that staff could not have done more to prevent the incident from occurring in the first place.

In their analysis of staff security behaviour based on observations and interviews, Wells and her colleagues (1998) categorised staff behaviour as good, neutral, bad and 'ugly'. Good behaviours included intervening early and calmly, being patient and non-aggressive but assertive. Neutral behaviours were those that were ineffective but did not involve actual aggression by staff, such as a lack of planning and coordination among staff, allowing escalation, and allowing regulars to return to the drinking establishment despite their involvement in aggressive incidents on numerous previous visits. Bad behaviour was defined as being unfair, using poor judgment and lacking control over patrons to the extent that others were harmed or at risk of being harmed. Ugly staff behaviour involved gratuitous aggression, sexual harassment and provoking behaviour. The incident in Box 6.5 shows restrained behaviour on the part of the staff that would have been defined as 'good behaviour' by these criteria.

The behaviour of staff in Box 6.5 illustrates how force was used in a restrained way to separate fighting patrons. Equally noteworthy is the fact that the two staff members acted together in handling the situation and ensured that one man was removed from the premises well ahead of the other, thereby minimising the risks of violence at the door or in the area immediately outside. However, there was also evidence of a lack of prevention, reflected by allowing patrons to ignore the no smoking rules, the length of time it took to respond to the fight and the remonstrations by the fighter's friend that the fighter be allowed to remain in the bar (suggesting that the patron had the expectation that the fighting behaviour would be tolerated – or at least not lead to ejection). The following incident in Box 6.6 provides an example of how violence escalated out of control because preventative actions were not taken and because there were insufficient staff to handle the large number of patrons involved.

It is clear that the incident in Box 6.6 occurred in a poorly managed establishment for the situation to reach this level of danger and instability. In this incident, the punching by staff may have actually been necessary for self-defence. However, there are numerous examples in this book as well as in published research of excessive or gratuitous aggression by staff. In the following section, we discuss some of the issues related to why security staff behave aggressively.

Implications of the growing role of security staff in licensed premises

As mentioned at the beginning of this chapter, the division of labour separating servers from security, and the proliferation of large-scale

Box 6.5 Restrained intervention by staff into wrestling match between two patrons
(Toronto)

The dance floor was really crowded in the main room. There were many empties on tables, as well as empties and garbage on the floor. Patrons were smoking despite the room being designated non-smoking. The crowd was very much into the metal, alternative and hip hop sets played by the DJs and people were dancing boisterously, at times jumping up and down and bumping into each other in fun. Many people seemed to be stumbling and swaying, holding drinks while dancing. It was very hard to see what was going on due to flashing lighting that created a strobe light effect on the movements of the customers.

The crowd opened up and two male patrons were observed struggling, one holding the other in a headlock. The two men wrestled each other into a hallway and out again, still entangled in each other's arms, but with the man no longer in the headlock. Up to this point, no other customers had become involved, although many had noticed what was happening. Some had moved out of the way while others had followed to watch the fight. At this point, a man tried to pull the two wrestlers apart with the help of two staff members while a third staff member looked on as back-up. The two staff held the two wrestlers who were struggling to get back at each other, but the staff were able to put some distance between the two fighters. The male patron who had intervened spoke to one of the fighters and helped the staff member to hold him back. The other staff moved the other fighter toward the exit. The man who had intervened seemed to be arguing with the staff against ejecting his friend, waving his arms and holding them out in a 'but why?' manner and appearing to exude righteous anger. The staff member replied calmly but firmly, and after about 30 seconds, the intervener turned away and walked toward the exit, seemingly unsatisfied and annoyed.

clubs where people obtain drinks from serving bars, may be at least partly contributing to increased risk of aggression. In particular, strategies for prevention, such as servers being able to monitor intoxication and incipient conflict, staff developing a rapport with patrons that can help to make those in a conflict more likely to be

Box 6.6 Beer bottle brawl
(Toronto)

A group of about fifteen male patrons and three security staff were crowded together between the dance floor and the bar. The left side of the group began pushing the right side of the group. After the pushing had gone back and forth three or four times, one man raised his right hand and forcefully threw a beer bottle which hit the left edge of the bar and shattered. Another bottle was thrown, striking one man on the head and knocking him unconscious. After that, others started throwing bottles. The lights were then turned on, and the DJ stopped playing music. One of the female serving staff was seen standing with a cut arm while another was bringing her ice. Two friends helped one man up from the floor. There were shards of glass from beer bottles all over the area.

Two minutes later, as staff were escorting two men out of the bar, another brawl began. The brawl involved at least 20–30 of the 60 male patrons in the bar. It was difficult to see clearly who was doing what because there were many people involved. The security staff were punching and pushing defensively as they were getting punched and pushed themselves. Both sides of the mob were trying to get at each other. The fighting lasted for about two minutes. After the fights were under control, the security staff escorted another two men out of the bar. The observers left at 1:50 a.m. rather than staying until 2 a.m. closing because they did not feel safe. As they left, eight police officers were entering the bar to investigate.

compliant, and staff being able to elicit support from other patrons in resolving situations peacefully, are less likely to be available in contemporary large clubs than they were in old style bars (where people were served drinks at tables) and in smaller establishments.

However, it is probably not only the structure of the drinking setting that affects aggression by security staff. There is a growing literature on security staff (Hobbs *et al.* 2002, 2003, 2007; Lister *et al.* 2000, 2001, Monaghan 2002, 2003, 2004; Wells *et al.* 1998; Winlow 2001; Winlow *et al.* 2001) that suggests that the attitudes and behaviour of security staff also contribute to aggression. This literature, based largely on ethnographic and interview research with security staff, provides a rich and complex description of those who operationalise the security role. As described by Hobbs and his colleagues (2002: 359), security staff operate unambiguously within a culture of violence:

... the environment within which bouncers work is often chaotic and saturated with aggression, egoism and intoxication, establishing a context within which physical violence becomes both a constant threat to door staff and a tool of their trade. The various control strategies utilized by door staff all have violence, either its potential as suggested by body shape, demeanour and verbal aggression, or its actuality, at their root.

Interestingly, a recent interview study of female doorstaff in the UK (Hobbs *et al.* 2007) found that the culture of masculinity and violence appeared to apply to some female security staff as well. However, findings from that study also indicated that the use of female security staff may lessen the focus on male ego and honour in some circumstances. As described by one club owner:

With a drinking crowd, they can be very aggressive, in your face and a woman can defuse a situation far quicker. If you've got a woman, she can talk them down ... With men it's all about image, it's about showmanship, and then he becomes aggressive. The doorman has to be in charge of his venue, he has to show metal, and he has to show his balls. (Hobbs *et al.* 2007: 25)

While it is difficult to know whether there was more or less violence before the use of security staff became widespread, there are a number of aspects of the job role that suggest that the present trend may be introducing a cycle of violence rather than controlling or reducing violence in the night-time economy. Perhaps the most critical issue for security staff is the focus on honour and respect:

Aspects of honour and personal integrity appear in all of the strategies discussed by bouncers and acceptable levels of disrespect, dishonour and discourtesy are negotiated and renegotiated by door staff... (Hobbs *et al.* 2002: 359)

This culture of honour among security staff involves taking everything personally and responding to violence with violence, as described by one interviewee:

It might be a job but it's me who's going to take the dig and, job or no job, you're not just going to stand there are you? Fucking right you're not. When stuff like that happens you forget it's work, it's not work, it's you against some cunt who wants to do you over. (Lister *et al.* 2000: 387)

Similar concerns with honour were noted by Tomsen (1997) in his ethnographic analysis of aggressive incidents in drinking establishments in Sydney, Australia, observed as part of the Sydney qualitative study (Homel, Tomsen and Thommeny 1992: 95):

This and similar incidents signalled that this explanatory model of public violence as the outcome of heightened concern with male honour can also be applied to the actions of doormen and many supervisory staff. The masculinist elements of these occupations appear to create a very great sensitivity to personal slights, and can promote violent responses to them. At least one third of the serious assaults recorded in this study were perpetuated by them. They were responsible for the majority of serious injuries (often involving significant facial and head wounds) that were inflicted on drinkers too intoxicated to defend themselves.

Another important issue in the role of security staff in aggression is the apparent lack of awareness by security staff of their own contribution to violence. As described by the following interview subject, security staff see the patrons, not themselves, as the source of all violence:

People don't realise how fucking mean and nasty the world can get when it's got a drink inside him. We stand there and the dregs of the universe are out on the piss, now we are on our own and there is no way that anyone understands ... (Winlow *et al.* 2001: 536)

The notion that people do not appreciate the difficulties of the security job and that police unfairly target security staff was echoed by door staff interviewed as part of an intervention study in Cardiff, Wales (Maguire and Nettleton 2003). There is no question that security staff are subjected to a considerable amount of provocation from patrons. An important aspect of effective security work is developing strategies (using both individual techniques and teamwork) to avoid losing one's temper in frustrating and provoking situations with patrons (for example, as included in the *Safer Bars* training described in Chapter 8). As noted by one security staff member, interviewed in the research by Hobbs and colleagues (2003: 119), '... what a lot of people fail to realize is that it is hard to politely escort somebody to the door seconds after they have punched you in the mouth.'

While security staff see the job as a difficult one because of violence caused by patrons, it is clear that these violent encounters also have benefits for staff. Ethnographic research suggests the dangers and violence associated with the job create a strong sense of camaraderie and loyalty (Winlow *et al.* 2001). In addition, there is clearly some enjoyment and excitement involved in job-related violence, as is evident from the following two quotes, the first from a male security staff member and the second from a female:

> ... I went over to this man, grabbed hold of him and pushed him out. I hit him on the back of the head as he left but I didn't do anything else because he was drunk. They've got to have some fight in them haven't they? Otherwise it's no fun. (Monaghan 2002: 421)

> There was once we were in a bit of a fight, and someone hit me over the head with a bottle as I was trying to pull these people apart ... things like that happen all the time. You get a lot of bruises and stuff, but when your adrenaline's running and you go in to something you don't feel it as much, you don't feel the pain ... (Hobbs *et al.* 2007: 33)

Finally, there is some evidence that the security profession in some jurisdictions has attracted 'bad apples' and has been taken over by organised crime and drug dealers (Hobbs *et al.* 2003; Lister *et al.* 2001; Morris 1998). In terms of bad apples, it is not surprising that a profession that involves violence will attract at least some individuals who use the position to exercise power and gratuitous violence with at least some impunity (Lister *et al.* 2000). The following incident from the London, Ontario study shows one case of a pathologically violent person abusing his position as a security staff member.

Although licensing and registration have been adopted in many jurisdictions to combat exactly the type of staff behaviour described in Box 6.7, the effectiveness of these forms of regulation has yet to be demonstrated (Hobbs *et al.* 2002; Lister *et al.* 2001; Prenzler and

Box 6.7   Bruce [the bouncer] is a scary boy
(London, Ontario)

A security staff member was observed throwing a male patron to the ground, holding the patron in a headlock, and punching him several times. The staff member then dragged the man toward the exit. Customers moved out of the way to let them both through. The man was fighting back at the staff by punching and lashing out with his arms and breaking away near the exit. The staff member appeared really angry and was lashing out very aggressively at the patron. He grabbed the patron's shoulder and shoved him toward and out the exit door which had been opened by a second security staff. The rest of the bar staff just stood around as the incident took place, close enough to jump in, if needed, but not actively involved. Observers spoke with one of the security staff after the incident ended and asked him what had happened. He said he had no idea, but guessed that the customer probably looked wrong at the security staff involved. He said the staff member (Bruce) is a 'scary boy' and he sometimes just snaps. He also said: 'He [Bruce] has been dropped on his head one too many times'.

Hayes 1998). In fact, in the course of her work with licensed premises in Queensland, Gillian McIlwain (personal communication) observed that she had previously encountered one head of security during her research at a prison several years before, where he had been serving an eight-year sentence for rape and violence. This man had obtained his security licence and worked in licensed premises prior to being convicted of the crime, and was therefore able to return to this job after leaving prison without being screened again for licensing. Thus, although working as a security staff member in Queensland requires a licence, there appeared to be no revocation of a licence for criminal behaviour. Even effective licensing, however, cannot address all problems. The casual acceptance of Bruce's violence by other staff and management in the incident in Box 6.7 suggests that it is important to change the culture of permissiveness toward violence in drinking establishments, and to ensure that highly aggressive individuals are not employed as security, whether or not they have a criminal record.

The purpose of this discussion, highlighting some of the problems related to the role of security staff, is not to further demonise an already 'demonised occupation' (Monaghan 2003). Rather the purpose is to demonstrate that, just as Zimbardo's experiment resulted in some appalling and violent behaviour when normal young men were assigned the role of guards, the situational demands of the job of security staff may also be influencing how the role of managing violence in licensed premises is currently being understood and performed. Notwithstanding the violence inherent in their role and the fact that numerous examples of aggressive and inappropriate behaviour by security and other bar staff can be found, it is important to note that both observational and interview research indicate that the majority of persons who work in drinking establishments are not prone to violence and interact with patrons in caring and ethical ways. Nevertheless, in addition to screening out the bad apples and preventing the job from being hijacked by organised crime, those interested in the prevention of violence in drinking establishments need to work towards a redefinition of the context and culture of violence in which staff, particularly security staff, work.

Strategies for improving the role of staff in preventing aggression

The four strategies for reducing situational precipitators defined by Wortley (2001: 65) are particularly relevant to staff behaviour: (1) controlling prompts (that is, reducing cues that elicit aggression), (2) controlling pressures (that is, reducing social pressure to behave aggressively), (3) reducing permissibility (that is, raising expectations for self-control and lowering acceptability of aggressive behaviour), and (4) reducing provocation (that is, reducing situations that cause frustration, emotional arousal, etc.).

(1) Controlling prompts

Observational and ethnographic studies suggest that door staff often transmit cues for macho, competitive and confrontational behaviour, apparently based on the perception that this is the way to achieve compliance – that is, to establish right from the start who is 'top dog'. However, there is no evidence from any research to date that this approach by door staff actually improves compliance, while there is plenty of evidence that it precipitates challenges and conflict. This suggests that one strategy for preventing aggression would be to reduce prompts attributable to staff dress, attitudes, demeanour or behaviour.

(2) Controlling pressures

Making it easier for people to do the right thing is an important situational prevention strategy and one that is particularly relevant to drinking establishments. At least two major strategies could be included under this heading: treating patrons with courtesy and respect, and making it easier for patrons and staff to withdraw from conflicts without losing face. Boxes 6.3 and 6.5 included incidents where staff acted courteously but firmly, resulting in problems being resolved without violence. This approach facilitates compliance by patrons, not only by reducing pressure on them to behave aggressively, but it also incorporates other situational crime prevention strategies such as reducing provocation (Wortley's fourth strategy) and assisting compliance (Cornish and Clark 2003). By contrast, 'scary boy' Bruce in the incident in Box 6.7 allowed the patron no real option other than to respond aggressively.

Fostering a culture among male staff and patrons in which fighting is not essential for manliness is also important. For example, in his research on young male drinkers and security officers in regional New South Wales, Australia, Tomsen (2005: 294) found 'an unexpected stress on safety' and the belief that it was possible to withdraw from some conflicts with male honour intact, and indeed with honour possibly reinforced.

(3) Reducing permissibility

The importance of clear rules that are understood and enforced was demonstrated in the example in Box 6.3 where staff refused to accept the persistently rowdy behaviour of patrons, thereby making clear the limits of the establishment. These staff also maintained good humour and acted firmly but fairly, demonstrating that breaching the limits had real consequences. A lack of rule enforcement or a lack of consistent rule enforcement, however, has been noted with regard to other behaviour in the bar, most often with respect to sexual aggression, as in the following example where staff did nothing about blatant sexual harassment and aggression:

> During peak hours, most frequently on ladies' night, small groups of moderately intoxicated males would informally organize into a sort of gauntlet located along a heavily travelled pathway from the main bar to either the restrooms or a smaller bar area ... until up to 20 to 30 men were in control of each side of the pathway ... the males would first initiate a restriction of

the pathway then freely grope, grab or fondle selected females – typically on the buttocks or breast ... At least one bar fight emerged as a result of organized sexual aggression during the observation period – although many more verbal confrontations took place. It is noteworthy that there was no intervention by the South Bar bouncers or bar staff during these incidents, although conversations with female customers during the observation revealed that several had complained to the bartender. (Fox and Sobol 2000: 443)

The importance of rules and consequences derives from research into the moral neutralisations that offenders use to justify illegal or harmful actions to themselves and others (Sykes and Matza 1957). Common justifications include sentiments such as 'everybody does it', 'she was asking for it', or 'I did no real harm'. For permissibility to be reduced effectively, rules should apply to staff as well as patrons. In this regard, Hobbes and his colleagues (2003) have proposed an interesting variation on moral neutralisation theory in their ethnographic study of bouncers. They point out that door staff 'do not have the luxury of engaging in *post hoc* neutralisation' after using physical force, 'for to do so would constitute a recognition that the action was impermissible'. Instead, staff use four types of excuse to distance themselves from blame and 'to placate the demands of personal honour, professional competency, and ultimately of commercial order' (Hobbs *et al.* 2003: 153). These excuses include: (1) accident (injuries caused to customers by staff are accidental); (2) defeasibility (injuries are caused by a lack of critical information such as believing the person has a knife, rather than deliberate intent to injure); (3) biological drives (bouncers are a breed apart who can't exercise as much self-control as other people); and (4) scapegoating (the victim's behaviour forced the security staff to act in an injurious way). The excuses offered by Hobbes' door staff do not sound very different from the explanations offered by burglars and robbers who injure those who get in their way (Indermaur 1996) and are equally specious and unacceptable: security staff who use gratuitous or disproportionate violence need to understand that their behaviour is criminal.

In summary, having clear rules and removing excuses (Cornish and Clarke 2003) are major tools for situational prevention. Even within the generally permissive environment of the commercial drinking establishment, setting clear and consistent boundaries on acceptable behaviour for both staff and patrons can go a long way toward reducing aggression.

(4) Reducing provocation

An important aspect of rule setting is that rules be implemented fairly. The example in Box 6.2 illustrated how aggression in queues could be provoked by unfair and arbitrary behaviour by door staff. Avoiding disputes (Cornish and Clarke 2003) is a related technique that applies both to rule enforcement and to interventions between patrons who are fighting. For example, observational studies have documented numerous incidents of ejected patrons hanging around outside, baiting and challenging the staff who ejected them. Staff using respectful and face-saving strategies could have avoided some of these challenges in the first place. However, even when the patron's challenging behaviour was unprovoked, avoiding becoming involved in the dispute with the patron will prevent escalation. Similarly, when intervening in an ongoing conflict, staff can avoid escalating the situation by avoiding becoming embroiled in an argument over who is at fault and focusing on resolving the situation. Reignition of the dispute (as occurred in the beer bottle brawl in Box 6.6) can be avoided by separating patrons who are fighting and ejecting them separately with sufficient time between ejections to minimise the chances that the fight will continue or escalate outside. A further general tactic is of course to intervene early in the course of a conflict or problem situation.

There are a number of other techniques and strategies that can improve the ways that staff prevent and manage problem behaviours, including planning and coordination, adopting methods for keeping control of their own emotions and temper, and so on. These are described in more detail in Chapter 8, where we discuss the *Safer Bars* training program. The emphasis of this section has been on what staff can do on the job, recognising that management policies that determine the overall settings, such as club atmosphere or staffing levels, are beyond the direct control of most staff. In later chapters, we discuss ways to implement these recommendations, including careful hiring practices, good training programs including formal training and staff meetings, codes of practice, house rules, appropriate supervision and other management techniques. The suggestions in this section are based on the assumption that management has hired sufficient numbers of staff and has screened employees to ensure that those working in the establishment are motivated to prevent rather than incite or cause violence.

Changing the framing of security and serving staff culture

In Chapter 2, we described how licensed premises are unique drinking settings, in that there are people present whose job it is to look after the drinkers – that is, the setting has built-in guardians and place managers, to use constructs from routine activity theory. Given this guardianship, it is ironic that, as we noted in Chapter 1, licensed premises have been identified in a number of studies as high-risk locations for violence. This finding suggests a need to redefine the staff role to be one of guardians, instead of perceiving staff, especially security staff, as authoritarian guards or enforcers. As suggested in previous analyses of bar staff behaviour in the Toronto study:

> ... it might be useful to introduce the constructs of guardian, handler and place manager into bar staff training programs as a way of fostering behaviors and interventions that use the minimum of force required. At present, bar staff may be more likely to see themselves as enforcers rather than protectors; therefore, a change in orientation might foster less aggressive approaches to conflict situations. In addition, communication to bar staff and managers of their legal liabilities for the well-being of patrons may serve to strengthen the role of protectors. (Graham, Bernards *et al.* 2005: 765)

One strategy for enhancing the guardianship versus enforcer role might be to first ensure that all rules are sensible and necessary and, secondly, to reframe rule enforcement to focus on hospitality in the form of protecting the safety of staff and patrons and maintaining a pleasant and fun environment, rather than on the bad behaviour of some patrons. The quote from Hadfield (2006), reproduced in the first section of this chapter about the licensee of a regulars' pub who gets potentially rowdy patrons on side when they first enter, shows one way that this orientation can be achieved.

Another way to foster a less confrontational, less guard-like staff culture is to make roles less rigid and less gendered. That is, all staff in the drinking establishment should be made responsible for ensuring the safety of patrons and staff, not just security staff. So if a fight develops among patrons, it is as much the fault (and responsibility) of the shooter girl or bartender who served them their last drink and observed that they were pretty intoxicated and argumentative as it is the fault of the security staff for not intervening sooner. Moreover, the server (whether male or female) should feel personally capable of telling the persons involved that if they do not calm down they will be asked to leave.

Finally, most strategies for preventing and managing aggression in current use by staff of licensed premises are based on personal experience, folk wisdom and stereotypes. Although there is a growing body of knowledge about the nature of staff behaviour and its impact on violence, more research is needed to identify effective staff practices that can be adopted in a variety of settings. Existing training programs (described in Chapter 8) were developed from observational research, general training programs for managing conflict, and from other sources such as situational crime prevention theory. However, research focusing on specific changes in staff practices (such as the impact of friendly, fair door staff *vs* door staff whose main concern is establishing who is boss) is needed for widespread implementation of good practices. This kind of knowledge base has been established for other professions and needs to be developed for those who work in drinking establishments.

We have referred elsewhere in this book to the potential for bad staff practices to lead to aggression and disorder in the streets by allowing problems to develop inside the establishments that then get pushed to the outside. On the other hand, Forsyth and colleagues (2005) have argued that staff practices that are effective for the particular establishment, that is, those that result in the ejection of trouble-makers or keep them from entering the premises in the first place, may contribute to aggression in the outside environment. Both Hobbs (Hobbs *et al.* 2003: 104) and Forsyth have noted that while there is a 'private army' of security staff overseeing problems within establishments, there are usually relatively few police officers or private security personnel available to deal with disorder and violence in the surrounding streets. In the following chapter, we explore what happens outside drinking establishment, and how this relates to staff behaviour, the social and physical environment within the premises, and the larger geographic and social contexts in which drinking establishments are located. We also outline some of the ways in which new governance structures and public space management techniques are being developed to maintain public order and preserve amenity.

Chapter 7

Spilling out the doors: the ecology and governance of violence in the licensed environment

King Street, Melbourne, early 1990s. Chaos and aggression were the immediate impressions. Crowded, chaotic, congested, lots of intoxicated males, one man was violently kicked and bashed by three others while many people looked on. Private buses with approximately 30 males on each had arrived and parked on King Street. Being refused entrance into the nightclubs these men gathered on the streets, big hassles here. On four separate occasions, we were asked our purpose by groups of very drunk males. Having felt reasonably safe in most of the audited areas, this impression was drastically changed as the social impact started to take its toll. With the social conditions prevailing, it was very difficult to feel safe or that there would be anybody else concerned for the safety of SELF/others. The first thing we saw was the fight mentioned earlier. This sensitized us to the dangers of the combinations present. Hot dog stands, buskers, taxis waiting, queues ... all congesting the traffic on the roads and footpaths, all increased our feeling of uneasiness. To survive, it was necessary to be able bodied, male and young.

(Safety Audit Report, West End Forum 1991: 55)

The Melbourne West End study in the early 1990s highlighted a problem that has become, if anything, more pronounced and widespread in recent years. Disorder, crime and violence on the streets of many city entertainment areas have gone beyond the tipping point of public tolerance, emerging as a major political issue. In this chapter, we review what is known about the ecology of these environments that makes them unsafe, building on an analysis of the interconnections between the internal and exterior environments of drinking establishments as well as on environmental criminology concepts. We also describe the governance of public spaces – that is, the processes and systems designed to maintain safety, amenity and good order – with a particular focus on different kinds of local partnerships. We also propose, in the final section of this chapter, an agenda for empirical research based on environmental criminology principles to address the paucity of rigorous research on the effectiveness of public space governance systems.

The connections between what happens inside and what happens outside

Aggression in the areas outside licensed premises is linked to specific premises through a number of mechanisms:

(a) clashes between groups emerging from or congregating outside different establishments;
(b) ejection of troublesome or aggressive patrons;
(c) unfair, confrontational or officious entry practices;
(d) aggression between staff and patrons who have been ejected;
(e) movement between establishments or different parts of the same establishment;
(f) crowds gathering to watch and sometimes participate in conflicts.

The Toronto study (Graham, Bernards *et al.* 2006) found that both frequency and severity of aggression were associated with the number of people hanging around outside after closing, controlling for other risk variables. Conflict or potential conflict between different social, racial and ethnic groups is one aspect of aggression in areas around drinking establishments. For example, in a study of stranger-on-stranger outdoor assaults in the centre of a Swedish city in the late 1970s, Wikström (1995) observed that these crimes clustered around certain licensed establishments, and that the conjunction of alcohol-intoxicated people from different social backgrounds tended to cause friction which sometimes developed into violence. Similarly, in his study of Glasgow pubs, Forsyth (2005) noted that the mix of people engaged in conflicts on the street suggested clashes between different groups, in contrast to incidents inside establishments where combatants tended to be more homogeneous.

Although just the presence of people outside appears to be associated with risk of aggression, entry and ejection practices by door staff and security staff are probably the mechanisms by which licensed establishments exert their biggest direct influence on the 'ambiguous and chaotic culture of the night' (Hobbs *et al.* 2003: 37), at least in the spaces immediately surrounding bars and clubs. This was demonstrated in the Toronto incident at the beginning of Chapter 1, in which the ejection of two men who were arguing turned into a street brawl, with several men being injured. Another brawl outside the premises, described by an interviewee in a London, Ontario study (Chapter 3, Box 3.1), began when two groups of men exchanging insults were pushed out the door by security staff.

Door entry practices can also contribute to street violence, as in the incident in Box 6.2 (Chapter 6), in which arbitrary decisions about who could or could not enter a bar ('Line-ups are club policy') fuelled anger and hostility toward door staff. Common grounds for discrimination on the part of door staff include gender (with women being more likely to be admitted) and friendships between staff and particular patrons.

The role of staff outside the premises can be critical, both in their management of patron conflict and dispersing crowds, but also in their own aggressive behaviour, as illustrated in Box 3.2 (Chapter 3) where the security staff member eventually punched the man who was taunting him. As we noted in Chapter 6, the street violence in this and other incidents might well have been avoided altogether by using a more respectful method of ejection, or by not serving patrons to intoxication in the first place. The Sydney suburban incidents in Box 2.5 (Chapter 2) provide extreme examples of staff apparently using the immediate environs of the disco as a convenient place to use violence to preserve their male honour and settle scores. Certainly, there seemed to be few management controls on movement into and out of the premises in this and other establishments visited in the Sydney study, which facilitated the sense of 'carnival' in the surrounding streets:

> Fights that moved outside the venue or resulted from a rough ejection, could be observed on the pretence of buying a hotdog, getting fresh air, or simply waiting around for a taxi. In many locations milling around to wait and see some of this action is a common practice that nobody questions. It is generally understood as comprising one more element of the night's entertainment. (Tomsen 1997: 97)

Steve Tomsen, who conducted extensive qualitative observations for the Sydney study (for example, Boxes 2.5 and 6.1 in Chapters 2 and 6), documented other occasions of street carnival and also 'power contests' between patrons and staff, illustrating how the internal and external environments can influence each other. On one visit to the establishment described in Box 6.1, ejected or departing patrons seemed to rebel against the repressive, officious, petty supervisory practices of floor staff within this club by delighting in viewing or participating in lengthy group brawls and regular fights outside the front door. The creation of the entrance area as a hot spot for disorder and violence was exacerbated by the door staff practice of refusing entry to non-members of the club, even though they had pre-paid tickets for the discotheque. By midnight, this practice had generated a crowd of angry people milling around on the front steps. Occasionally, doormen intervened to separate fighters involved in fights and brawls, but in most instances the carnival atmosphere outside was allowed to thrive without intervention from club security or public police.

Even apart from problems created by entry and ejection policies, it is apparent that the atmosphere or events inside a bar can precipitate the transfer of crowds to the outside and cause associated problems. The narrative in Box 7.1, for example, shows how uncomfortable conditions inside the disco encouraged patrons to seek relief outside in the beer garden and on the streets, with associated problems and violence.

The policy of ejecting troublemakers, or encouraging combatants to take their dispute outside, is based on the (often mistaken) belief of security and door staff and management that they have no responsibility for what happens away from their front doors (Victorian Community Council Against Violence 1990). Although it is clear that pushing combatants outside the establishment and into harm's way could result in legal problems for the establishment, if not the staff personally, in many jurisdictions (as noted in the *Safer Bars* program described in Chapter 8), staff responsibility for street conflicts that did not emanate from their own establishment is more ambiguous. Observational research suggests that security staff do not generally intervene in fights in car parks or streets unless the fight approaches the entrance to the bar or could harm the establishment's reputation.

The 'no responsibility' attitude of staff is only moderated, a little, at closing time. Most establishments are mindful of noise complaints and therefore encourage patrons to 'leave quietly'. They also require

Box 7.1 Better entertainment outside than in!
(Sydney qualitative study, condensed from observer notes by
Steve Tomsen)

> The crowd grew bigger towards 12 p.m. ... Due to the low
> lighting, very loud music, lack of seating, lack of ventilation,
> crowding, and high movement and bumping, this was a very
> uncomfortable occasion. ... There was a large crush during
> breaks in the music as hundreds of patrons attempted to get out
> to the beer garden for relief from the crowding, poor ventilation,
> and later I noticed, from the noise of the group they had paid to
> hear. There was slight rain but a rowdy gathering of about 200
> people, which became constant, built up outside the door. These
> patrons were mixing with people without tickets and others who
> had been ejected through the night. There was high movement
> in and out of the disco next door ... The action outside was
> added to the entertainment provided by the aggressive bouncers
> on the door. These bouncers were observed removing patrons at
> least four times. ... leading to several violent incidents in the
> immediate surroundings.

patrons to finish their remaining drinks or leave without them, if
not for home then somewhere else. But it is the 'somewhere else'
that is frequently the problem. If all establishments in the area close
at the same time, then large numbers of (often) intoxicated patrons
head simultaneously for the taxi ranks, car parks, bus or railway
stations, or fast food outlets and hotdog stands. Many patrons just
'mill around' looking for something to do or for a ride home. If, on
the other hand, some clubs or bars remain open after others close,
many patrons forced to leave one establishment will go to a later
closing one, postponing the challenges of getting home till even later
in the evening, and often moving conflict and problem behaviour to
these late-night venues (Chikritzhs and Stockwell 2002).

The ecology of the public spaces around drinking establishments

In his studies of pubs (2005) and clubs (2006) in Glasgow, Forsyth
identified a large amount of street disorder and violence, particularly
after pub closing. Indeed, Forsyth noted that, in the pub study,
patrons observed more incidents of aggression (some quite serious)

on the streets on their way home than they had observed in the much longer period spent inside the pubs. However, as the examples in the previous section illustrate, events inside licensed premises are clearly connected to events in the immediate environs. For example, many incidents of aggression and violence on the streets have their origins in events that occurred earlier inside a drinking establishment. The fact is that it is often in the interests of managers to transfer trouble to the external environment as quickly as possible, and, in some cases, management is so lax that patrons and staff involved in violent incidents move freely to the street and back into the establishment again. When incidents do occur inside bars, they are routinely dealt with in-house, with police being called only when circumstances reach a level of seriousness that makes some involvement from the authorities unavoidable, with the concomitant risks of investigation and possible operating restrictions. The formal crime statistics on violence associated with drinking establishments are, therefore, likely to be incomplete and inaccurate.

In terms of the human ecology of entertainment areas, the precise ratio of interior and exterior violent incidents is perhaps not critical. More important are the processes that connect events in the two locations, and how various 'hot spots' and 'burning times' for aggression and violence are related to features of the physical environment and to the ebb and flow of human populations across time and space. At a deeper level of analysis, we need to understand not only the effects of the built environment and the social uses of physical space, but also the *symbolic landscape*, the features of entertainment areas that signify the shared experience of time out from day-to-day responsibilities and ordinary states of consciousness (Hadfield 2006). Licensed premises and the pleasures that they promote fundamentally shape the night-time entertainment experience and, directly or indirectly, generate many of the aggressive and violent incidents that are the focus of this book, whether these incidents occur on the dance floor or at a fast food outlet on the street.

The spatial and temporal distribution of violence related to drinking establishments

The ecology of violence in downtown entertainment districts can be investigated at a number of levels. One obvious approach is to examine where and when incidents occur. As part of the Surfers Paradise Safety Action Project, analyses were conducted on records maintained by security firms patrolling the public spaces in Surfers Paradise, a major tourist and entertainment area located on Queensland's Gold Coast

(Homel *et al.* 1997). The Surfers Project, described in more detail in Chapter 8, was an intervention conducted in 1993 to reduce violence by using community action techniques. The security data comprised 948 street incidents (some violent but most non-violent and minor) observed in 1992 and 1993. The extracts from the records shown in Box 7.2 illustrate the nature and location of typical incidents, most of which did not involve police.

Qualitative analysis of these security records revealed patterns that are typical of similar areas in the UK (Burrell and Erol 2006; Hadfield 2006; Nelson, Bromley and Thomas 2001; Tuck 1989) and elsewhere. Peak times were invariably between 10 p.m. and 3 a.m. on weekend nights, coinciding with peak crowds, high levels of intoxication, and considerable movement into and out of venues. Instances of incivility and public nuisance were extremely common. Not all of these incidents were necessarily alcohol-related (for example, the street kids with the skateboards or the buskers in the examples above). Common locations of violent incidents include taxi ranks, car parks, bus stations, food outlets, sporting venues such as football grounds, main pedestrian thoroughfares such as arcades, and the front steps, entrances and the immediate environs of licensed premises.

Tuck's (1989: 52) study of disorder in regional areas of the UK distinguished 'clustering' and 'congestion' within entertainment centres. She defined cluster points as outdoor locations where people gather and remain for a period, while congestion points are on thoroughfares where large groups of people are likely to be moving from one area to another and where they might collide. Bus stations, taxi ranks and food outlets are examples of cluster points, while the areas in front of clubs may be congestion points as crowds leaving at closing time interact with crowds leaving other venues or moving through the street to another attraction.

Using the Surfers Paradise security data, Macintyre and Homel (1997: 98–99) analysed 119 violent incidents involving security that occurred inside or in the immediate vicinity of the 22 drinking establishments in the one kilometre square area (shown in Figure 7.1). From Figure 7.1, it is apparent that there were cluster points strung along the central thoroughfare of Orchid Avenue where the majority of nightclubs were located, with four (18 per cent) of the 22 nightclubs accounting for 64 per cent of the 119 incidents. These cluster points probably became points of congestion in the late evening, especially outside clubs 15, 16 and 19. At the other end of the scale, nine nightclubs (41 per cent) accounted for only 3 per cent of the total number of incidents.

Box 7.2 Security incident records
(Surfers Paradise)

Incidents of violence

Friday night, 11.45 p.m. Fight on steps of [Nightclub N1]. Three males onto one, fight ended after a few minutes.

Friday night, 12.15 a.m. Opposite Orchid taxi rank, same three males involved in fight. Neither police nor security attended either of the two fights.

Friday night, 4.17 a.m. Fight outside Taxi Pizza Shop stopped by security. Fight continued outside bank. Security attended and called police. No arrests made, persons known to [security staff].

Thursday night, 3.00 a.m. Two males fighting in Beach Road were pulled apart and separated. One went back into [Nightclub N4] as he was known to the staff of the club.

Saturday night, 1.30 a.m. Found blood and broken glass in the arcade next to [Nightclub N4]. People involved could not be seen anywhere. Security in the club said a fight had happened over an hour ago. They were not involved.

Noise and 'public nuisance' incidents

Saturday night, 10.15 p.m. Group of males sitting on the benches outside Hungry Jacks [Burger King in the US] were told to quieten down by police.

Saturday night, 11.50 p.m. Buskers outside the Dolphin Centre were told to turn the volume down on their amplifiers as they were making too much noise. They were also told to move away from the shop.

Friday night, 11.00 p.m. Drunk male was in the middle of the road in Orchid Avenue with his pants down and bottle of alcohol in his hand. Police took him away.

Wednesday night, 12.15 a.m. Street kids were riding skateboards on the beach side of the Paradise Centre. It was next to the shop windows that is why I told them to stop. They stayed around the area. I asked the staff at the Sushi Restaurant to call me if they started again.

Other researchers using different methodologies (for example, Brantingham and Brantingham 1999; Sherman, Gartin and Buerger 1989) have noted similar concentrations of violent incidents in hot spots. Thus, consistent with our analyses in earlier chapters (especially Chapter 5 regarding environmental risk factors), it is clear that while licensed premises generate a high percentage of problems and give

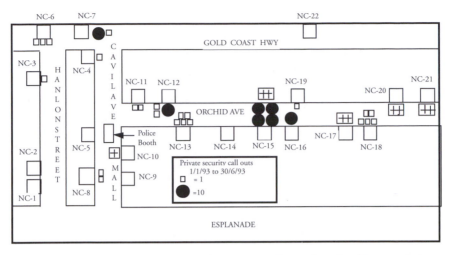

Reproduced with permission.

Figure 7.1 Surfers Paradise nightclub area showing security call-outs for 1 January 1993 to 30 June 1993

downtown entertainment areas their distinctive character, not all such premises are equally troublesome (Briscoe and Donnelly 2001).

The relationship between violence and the density of drinking establishments

In studying the social ecology of entertainment areas, we need to know whether the high levels of violence and associated incidents are simply a product of the presence of a large number of outlets in a small area, or whether there are interactive or synergistic effects whereby the whole is more than the sum of the parts. In other words, does geographical propinquity of establishments to each other compound the individual effects of individual establishments, or is the problem simply the sum of these effects?

If the number of establishments is the only issue, then we need to focus on limiting the number of drinking establishments in a given area and reducing the harms associated with each. If there is an effect of a large number of establishments over and above the effect from each, then we need to understand the nature of the synergies or interactions and devise appropriate preventive measures that can be used in addition to limiting the numbers. For example, if the specific locations of licensed premises generate congestion points in a busy thoroughfare that contribute to the formation of violence hot spots, as suggested by the Surfers Paradise data, then prevention of violence and other problems might be enhanced by focusing on such issues as premises entry and exit strategies and timing, management of pedestrian movements outside premises, the location of fast food outlets and transport hubs, and targeted law enforcement.

Unfortunately, the extant research literature does not permit an easy answer to the theoretical, evidential and policy problems posed by the phenomenon of outlet density. The bulk of evidence, however, suggests a positive relationship between outlet density and violence. A recent review by Livingston, Chikritzhs and Room (2007) concluded that there was a positive relationship between density of alcohol outlets and violence, although the specific relationship between on-premise drinking establishments and violence was not always found or was conditional on other neighbourhood factors such as poverty (Gruenewald, Freisthler *et al.* 2006). More powerful evidence linking outlet density to violence has emerged in a recent longitudinal study (Gruenewald and Remer 2006) that examined the effects of changes in outlet densities on violence rates across 581 zip code areas in California, with a positive association found between violence and density of both bars and off-premise outlets and a negative association found between violence and density of restaurants. The differential findings for bars versus restaurants highlight the importance of examining type of establishment, rather than assuming the same effect from all licensed premises.

The research tends to refute arguments, frequently proposed by industry interests and government regulators, that improving consumer convenience by increasing the number of bars (and deregulating hours of opening) at worst redistributes violence and other problems without increasing the overall level of harm (Babb 2007) and, at best, might reduce the level of harmful behaviours by civilising drinking contexts (see discussions by Babor *et al.* 2003; Hadfield 2006; Plant and Plant 2005; Stockwell and Gruenewald 2004). In fact, a recent longitudinal study of restrictions on opening hours in Diadema, Brazil found a significant decline in homicides when hours of operation were made more restrictive, with the law allowing 24-hour sales at drinking establishments changed to require bars to be closed between 11 p.m. and 6 a.m. (Duailibi *et al.* 2007).

However, even the longitudinal population research of the kind carried out by Gruenewald and Remer (2006) fails to disentangle the cumulative effects of an increase in the number of outlets from possible synergistic effects in small areas. This is because the population unit of analysis does not permit the analysis of contextual effects that is needed to better understand the underlying social processes linking the number of drinking establishments to the level of violence. Moreover, as Stockwell *et al.* (2004) note, the concepts of availability and harm are multi-faceted, and reducing alcohol-related harms may require analysis of the relationships between specific types of availability and specific types of harm. For example, the local impacts on one problem, such as violence, may be different from the impact on another problem, such as motor vehicle crashes. In addition, levels of alcohol-related harm vary with different types of outlet, and the effects of modifying outlet density appear to vary according to the type of alcohol product (Ludbrook, Godfrey *et al.* 2002).

An innovative study by Richard and Carolyn Block (1995), using geospatial mapping techniques, illustrated how a form of local data, namely the exact geographical locations of incidents of crime and violence and of licensed premises, could be used to address some of the ecological processes triggered by a geographical concentration of licensed premises. They began by nesting (1) specific situations, (2) places or locations, and (3) spaces or geographical areas in a conceptual hierarchy. They geocoded licensed premises in Chicago (including not only taverns but also 'corner package goods stores' that sometimes function as taverns, especially in poor areas), then matched these with a geocoded set of police crime incidents designated as 'tavern or liquor store location'. By overlaying maps of liquor licences and crimes occurring in licensed premises, and relating these to densities in census tract areas, they were able to show that there was only partial overlap between areas with high densities of licences and high rates of violence or crime occurring in taverns or liquor stores. In fact, there were several major areas in the city with high concentrations of licensed premises but no evidence of concentrations of violent incidents occurring at a tavern or liquor store. Conversely, there were several areas with high concentrations of violence in licensed premises but low concentrations of premises. That is, while locations with high density of alcohol outlets could be hot spots for violent incidents, there could also be high rates of violence associated with a single isolated outlet (as found in some of the suburban premises in the Toronto study) and low rates of violence even in areas with a high concentration of outlets.

In summary, despite evidence linking violence and higher density of alcohol outlets, the issue of density is complex, and the congregation of premises does not always result in an increased risk of violence. While Livingston *et al.* (2007) identified a number of risks associated with 'bunching' of premises, they also noted some advantages, such

179

as focusing police and transportation efforts toward a specific area. Moreover, Forsyth (2006) found, in the Glasgow club study, that while congested areas increased the likelihood of violence for males, females considered congested areas to be safer than areas with less pedestrian traffic. Similarly, women in focus groups in Buffalo, New York (Parks *et al*. 1998) identified dangers associated with being alone in deserted parking lots and other low traffic locations.

Governance of the licensed environment

In most countries, there is no group or authority that has a monopoly on responsibility for the public areas around drinking establishments. One obvious candidate for managing public spaces is the local government or city authority, but in practice they tend to be only one player among many, including the liquor and hospitality industries on the one hand, and various state agencies with a responsibility for liquor licensing and public safety on the other. Therefore, local governments often participate in partnerships of various kinds, usually involving licensed premises, police, local community groups, local businesses, as well as other organisations, including national organisations such as the UK Civic Trust that promote a partnership approach.

Local partnerships, a form of what Wood and Shearing (2007: 13) call 'nodal governance', have emerged in the last few decades as a key tool for crime prevention in the UK and other countries (Fleming 2006; Hope 2001). 'Governance' suggests the notion of 'steering' rather than 'rowing', in that government takes place through 'the efforts of others' (Grabosky 1995: 528), these 'others' being industry and community groups and government and non-government institutions that interact and negotiate as nodes within loose networks rather than through the traditional hierarchical, top-down approach of government (Homel 2007).

Unfortunately, partnerships have not solved the problems of evidence-based governance (Armstrong *et al*. 2006). The frequent absence of a body responsible for managing the whole space around licensed premises creates a vacuum in terms of who collects data and monitors trends, addresses problems, sets policy, and coordinates the activities of so many players who often have conflicting interests. As a result, strategies for handling problems related to drinking establishments vary greatly both within and between countries, and are often highly controversial and of dubious effectiveness.

The role of licensed premises in partnerships varies widely: sometimes licensees or representatives of their association (if there is one) are primary partners or have an indirect role through membership in a community forum. In other cases, particularly where regulatory agencies are the prime movers, licensees may simply be the target of intervention and have no influence in program design. The police role also tends to vary greatly. At one extreme are 'third party policing' models, in which police initiate action by partnering with or coercing other groups to solve problems through civil law proceedings or though administrative or regulatory methods (Mazerolle and Ransley 2006). At the other extreme are partnerships where police play a limited role (perhaps through providing resources for the training of bar staff) or even no role at all. In between are a variety of models in which police play a vital, but not necessarily dominant, role.

Examples of governance models

Concierge government

In this model, the alcohol and hospitality industries take a lead role. The term 'concierge government' has been proposed by the US-based Responsible Hospitality Institute (RHI) (2006), an organisation set up and underwritten by the Wine and Spirit Wholesalers of America, the Distilled Spirits Council, Diageo (premium drinks manufacturer), and the National Beer Wholesalers Association, with the financial support of the National Highway Traffic Safety Administration. The RHI's goals are to promote alliances between government and city authorities and business to create 'a vibrant dining and entertainment economy'. According to the RHI, the hallmark of concierge government is to ask, 'How can we assist you to succeed?', rather than saying, 'You can't do that' or 'Figure it out yourself' (2006: 8).

> Centralizing permitting and licensing functions, creating online application processes with access to simplified summaries of rules and regulations, periodic seminars on the process of opening a business, with representatives from key agencies available to answer questions, qualified staff to serve as a liaison when conflicts arise are all of what is needed by a concierge government system. (RHI 2006: 8)

Thus concierge government is designed to resource business, especially leisure and liquor retail interests, to take the initiative in creating civilised, European-style entertainment areas in partnership with regulatory authorities.

Grass-roots neighbourhood mobilisation
Often in opposition to the hospitality industry, this type of partnership involves the formation of a neighbourhood group to control the licensing and location of drinking establishments and the management of these establishments (see, for example, Cusenza 1998). These partnerships tend to be focused primarily on licensing and less on the comprehensive management of the space around premises.

Government-led partnerships with community or business groups
These involve the creation of coalitions or alliances between government and community or business groups with a view to preventing violence and alcohol-related injuries and promoting public amenity. Government personnel (such as those working in the drug and alcohol sector) play a lead role, either on their own initiative or through their organisation. An example is the Melbourne West End Good Neighbourhood Forum, developed by Melbourne City Council West End Forum (1991).

Pubwatch
Pubwatch schemes, as they operate in the UK, provide a communication and information sharing network for operators of drinking establishments, to enable them to warn each other about problems of disorder as they occur and to monitor the activities of patrons who are potential troublemakers, perhaps banning persistent offenders (Hadfield *et al.* 2005a; MCM Research 1993). These schemes sometimes receive support and resources at the national level but have as yet not been evaluated.

Alcohol accords, licensing forums, and other partnerships with the
comprehensive regulation of licensed premises as the central focus
These are voluntary agreements without specific legislative backing, mainly concerned with the practices of licensed premises and negotiated by licensees and police, local government, community groups, health agencies and other interested parties (see, for example, New Zealand Department of Prime Minister and Cabinet 2000; Vaughan 2001). The focus in accords or forums is on preventing harms generally, although violence and disorder is a major focus of this approach. In some accord models, police initiate or dominate the partnership, but in other cases a government department takes the initiative. In a few cases, local licensees have initiated an accord (Haak, Coase and Tanjic 2003). In many other cases, no one agency dominates, although

the involvement of police and licensees is always critical. Alcohol or licensing accords have proliferated in recent years, primarily in Australia and New Zealand. Although not called 'accords' in other countries, 'local licensing forums', such as the one included in the TASC project (Tackling Alcohol-related Street Crime) (Maguire and Nettleton 2003) in the UK (Hadfield *et al.* 2005a: 616), are similar in partnership structure and philosophical approach to Australian and New Zealand accords. The evidence regarding the effectiveness of accords is discussed in Chapter 8.

Crime and disorder reduction partnerships

The UK Crime and Disorder Act 1998 placed an obligation on local authorities and the police, in partnership with other agencies, to develop and implement strategies to tackle crime and disorder, including anti-social and other behaviour adversely affecting the local environment, as well as the misuse of drugs. Alcohol-related crime and disorder have become an important focus for these partnerships (Phillips *et al.* 2002), with problem-analysis and systematic data collection a first step (for example, Tierney and Hobbs 2003). While many of these partnerships include evaluation components, no results concerning their effectiveness are available at present.

Community action projects

These are partnerships arising from local community action or from a government response to widespread concerns in the larger community about alcohol-related problems. They are distinguished from grass-roots neighbourhood mobilisation, in that community action approaches tend to have a wider focus than just licensing, and involve the formation of partnerships with government agencies. Community action approaches are distinguished from accords in their focus on system capacity development in the formal regulatory and community sub-systems as well as on drinking establishments (Holder 1998; Homel *et al.* 2003). Community action partnerships often develop in response to a peak in problems and tend to encounter problems of sustainability after funding ceases or the problem lessens. Some key strategies and aims typical of community action projects are described in Box 7.3 below with regard to the Melbourne community action project (Melbourne City Council West End Forum Project 1991). Further evidence regarding the evaluation of community action projects is discussed in Chapter 8.

Box 7.3 The Melbourne West End Forum
(Victorian Community Council Against Violence 1990)

The Melbourne West End Forum arose from a recommendation of a government-funded group, the Victorian Community Council Against Violence, and was funded through the Ministry for Police. Although government-led, it qualifies as a community action approach because of the degree to which the community was involved.

The project relied on three main strategies in its focus on serious violence associated with licensed premises in the entertainment areas of Melbourne:

1. Use of safety audits and responsible server training to encourage safe practices and reduce excessive alcohol consumption;
2. Increased police presence to raise the risk of apprehension as an incentive to improved practices; and
3. Development of a Code of Practice by licensees to guide and encourage good management practices.

A high level of community involvement was achieved through public meetings, safety audits and five task groups focused on: town planning and urban design; traffic and by laws; venue management and cultural attitudes; policing; and transport. No quantitative evaluation was carried out, although qualitative evidence suggested a substantial short-term effect.

The local partnership approach largely begs the question: 'Can areas actually be managed at the local level in the face of the massive influence of government deregulatory policies and the power of leisure capital?' For example, Maguire and Nettleton (2003) noted that strategies such as improved club management and street policing may be of limited and short-term value if issues such as city or state planning policies and the marketing practices of entertainment organisations and breweries are not addressed. However, even though large-scale forces are important, it does not necessarily follow that local management strategies are without value in their own right. Crime problems are always the product of both proximal and distal causes and can usefully be tackled at both levels.

Social control strategies

The issues of urban design, regulatory systems, and local governance are intertwined, immensely complex and largely beyond the scope of this book. Our goal in this section is limited to a brief overview of some specific violence-reduction strategies and techniques that derive from one or more of these general approaches to the problems of amenity and safety. For a much more detailed review of strategies for the prevention of public disorder, crime and violence related to drinking establishments (within the UK context), the reader is referred to the work of Hadfield and his colleagues (2005b).

We have classified control techniques into three broad categories: local and licensing laws; policing strategies; and crime prevention through environmental design (CPTED).

Local and licensing laws

Local laws, ordinances or bylaws are made by local authorities to address matters such as controls on where and when people may consume alcohol in public areas. Local laws, if enforced by local police or other officials, probably have some impact on improving local amenity and safety, although there appear to be no evaluation data to draw on in this regard. There is better evidence regarding liquor licensing laws, with at least some research suggesting that legislative restrictions on the availability of alcohol through, for example, reductions in the hours and days of sale and in the numbers of alcohol outlets, reduce alcohol problems (reviewed in Babor *et al.* 2003), including sometimes violence (Duailibi *et al.* 2007). Given, however, that the general trend is toward deregulation and away from such legislative restrictions (Craze and Norberry 1994), governments seem to be turning to strategies designed to limit violence and disorder without reducing access to alcohol (Hadfield *et al.* 2005b). These strategies are as yet largely unevaluated. For example, in 2004, the Queensland Liquor Act was amended to impose a '3 a.m. lock out' on Gold Coast nightclubs in order to reduce problems associated with patrons moving from one establishment to another. 'The lock out prevents patrons from entering a nightclub after 3 a.m., [but] patrons can still drink within the facility' (Queensland Liquor Licensing Division 2007: 1). Police reported 'a substantial reduction in crime' after the lock out, with calls to ambulances and assault offences down significantly between 3 a.m. and 6 a.m. compared with the previous year; however, only one preliminary scientific evaluation of this policy has been published (Palk *et al.* 2007).

Policing strategies

Police call-outs to deal with disorder, violence and crime are, by far, the most common form of management strategy for problems inside and around licensed premises, reflecting the dominant philosophy of professional policing based on undirected patrolling, rapid response and post-incident investigations (Homel 1994; Moore 1995). It is noteworthy that the first book published by the US Department of Justice in their Problem-Oriented Policing series is devoted to the topic of assaults in and around bars (Scott 2004). It contains the following summary of police responses under the heading, 'Responses With Limited Effectiveness':

> Many police departments concentrate on the streets outside bars rather than the conditions inside bars. They do so by providing a heavy police presence outside bars and, in some instances, in the bars themselves, with regular on-duty patrols through the bars or off-duty police officers working there. The main result seems to be an increase in the rates of reported and recorded offenses, if for no other reason than the police witness offenses that might otherwise go unreported. Heavy police involvement through patrols and enforcement is not essential if there is sufficient community, peer and regulatory pressure on licensees to manage bars responsibly. The police are neither able, nor fully authorized, to regulate every aspect of bar management, but they can encourage, support and insist on responsible management policies and practices. (Scott 2004: 24–25)

Research suggests that police typically operate in a reactive and discretionary manner, are often delayed in responding to incidents, and frequently fail to make any arrests (Hadfield *et al.* 2005b: 671; Room 2005). One reason for delay is the large number of call-outs late on weekend nights and the relatively small numbers of police available to respond. However, anecdotal evidence suggests that there are also attitudinal issues that may come into play, such as the view that 'assaults are just excessive exuberance by young men or, alternatively, "just desserts" for drunken troublemakers' (Scott 2004: 2), or that 'such investigations are both time consuming, difficult to conclude successfully and often involve victims who have stepped out of line themselves ...' (Lister *et al.* 2000: 391).

A number of police approaches related to safety in and around licensed premises have been identified, in addition to the standard patrols and incident response. For example, in the UK and parts of Canada, police have required licensed premises to pay for extra policing related to problems caused by their patrons. In the UK, this approach is called 'polluter pays' (Hadfield *et al.* 2005b: 650–651). In addition, many police agencies are now devoting considerable resources to accessing a wide range of data for 'intelligence-led policing'. Examples include national databases on licensed premises, publications on risk factors and problem-solving for crime analysts (Clarke and Eck 2003), and 'last drink surveys' that make it possible to record systematically the general degree of intoxication of apprehended persons, and the location and time of their last drink (Hadfield *et al.* 2005b: 673; Wiggers *et al.* 2004). Researchers have used such data to identify and intervene in high-risk premises since the late 1980s (MCM Research, 1993). It is not known, however, the extent to which these systems are maintained and applied in practical enforcement contexts. Research on the potential effectiveness of policing approaches is discussed in more detail in Chapter 8.

Crime prevention through environmental design

In some countries, local authorities, police or community groups routinely carry out systematic audits of the physical environments of major entertainment areas to identify features of the environment that can be modified to improve public safety. Audits are based broadly on the principles of crime prevention through environmental design (CPTED), ideas pioneered by architect Oscar Newman (1972). Newman introduced terms such as 'defensible space', 'natural surveillance' and 'community of interest', aspects of which have since influenced situational crime prevention theory and urban planning and architectural design (Clarke 1997; Crowe 1991; Fennelly 2004).

Unfortunately, CPTED techniques are often implemented with little attention to systematic evaluation. Two exceptions, at least in recent years, have been street lighting and closed circuit television cameras (CCTV). Systematic reviews of lighting experiments (for example, Pease 1999) and a meta-analysis of UK and US experiments conducted by Farrington and Welsh (2002) have shown that improved street lighting can lead to reductions of the order of 20–30 per cent in recorded night-time and day-time crimes, although it is not clear from the analyses whether this can be achieved in city centre areas where, typically, there is a concentration of licensed establishments. A meta-analysis of 22 experiments on the effects of CCTV (not necessarily inside or near licensed premises), conducted by Welsh and Farrington (2002), suggested that CCTV can only reduce crime by a small amount and perhaps not at all in city centres. On the other hand, a study by Sivarajasingam, Shepherd and Matthews (2003), comparing the entertainment areas of five CCTV towns with five matched control centres two years before and two years after installation, found significant reductions in assault-related emergency department attendances in the intervention sites compared with the controls.

Towards a better understanding of the ecology of street violence related to licensed premises

Routine activities theory, described in Chapter 2, provides a useful backdrop to most of the relevant environmental perspectives on preventing street violence. Wikström (1995: 429) suggested that preventing crime in the city centre, and by extension in entertainment areas, 'is basically a question of influencing routine activities generating temptations and friction and of developing focused strategies of policing and surveillance'. Drawing upon situational crime prevention theory (summarised in Chapter 2), we might supplement the notion of friction with various forms of precipitation (especially provocation), and search for cluster or congestion points generated by the routine activities that draw large numbers of people into a small area, thereby increasing the incidence of precipitating processes. However, greater analytical precision is required if we are to understand better the dynamics of violence in the night-time economy. Accordingly, mathematicians/criminologists Patricia and Paul Brantingham (1993; 1999) have introduced a number of concepts that have helped to bring increased precision to aspects of environmental criminology.

A fundamental idea is the environmental backcloth, which refers to 'the uncountable elements that surround and are part of an individual and that may be influenced by or influence his or her criminal behavior' (Brantingham and Brantingham 2003: 6). The environmental backcloth includes the built environment – the locations of licensed premises, shops and businesses, the street layout, building design – but also the people located within the physical infrastructure, especially the ways that people use downtown entertainment areas and how these persons interact with and influence the shape of the built environment. For example, ecological labels, that is, the reputations popularly appended to specific places or spaces, are a critical part of the backcloth. The Brantinghams emphasise, however, that the backcloth is more than all of this, since it includes, at a minimum, the 'social, cultural, legal, spatial and temporal dimensions' (2003: 7). Moreover, the backcloth is constantly changing.

The importance of the idea of the backcloth is that it calls attention to the political, social, cultural and economic forces that drive the night-time economy and that create the specific environments within which crime and violence occur. Without some understanding of the changing dimensions of night-time city centres, an ecological analysis of street violence will be severely limited and soon out of date. Although, in recent years, deregulation and the expansion of the night-time economy in the UK appear to have gone much further in a very short period than in any other developed country (Room 2005), the same trend toward liberalisation is also occurring in other countries. It is therefore helpful to highlight the major elements of these trends as they relate to the shape of urban nightlife, drawing from Hadfield (2006: especially 138–9) in terms of the contemporary British nightlife scene and also drawing from the findings of researchers in other countries who have observed these streets after dark. These elements include the following:

1 Entertainment areas are very attractive, mainly to young adults interested in alcohol-oriented leisure.

2 Very large licensed premises not in entertainment areas (but often near transport hubs) that offer an exciting blend of intoxication, sex, and music and dance are also very attractive (Block and Block 1995).

3 In some countries, entertainment areas and individual premises are shaped, increasingly, by powerful market forces recently released from the shackles of the old-style regulatory controls of fixed closing times, restricted forms of entertainment, and limited numbers of licences.

4 Although market dominance by chains varies by country, the consumer experience in drinking establishments is becoming increasingly homogenised in many countries (for example, Grazian 2008; Purcell and Graham 2005; http://www.clubplanet.com/Venues/), similar to the 'series of homogenised "brand-scapes"' dominated by large national chains observed in the UK (Hadfield 2006: 48; also Chatteron and Hollands 2003).

5 The combination of a homogenised consumer experience and the associated spatial concentration of bars and clubs in areas not designed for massive crowds, as well as extensive patronage by

a specific population demographic (for example, young adults), serves to exclude families, older people, and even many young people with different tastes. As these areas acquire a certain kind of ecological label, these excluded groups increasingly avoid them.

6 The erosion of population diversity and the homogenisation of the types of establishments and the experiences that they sell, combined with growing rates of violence and a loss of general amenity, create a cycle that is self-perpetuating.

7 Sometimes, local daytime businesses not in the alcohol-oriented entertainment business can become increasingly alienated and hostile, as can local residents and organisations representing population groups (such as tourist and civic associations, political groups, and businesses interested in creating more European-style entertainment districts) who want to use these areas in different ways. Increasingly, towns and cities are looking to promote multi-use spaces or provide a 'split-use' economy – for example, restaurants for earlier in the day and evening and dance clubs for later at night (Responsible Hospitality Institute 2006).

8 All these forces combine to create place-space-time niches that are likely to be hot spots for crime and violence, although the specific ecological processes are complex and highly varied.

The analyses in earlier chapters address aspects of many of these processes as far as the actual premises are concerned, but we still require an analytical framework for making sense of the complexity of what happens on the street. The Brantinghams' 1993 analysis assists through the ideas of 'activity nodes', 'travel pathways', and 'edges', and, in later work, the concepts of 'crime attractors', 'crime generators', and 'hot spots' for crime or violence (Brantingham and Brantingham 1999). Activity nodes are sites where violent or crime incidents are concentrated. These are generally places where people cluster, and can include licensed premises of a certain type, fast food outlets, and transport hubs. Brantingham and Brantingham (1993) emphasise that, although nodes are amongst the strongest physical characteristics of crime, they exist partly because of participants' cognitive maps or images, making them also part of the perceptual landscape. Consequently, how specific places are perceived and used, and the reasons why they are perhaps 'honey pots' for young consumers (Hadfield 2006: 138), are critical problems for research.

Crime generators, crime attractors and hot spots are slightly different concepts but are closely related to activity nodes. Crime generators are 'specific sites or land uses or locales to which large numbers of people are attracted for reasons unrelated to crime' (Brantingham and Brantingham 1999: 17–18). These include licensed venues and entertainment districts, as well as a variety of other sites such as travel nodes. Crime generators produce crime by creating settings in which opportunistic violence arising from friction or other precipitating factors is likely to occur. In other words, incidents are mostly not premeditated but are the result of opportunity and unplanned aspects of social interactions.

By contrast, crime attractors are places that attract people intent on offending. Licensed premises and entertainment areas are attractive to many young people, but do not become crime attractors unless they are known as places to commit assault, pay back a score, or engage in other kinds of planned illegal actions. For example, young men intent on 'getting rowdy with the boys' (Burns 1980) may deliberately choose specific establishments and public spaces known for fights, illicit sex, or related activities (such establishments often have nicknames indicative of their reputation, such as 'The bucket of blood'). Notwithstanding this possibility, most violence in bars and the spaces around them occurs because large numbers of people attracted to these settings for entertainment become involved in incidents because of the heightened risk of friction and opportunistic violence.

Hot spots may develop in activity nodes, crime generators or crime attractors, but may also arise from more subtle processes involving the layering of 'crime potentials on the environmental backcloth':

> Generally crime hot spots are understandable when considered in terms of the environmental backcloth in conjunction with normal movement patterns, the distribution of crime generators and crime attractors, the situational characteristics of places and the content of ecological labels attached to different places. (Brantingham and Brantingham 1999: 19, 22).

Hot spots may also be analysed in temporal rather than spatial terms, giving rise to burning times such as the high-risk times for violence around closing time (Babb 2007; Maguire and Nettleton 2003).

Travel pathways link high activity nodes. Brantingham and Brantingham (1993) have suggested that violent incidents tend generally to occur at the end points of paths, especially at home, in other private settings, or at licensed establishments, while property crimes tend to be strung out along paths as well as near high activity nodes. However, research on violence specifically related to licensed premises (Forsyth 2005) suggests that violence along these pathways by intersecting groups leaving particular premises may be quite common, especially among men. Pathways are influenced by people's routine activities and knowledge of the physical layout of specific areas, as well as by the ways in which crowd movements are controlled by venues or by the authorities. Different groups' intersecting pathways may create cluster points or points of friction, and may also lead to the formation of new activity nodes such as fast food outlets.

Finally, as Brantingham and Brantingham (1993: 17) put it: 'The urban mosaic is full of perceptual edges, places where there is enough distinctiveness from one part to another that the change is noticeable.' Usually, we think of edges in physical terms as, for example, the boundaries of an entertainment district, but edges can also be temporal. Closing time is a temporal edge that illustrates the general point that edges may be characterised by high rates of crime or violence. Some activity nodes are also simultaneously at spatial and temporal edges, such as railway stations or taxi ranks. The combination of large crowds competing for limited transport at closing time at places that are on the periphery of the bright lights and are somewhat removed from formal surveillance is a well-known recipe for conflict and violence. Edges can also be created in a number of other ways, including through purely perceptual processes such as the boundaries of 'my group's territory' or the streets defining the specific cluster of nightclubs that are the 'in place' to be seen. The main point is that edges always contain a perceptual element and are zones of uncertainty or transition where there is a temporary (or inherent) loosening of controls and a heightened risk of conflict, violence and crime.

These environmental criminology concepts provide a useful framework for understanding the ecology of violence in the spaces around drinking places and designing strategies to prevent violence. For example, safety audits might be more powerful as a tool for prevention planning if they were linked explicitly to the concepts of environmental criminology discussed in this section, namely activity nodes, pathways, edges, hot spots, and burning times. Moreover, the data, which these audits generate regarding salient features of the physical environment, should be linked to systematic data on violence and injuries inside and outside licensed premises, as well as to data on the cognitive maps and subjective understandings of the users of night-time entertainment areas.

More generally, systematic research that actually undertakes these analyses for specific localities is now needed for the development of theory and practical application. Specifically, the following analytic activities are required:

1 A fine-grained analysis of how the features of the physical environment interact with the routine activities of users.

2 Analysis of the role of the perceptions of users – including their cognitive maps and the symbolic meanings and values they attach to specific places – in generating hot spots and burning times.

3 Research on how the social environment is shaped by legislation and the actions of regulators and big and small businesses.

4 A detailed analysis of how the physical, social and perceptual environments shape activity nodes, crime attractors, pathways and edges, and how these in turn contribute to the formation of hot spots and burning times.

This analysis needs to be overlaid on data on the licensed premises in the area, including data on their impact on the immediate surroundings. It also needs to incorporate a *temporal dimension* at the seasonal, weekly, daily and hourly levels. For example, some areas are particularly attractive at certain times of the year, for example Queensland's Surfers Paradise at the end of the school year in early summer when tens of thousands of school leavers arrive from all over Australia for two weeks of alcohol-oriented partying in clubs, apartment towers, the beach, and on the streets. A similar pattern occurs in the US at beaches and resorts where young adults congregate, especially during spring break. The entire centre of the city is effectively given over to the night-time economy for this period. More generally, the normal rhythms of the night in such areas, and the ebb and flow of the crowds, reflect the effects of the day of week, the routines of licensed premises, specific entertainment events, and how the regulatory environment varies across the week. These rhythms must be incorporated into the analysis of how the social, physical and perceptual environments interact.

To advance the research and theory building agendas, it will be necessary to draw on a wide variety of local data, including:

(a) geocoded police, ambulance, hospital and security databases;
(b) systematic observation of premises and their surroundings, particularly with a view to enumerating incidents of aggression

and violence and identifying activity nodes, edges and pathways;

(c) alcohol consumption and management data for individual premises;

(d) interviews with key players in the night-time economy (such as managers of licensed establishments, police and other regulators, patrons and other users of public space); and

(e) safety audits and planning maps that describe the physical environment in detail.

Generally, any data that assist in the understanding of 'environmental stress' and of the effects of human activity will be helpful, whether in the form of archival records, planning documents, interviews or direct observations (Elvins and Hadfield 2003). Although some of these kinds of data are already routinely generated in many countries as part of an attempt to better manage entertainment districts and the spaces around licensed premises, more comprehensive and systematic data systems are required (Tierney and Hobbs 2003).

The prevention of violence in the licensed environment

Violence inside and outside drinking establishments should be understood as a connected whole. The actions and reactions of door staff are pivotal to the relationship between events in the two arenas, suggesting that our proposals in Chapter 6 for involving staff in violence prevention strategies are as relevant to the external environment as to the internal.

Licensees and managers also play an important role in addressing the problem because they set policies relating to incidents beyond their doors. Given the connection between events inside and outside, one strategy for regulatory authorities would be to seek legislative support to give licensees *prima facie* responsibility for serious violence that occurs in the immediate vicinity of their premises when one or more of the protagonists can be shown to have been drinking at their establishment.

Our analysis of the ecology of violence in one sense produced no surprises. The times and locations of violence are generally well established, but what is less well established is an effective approach for addressing the problem. As we have noted in this chapter (and discuss further in Chapter 8), the governance approaches and social control techniques that are currently in use mostly lack empirical evidence of their effectiveness in preventing crime, violence and disorder. Forming partnerships that bring together individuals and groups who have perhaps not previously talked to each other may be a start for prevention, but it still needs to be demonstrated that these partnerships can actually reduce violence, and do so more effectively than agencies working alone.

Thus, there is an urgent need to move beyond approaches that are focused on process to ones that focus on outcomes. Improved lighting and CCTV are two popular measures that do have some evidential support, but their potential to reduce violence specifically in and around drinking establishments needs stronger experimental evidence. In terms of urban design, correlational and longitudinal evidence suggests that limiting the number of drinking establishments within a particular area could reduce violence (although this has yet to be tested as an intervention strategy). Given that more restrictive policies are very unlikely to be implemented, legislative amendments that 'tinker at the edges' (for example, restrictions on re-entry to establishments to prevent a lot of street activity) should be subjected to rigorous evaluation.

Although most of the focus of this chapter has been on areas where there are a number of drinking establishments in proximity to one another, it is clear from the research we have reviewed that drinking establishments that are geographically isolated from other licensed premises, and are perhaps nowhere near major entertainment areas, can also also be extremely troublesome and should also be the focus of prevention efforts. The ecology of violence in the vicinity of these places requires careful attention to determine whether problems flow solely from the establishment or are also a function of features of their external environment (such as, being located close to a transit station that is a node for drug dealing).

In summary, the development of effective strategies to prevent violence related to drinking establishments is most likely to be achieved by combining theoretical concepts, such as activity nodes, pathways and edges, with the systematic collection of relevant empirical data.

Chapter 8

Evaluated approaches to preventing violence related to drinking in licensed premises

Capone's Law. You can get a lot more done with a kind word and a gun than with a kind word alone. (Rawson 2002: 45)

'It should be a working together thing'. (Licensee in the Wellington enforcement experiment – Sim, Morgan and Batchelor 2005: 51)

There are all sorts of efforts being made around the world to reduce violence related to drinking establishments. These include such diverse approaches as government regulation of licensing hours (Duailibi *et al.* 2007; Plant and Plant 2005), hospitality industry-driven community partnerships in entertainment zones (Responsible Hospitality Institute 2006), encouraging safer practices with schemes such as the 'best bar none' award sponsored by the Home Office in the UK (http://www.crimereduction.gov.uk/tvcp/tvcp03.htm), and licensing and regulation of security staff (Lister *et al.* 2001; Prenzler and Hayes 1998). Most of these efforts have not been formally documented, fewer still have been evaluated and only a handful have been evaluated with sufficient rigour to draw conclusions about effectiveness. In this chapter, we focus on the minority that have been subjected to at least minimal outcome evaluation.

Voluntary programs for individual drinking establishments

Although there have been a number of evaluations of programs for training staff of licensed premises in responsible beverage service

(RBS) (as described in reviews by Buka and Birdthistle 1999; Graham 2000; Lang *et al.* 1998; Saltz 1997; Stockwell 2001; Toomey *et al.* 1998), these programs have not focused specifically on preventing violence. Training programs for security staff, offered in a number of countries by private security firms and others, often do focus on preventing violence as well as other issues; however, we could find no published outcome evaluations of these programs. The only program focused specifically on preventing and managing violence in drinking establishments for which outcome evaluation data are publicly available is the *Safer Bars* program, developed in Ontario, Canada and led by a team from the Addiction Research Foundation (now the Centre for Addiction and Mental Health).

The Safer Bars program

Safer Bars includes: (1) a three-hour training program for all staff and management focused on strategies for reducing and managing problem behaviour and aggression; (2) a risk assessment workbook for owners/managers to identify and address aspects of the environment of their particular establishment that may be increasing the risk of violence; and (3) a pamphlet that outlines the legal responsibilities of management and staff for violence prevention.

The content of the program was based on original observational and interview research, reviews of the relevant literature and consultations with staff, managers and owners of drinking establishments, police, a lawyer, community health professionals, civic leaders and liquor licensing officials. The initial program underwent a series of revisions based on repeated testing with staff and management of drinking establishments (Chandler Coutts, Graham, Braun and Wells 2000) before the program was finalised in 2000 prior to the outcome evaluation. A second edition of the program is being prepared at the time of writing (early 2008) in order to incorporate new research since 2000 and to address suggestions for improvement made by participants in the evaluation study.

The *Safer Bars* **training** is based not only on research on drinking establishments but also on knowledge related to communication generally, such as use of personal space and body language (Sears, Peplau, and Taylor, 1991) and techniques that were developed for police officers and others who work with violent individuals (Albrecht and Morrison 1992; Garner 1998). The training covers the following six broad areas related to preventing aggression and managing problem behaviour:

1 ***Understanding how aggression escalates:*** for example, recognising the early signs of trouble in order to intervene early, understanding that all bar staff (not just security staff) have a role in spotting potential conflict and preventing aggression.

2 ***Assessing the situation:*** for example, planning ahead to coordinate responses to problems, recognising the importance of having backup.

3 ***Keeping cool (that is, not losing one's temper):*** for example, knowing the types of people and situations that trigger one's anger, using teamwork to prevent a staff member from losing his or her temper with a patron.

4 ***Understanding and using effective body language (non-verbal techniques):*** for example, using body language to de-escalate situations.

5 ***Responding to problem situations:*** for example, focusing on resolving the immediate situation, using techniques such as giving clear options and avoiding humiliating the person.

6 ***Legal issues:*** for example, knowing legal obligations and restrictions.

The recommended format is for training to be delivered in groups involving all staff from the same establishment (including security and serving staff as well as managers) in order to facilitate communication and teamwork among staff; however, the training has also been used successfully in educational or training settings involving individuals from different establishments. The interactive format relies on group discussion to cover most of the material, with slides and video clips used to illustrate specific points. Because of the emphasis on group participation, the suggested maximum number of participants is 25. Some areas of the training use role play, and the legal section of the training includes a self-administered quiz. Each participant is given a copy of the *Safer Bars* legal pamphlet that summarises legal issues relating to aggression in bars ('Do you know the law?', Centre for Addiction and Mental Health 2000) and a workbook that contains instructions for the role play exercises and summarises major points from each section of the training.

The **risk assessment workbook** (Graham 1999), completed by bar owners or managers, includes 92 questions on which the owner/ manager can rate his or her bar with explanations describing how each item may contribute to the risk of aggression. The workbook covers reducing risks in the following areas of bar operation: entering the bar; maintaining a safe and friendly atmosphere; using layout to avoid risk factors such as bumping; physical comfort and safety; setting rules and keeping order; hiring, training and supervision of servers and bartenders; hiring, training and supervision of security staff; staff behaviours and practices that minimise problems; addressing risks specific to closing time; and other aspects of a safe environment. A sample section is shown in Box 8.1.

The goal of the risk assessment workbook is to reduce risks based on existing knowledge of aspects of the bar environment associated with a higher risk of violence and other problems. However, as described in the workbook, it is recognised that not all risks can be eliminated while maintaining the function of the drinking establishment. For example, although the presence of pool tables has been found to be associated with an increased risk of violence, pool tables may be a key attraction for some drinking establishments; therefore, the owners/ managers in those circumstances might opt to keep the pool tables and look to other areas for reducing risk, including making sure that pool tables are not in high traffic areas and that rules of operation minimise conflict over issues such as whose turn it is to play.

The **legal pamphlet** covers the major responsibilities of staff, management and owners in terms of preventing violence and managing aggression in order to ensure the safety of patrons and staff. Each issue is illustrated with a summary of a legal case. Although the cases are based on Canadian law, the issues tend to be generally applicable in that many countries have similar laws and regulations.

Outcome evaluation

A large-scale, randomised controlled trial of the *Safer Bars* program was conducted in large capacity bars and clubs (>300 people) in Toronto, Canada between November 2000 and June 2002. The pretest began with observations in all 118 eligible establishments in the Toronto area. Of these, 38 establishments judged at risk of aggression were selected for the outcome evaluation, with 26 randomly assigned to receive the *Safer Bars* program and 12 to serve as controls. The participation rate of 84 per cent of staff in 18 of the 26 selected establishments was higher than the rate usually obtained in voluntary server training programs with licensed premises (for example, Saltz and Staghetta 1997; Stockwell 1997) and was achieved partly by paying persons who worked in the hospitality industry to recruit bar management, as well as by paying staff and managers to participate in the training.

Box 8.1 *Safer Bars*: 'Assessing and Reducing Risks of Violence', 'Part A. Entering the Bar'

A Entering the Bar

Do you...	Never or almost never	Seldom	Some of the time	Fairly often	Always or almost always	Explanations
			Check one ✓			
1 Make sure that people are not intoxicated before they enter the bar?	①	②	③	④	⑤	**1** Intoxicated people are more likely to cause problems. Keeping them out in the first place will be easier than handling problems they may cause later inside the bar.
2 Keep track of the number of people inside the bar on a busy night?	①	②	③	④	⑤	**2** Overcrowding is associated with violent behavior.
When you have a lineup do you (or your staff)... *If you never have lineups to enter the bar, go to Section B.*						
3 Tell the people in line how long they'll have to wait?	①	②	③	④	⑤	**3** If you tell people how long they will have to wait, it shows that you are concerned about their comfort. It also reduces frustration, because people can choose either to wait or to go elsewhere.
4 Supervise the lineup so that people can't drink alcohol while waiting in line?	①	②	③	④	⑤	**4** If customers drink in line, they are more likely to be intoxicated when they get into the bar. Allowing people to drink in line also suggests that the bar will put up with illegal or unruly behavior.
5 Prevent people inside the bar from talking with or bothering people waiting in line?	①	②	③	④	⑤	**5** Contact between people in line and those inside the bar sometimes leads to problems such as people inside the bar passing drinks to those in line outside the bar or sneaking people into the bar.
6 Tell young people ahead of time or have a sign posted about the kind of "proof-of-age" ID they will need to enter the bar?	①	②	③	④	⑤	**6** Young customers should know before they get to the door that they will need proper ID to enter. Problems can occur at the door if someone has waited in line for a long time and then is not allowed in.
7 Prevent people from cutting ahead of others in the line? How? ▷	①	②	③	④	⑤	**7** If you allow people to cut in line ahead of others, you are giving the message that it is okay to break rules.
8 Use special passes or favoritism to let certain people into the bar ahead of others?	①	②	③	④	⑤	**8** When people in line see others given "special" treatment, they feel that customers are not treated fairly. This may make them less co-operative with staff.

Higher scores on questions 1 to 7 and a lower score on question 8 indicate lower risk of violence.

The primary evaluation data (number and severity of aggressive incidents observed during each bar/club visit) were collected by male-female pairs of trained observers, who conducted observations in study bars/clubs on Friday and Saturday nights between midnight and 2 a.m., including 355 nights of observations in the experimental and control premises as part of pretest data collection between November 2000 and June 2001, and 379 nights of observations from December 2001 to June 2002 for collection of posttest data. Between April 2001 and March 2002 (but mostly from July to November 2001), a total of 522 staff, managers and owners participated in the training (including five establishments that participated as part of a pilot study). Follow-up interviews were conducted with the owner/ manager of each participating bar/club one year after their staff participated in the training.

The approximately 140 observers hired to conduct the observations were given a general description of the project, but were not told about the design or intervention aspects of the study. Each observer was provided with a training manual describing observation and data collection procedures and participated in approximately 25 hours of training over two weekends. (Forms used in the data collection and the training manual used for pretest observations can be found at http://publish.uwo.ca/~kgraham/safer_bars.html.) The training included extensive focus on ethical and safety issues as well as on recognising and documenting aggression. Aggression data included detailed narrative descriptions of all incidents and quantitative information on all participants in each incident. The observers also rated various aspects of the barroom environment. Additional details regarding design and measurement are available in published papers from that study (Graham, Bernards *et al.* 2005, 2006; Graham, Osgood *et al.* 2004, 2006; Graham, Tremblay *et al.* 2006; Purcell and Graham 2005).

The outcome evaluation examined the effect of the program on moderate and severe aggression (moderate aggression included behaviours that caused discomfort, such as shoving or grabbing, while severe aggression included behaviours causing pain or injury, such as kicking or punching). Results indicated a modest but statistically significant effect, with the number of moderate/severe incidents of aggression dropping from 18 incidents per 100 nights of observation during the pretest to 13 incidents during posttest observations in bars/clubs that received the *Safer Bars* program, while control establishments showed a slight increase (Graham, Osgood *et al.* 2004).

The data analysis found no measurable reductions in environmental risks and no mediating role of environmental changes accounting for reductions in aggression, suggesting that the reduction in aggression was likely mostly due to the training. The importance of the training was also supported by the finding that there was less posttest aggression in establishments that had a lower turnover of *Safer Bars*-trained management and security staff.

Evaluation of the training
The study included evaluation of the effects of the training on knowledge and attitudes, using a 10-item, true-false certification test that was administered immediately prior to and following the training session. This test covered all six sections of the training and used the most reliable and discriminatory items identified during the pilot testing, including the following:

- 'If people start a fight in the bar, the safest thing legally is to tell them to take it outside' (false – bar owners and even bar staff can be held liable for injuries if they eject someone who is likely to be attacked or face the risk of death or injury).

- 'You should always try to find a way for a customer who is causing problems to "save face" (keep their pride)' (true – it is easier to get someone to obey staff if the person is given a face-saving way out of the situation).

Figure 8.1 shows the pre and post scores on the knowledge/attitude test by years of experience of the participant. The dark part of the graph shows the average score on the test before the training; the lighter coloured extension shows the average score following the training (that is, the lighter part of the bar shows the average improvement in score from the pretest). As shown in this figure, participants who had the most experience tended to score highest on the pretest, while those with the least experience scored lower initially but did as well as the more experienced staff on the posttest.

The evaluation also included feedback from training participants and follow-up interviews with owners/managers one year after the training. Reactions to the training were extremely positive, with 98 per cent of those who completed the feedback form (89 per cent of all participants) responding that they would recommend the training to others. All aspects of the training were rated highly, especially the legal section (rated 9.0 on a scale of 1 – not at all useful – to 10 – extremely useful) (more details about the training evaluation

Years of experience

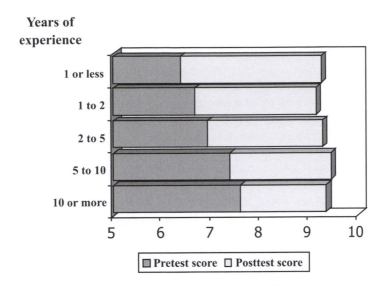

| | 5 | 6 | 7 | 8 | 9 | 10 |

■ Pretest score ☐ Posttest score

Figure 8.1 Average scores (out of 10) on the certification test before (dark coloured bar) and after (light coloured extension of the bar) *Safer Bars* training by years of experience in the hospitality industry

can be found in Graham, Jelley and Purcell 2005). Although high ratings of the usefulness of a program do not necessarily mean that the program will be effective, these ratings are important because a training program that lacks practical relevance from the perspective of the participants is unlikely to result in positive changes in behaviour. Hobbs, Lister and their colleagues (Hobbs, Hadfield, Lister and Winlow 2002; Lister, Hadfield, Hobbs and Winlow 2001) have particularly noted the problem of training relevance with regard to existing programs for security staff in the United Kingdom.

Implications and limitations
The *Safer Bars* evaluation was important because it demonstrated, using the most rigorous design possible, a measurable impact of a stand-alone voluntary program to reduce aggression in drinking establishments. A key factor in the success of the *Safer Bars* program was that it was based on extensive observational and interview research, documenting the nature of barroom aggression and good and bad strategies used by staff to prevent or manage problem behaviour. Another important aspect was the iterative process of testing and refining the training to maximise its relevance and useful-ness for staff. This ensured that the content of the training clearly reflected the nature and diversity of aggression-related problems

occurring specifically in the licensed environment. Thus, while conflict management strategies were drawn from the broader literature, the training itself focused explicitly on problems specific to drinking establishments, and engaged staff in discussion of the best solutions and strategies for addressing these particular problems.

Despite the success of the program, it is important to note that the reduction in aggression was modest. One reason for the fairly modest impact of the program was the relatively low level of aggression in many of the large capacity bars and clubs in Toronto at the time of the pretest, much lower than found in previous research in a smaller city in Ontario (Graham and Wells 2001b) and in studies conducted elsewhere (Homel and Clark 1994). A second explanation for the modest impact might be the short duration of the training. Three hours was identified as the maximum time that bar owners and staff in Ontario, Canada were willing to participate in this type of training program at the time of the study. However, as we describe later in this chapter, other studies that have involved more pressure from the police and other regulatory bodies have been able to implement longer programs (for example, Wallin et al. 2003) that may be able to achieve an even greater impact on the skill level of staff. In addition, as more emphasis is placed on training and safety and as training programs are able to demonstrate positive effects, there is likely to be an increased willingness by staff and managers to participate voluntarily in training programs of longer duration.

High staff turnover may also have reduced the impact (about 40 per cent of the originally trained staff were no longer working at the participating establishments one year later). Thus, training programs for staff of licensed premises need to be ongoing in order to ensure a minimum level of skills and knowledge for all staff (Buka and Birdthistle 1999). In addition, although targeting problem establishments and increasing the duration of training may increase its impact, these gains may be at least partly offset if implementation follows a typical pattern of programs becoming less rigorous and less effective when they are implemented on an ongoing basis in the real-world, outside of the careful monitoring of a research project (Toomey et al. 1998). This highlights the need for quality control systems that can safeguard program integrity. Such systems are probably best developed, controlled and maintained by the industry, in partnership with regulatory agencies and supported by ongoing research and development (Nutley, Walter and Davies 2007).

The analyses revealed that the training (not reducing environmental risks) was probably the key factor in the reduction of aggression.

This suggests that the role played by staff and management may be more important than that of the environment. However, the lack of environmental change could also be due to low motivation of owners/managers to change environmental risk factors or the lack of opportunity to implement major environmental changes in the short time period between the risk assessment and posttest observations. It highlights the need, as we discuss in more detail in Chapter 9, for additional research on the potential impact of environmental changes on reducing violence.

Police enforcement

There is no question that police have a key role in the prevention and control of aggression in drinking establishments, partly because it is their job to enforce many of the laws and regulations that govern the operations of licensed premises, and partly because they must respond to violence that escalates beyond a level that can be controlled by bar staff (Doherty and Roche 2003; Scott 2001; Smith, Wiggers, Considine, Daly and Collins 2001).

The power of enforcement on the operations of licensed premises was demonstrated by a study in a county of Michigan, US of the effects of enhanced enforcement of serving practices (McKnight and Streff 1994). The project began with an education program for licensees, describing the planned enforcement activities. The enhanced enforcement (involving about 10 personnel hours per week) included intensive undercover police operations to watch for and cite staff who served alcohol to intoxicated persons (with half of the efforts focused on 10 establishments known to account for the greatest number of drinking drivers). Reports were also sent to licensees that had been visited but whose staff were not cited, to let the licensees know that their establishments had been visited. All these strategies were underpinned by media publicity.

The evaluation showed a greater reduction in the enforcement county than in a nearby comparison county in both refusal of service to intoxicated persons (as measured by service to 'pseudo patrons' – actors hired on the project to pretend to be intoxicated) and arrests for 'driving while impaired' (DWI). Moreover, cost-benefit analysis indicated that the benefits of enhanced enforcement greatly exceeded the costs (Levy and Miller 1995). McKnight and Streff noted that media publicity and pre- and post-visits to licensees were a critical aspect of the success of the project. This finding is consistent with the general consensus that deterrence is fundamentally a communication process; that is, while furtive law enforcement may increase arrests, such enforcement cannot influence the larger population of potential offenders unless the legal threat is effectively conveyed to them (Homel 2004).

Policing interventions directed specifically toward reducing violence and other problems related to licensed premises have used both randomised and targeted strategies. Randomised enforcement focuses on all or most licensed premises in an area, using highly visible enforcement of licensing laws delivered according to a randomised schedule. Targeted enforcement uses data on the location of drinking prior to assaults or other offences in order to target problem establishments. These approaches are not mutually exclusive, and often both are used, as in the McKnight and Streff study (1994) where enhanced enforcement included both random visits as well as a greater number of visits to problem establishments.

Randomised enforcement

The Torquay experiment

The now classic study by Jeffs and Saunders (1983), conducted in the summer of 1978 in the English seaside resort of Torquay, is often the starting point for those studying the effects of law enforcement on violence and other offences in and around licensed premises. The project began with a visit to premises in May 1978 by the seasonal Task Force Commander and a police sergeant. They warned every licensee of the new policy, which involved uniformed police visiting 'all licensed premises in the harbourside area considered to be potential sources of, or targets for, public disorder' (1983: 69). Police visited establishments at random intervals two or three times a week over a five-month period, conspicuously checking for under-age drinkers or intoxicated patrons. Officers were instructed to conduct visits amicably while, at the same time, checking thoroughly for transgressions. A control town was selected that was in the same tourist region but where no special enforcement was carried out during the same period.

Police statistics on crime and public order offences were analysed for the years 1977, 1978 (the time of the intervention in Torquay) and 1979 for both areas. Compared with the control area, there was a decline of approximately 20 per cent in all arrests in Torquay from 1977 to 1978, with a reversion to baseline levels the following year (1979). Although a specific effect on violent offences was not observed, there was a marked effect on public order offences known to have the strongest association with alcohol. It is noteworthy that the decline in arrests was achieved despite the potential for a rise in overall arrest rates due to the increased presence of police as part of the intervention. The decline therefore suggests a genuine reduction in offending.

There are six aspects of the Jeffs and Saunders experiment that merit special comment. First, despite their remark in their report that the experiment required only 'a comparatively minor alteration in police practice' (1983: 74), the visits to every targeted establishment two to three times per week for the summer months probably required a considerable amount of effort on the part of local police, especially because the visits had to be made at random rather than following a set routine. The second key element was the unpredictability of timing, which made it difficult for staff or patrons to plan to limit compliance to the duration of visits. Thirdly, the visits were very thorough and not rushed, reducing the chances that offences could be concealed. Fourthly, the visits were not at all furtive but were very visible to patrons and staff, ensuring that the high risk of getting caught was apparent. Fifthly, the thoroughness and visibility of visits emphasised that 'good orderly conduct' was the responsibility of *both* staff and patrons (1983: 69). Finally, the whole operation was apparently conducted in an amicable manner, with managers warned well in advance that the new policy was on its way. The police stance was one of friendly cooperation described as follows: 'The licensees were reminded of their responsibilities under the licensing legislation and full co-operation in facilitating the observance of the law was agreed between the licensee and the police' (1983: 69). At the same time, it was clear that this was entirely a police initiative.

The Torquay experiment probably worked, albeit with a modest impact overall and apparently little or no effect on violence, because it was an excellent operationalisation of both deterrence theory and the theory of responsive regulation. As noted above, deterrence works when there is effective communication of a legal threat to the population of all potential offenders. In addition, deterrent effects are optimised when enforcement is unpredictable, highly visible, well publicised, apparently ubiquitous, and not able to be easily evaded by offenders (Homel 1988; 2004). The element of unpredictability and keeping people in the dark as to their real chances of detection is critical.

The apparent lack of effect on violence of the Torquay experiment may have been due to its exclusive focus on alcohol serving. As we have described throughout this book, alcohol intoxication is only one risk factor for aggression in drinking establishments. A surprising aspect of the study is the lack of carry-over to the following year. The authors argued that the program helped police overcome their reluctance to enforce provisions of the Licensing Act due to factors such as 'ignorance of, or mistaken belief about the law, a lack of knowledge about the effects of drink, and failure to see much harm in drinking' (1983: 75), all factors that would have been expected to improve as part of implementing the program of enhanced enforcement and continue to affect police behaviour after the program ended. Similarly, if the program had made licensees more conscious of their legal obligations, a carry-over in changed practices might have been expected the following year. However, the study found a reversion to baseline one year after the intervention, suggesting that the experiment's impact was restricted to immediate deterrent effects that were not sustained.

The Brighton replication

Stewart (1993) reported a replication in 1986 and 1987 of the Torquay experiment in Brighton, a popular seaside town in the south-east of England, including a more intensive intervention by the Sussex Police, for example publicising the project with industry groups and even writing to the area managers of breweries when offences were detected in premises supplied by their companies. The idea was that breweries might respond by encouraging better standards of management in bars and clubs. The breweries' response was surprisingly positive, and they actually provided a wide range of practical advice to licensees. A significant decline in alcohol-related arrests of 14 per cent in 1987 (while total arrests increased by 9 per cent) and qualitative data from nightclub managers, breweries and police suggested a major positive impact of the project. However, these results are difficult to interpret because no control area was selected for comparison. Nevertheless, the thoroughness of the Brighton replication, combined with its innovative industry focus, makes it a useful resource for future interventions.

The Sydney replication

A replication of the Torquay experiment in Sydney, Australia (Burns and Coumarelos 1993; Burns, Flaherty, Ireland and Frances 1995) was unable to find support for the impact of this type of program on reducing violence associated with licensed premises. The design was considerably improved from the original Torquay study. Ten police patrols (corresponding to different districts across the metropolitan area) were selected. These districts had relatively high and stable crime rates and sufficient beat police to carry out the intervention. These 10 patrols were matched in five pairs according to selected socio-demographic characteristics of the populations they served, with one patrol from each pair randomly assigned to the experimental group and the other patrol from each pair assigned to the 'business as usual' control condition. All patrols agreed that they would not undertake any other new initiatives during the course of the study, and beat police in the control condition were kept 'blind' to their control status. Prior to initiating the visits to the premises selected for the intervention because they were known to the police as 'troublespots', police in the experimental condition met with licensees to encourage them to work cooperatively with the police and remind them of their legal obligations not to serve intoxicated or rowdy patrons. The experimental period of six months was broken into a two-month, pre-intervention period of business as usual, two months intervention, and two months post-intervention. Schedules drawn up by beat sergeants provided for visits of 10 minutes duration to each establishment two or three times per week, with an emphasis on friendly interactions while on the premises.

Contrary to expectations, the number of recorded assault offences was *highest* during the intervention phase compared to the pre- and post-intervention phases for the experimental patrols, while the opposite was true for the control patrols. Other offences followed a similar pattern. The change in the rate of assault-related hospital admissions for the intervention period compared to the pretest showed no significant differences between experimental and control areas. The authors speculated that the police visits themselves may have generated the increase in recorded offences during the intervention phase, simply because more police were present in and around troublesome premises for longer periods and were therefore able to observe more offences than they would have under normal circumstances. They also suggested that the intervention period of two months may not have been long enough (the Torquay intervention took place over five months), and that imperfect compliance by police with the experimental design (78.5 per cent of scheduled visits to 49 establishments were actually made) may have reduced the impact. In addition, it is likely that 10-minute visits were not adequate to establish relationships, create a highly visible presence (particularly in very large, crowded venues), and accurately observe malefactions across the whole establishment. Burns and her colleagues (1995) also observed that no licensees were prosecuted during the course of the intervention. This lack of prosecution may have limited the deterrent effect of the intervention. Finally, it may be that, like the Torquay study, the focus on serving underage and intoxicated persons was insufficient to produce a measurable effect on violence.

The Wellington enforcement experiment

A replication of the Torquay experiment was conducted recently in New Zealand (Sim, Morgan and Batchelor 2005). The main features of the study design and the results are presented in Box 8.2. These included comparison of two intervention periods of heightened policing with three periods of normal policing, the use of multiple outcome measures including crime and hospital statistics, and qualitative data from observations of police visits to licensed establishments. The study found that the intervention periods were associated with modest improvements on some of the outcome measures.

Box 8.2 The Wellington enforcement experiment
(Sim, Morgan and Batchelor 2005)

Design
- A combined regulatory approach involving police, the Wellington District Licensing Agency, and the Regional Public Health Team.
- Two six-week periods of heightened police presence in licensed premises (mainly from 8 p.m. till 4 a.m.) in the city area of Wellington were compared to three periods of no intervention (one month prior to the first intervention, two months between interventions, one month following the second intervention) thus resulting in an ABABA design (where A reflects control conditions and B reflects experimental conditions).
- The enhanced enforcement included visits by a combination of police teams (including specialised liquor policing units) in order to identify intoxicated or underage patrons in 60 bars on 244 occasions for up to 30 minutes per visit for the first enforcement period, and 76 bars on 233 occasions during the second intervention period.
- During the intervention periods, public health and licensing agency officials made day time visits to 111 premises to discuss compliance issues with bar managers and to inspect host responsibility practices.
- Police and regulatory officials focused visits particularly on twenty premises identified as problem bars by data from

the Last Drink Survey, a routine data collection instrument used by police since 1999, to ascertain whether apprehended persons had been drinking, their level of intoxication, and the locations where the persons had consumed their last drink prior to the offence.

- Outcome evaluation was based on time series analyses using several sources of weekly data: police incident statistics for violence, disorder, property damage and breaches of liquor licensing laws; injury presentations to Wellington Hospital emergency department; ambulance attendances at assaults and alcohol-related incidents.
- Process evaluation used qualitative data from focus groups with police, bar owners and managers as well as unobtrusive observations of the environment and server and patron behaviour before, during and after police enforcement.

Results

- Higher than usual numbers of intoxicated bar patrons were detected during both enforcement periods, although fewer than usual extremely intoxicated patrons (based on a 5-point rating scale) were detected in the second period.
- Violent offending and overall alcohol-related offences decreased during the enforcement periods, but the trend was not statistically significant.
- Emergency department presentations were not significantly lower during enforcement periods.
- If lag effects (two weeks) were taken into account, there was a significant reduction related to the enforcement periods in disorder offences and intentional injury incidents attended by ambulance officers.
- Observations by researchers during the police visits found:
  o generally more attention to serving practices (for example, increased signage relating to underage drinking and intoxication) during the periods of heightened enforcement;
  o positive changes in server and patron behaviours when police were present although this often reverted to pre-visit 'normal' behaviour once police left;
  o supervisors and security staff became more compliant during police visits;
  o police tended to focus disproportionately on young, male patrons.

> • Police became less 'authoritative' and adopted a more educative and friendly stance in the second enforcement period when the focus was broader and not just on problem premises. However, licensees and industry representatives complained of a deterioration in the relationship between drinking establishments and police due to the heightened attention and indicated that they wanted a more cooperative approach from police including better communication with patrons: *'It should be a working together thing'*. (2005: 51)

Although the study encountered difficulties with confounding factors, such as the occurrence during the study of a street-focused policing operation targeting youth drinking and violence in public places ('Operation Hurricane') and did not use a control area, its otherwise sophisticated design and relative success reinforces the potential for randomised enforcement to be an effective strategy for the prevention of violence and other alcohol-related offences in and around licensed premises. The drop in intentional injuries based on reports by ambulance attendants, and the corresponding non-significant (but clear) trend in police assault data, combined with the qualitative process data, provide some of the best evidence available that an enforcement approach may be able to achieve at least some reduction in violence. Moreover, the study's thoroughness of implementation, its interrupted time series design using weekly data, and the quality and range of data collected on both outcomes and implementation processes set the standard for future projects of this type.

The authors identified the following lessons from the study:

1 The need for the police to adopt a more cooperative, less confrontational, stance with bar staff and managers.
2 Appreciation of the quite real problems bar staff face in complying with licensing law in large, crowded, noisy and dimly lit venues.
3 The need to deal with the reluctance of the authorities to take action against licensees who persistently offend (only two were prosecuted during the period of the study).
4 The value of an inter-agency regulatory approach, involving police visits supported by educative, compliance-oriented visits by health and licensing staff.

Implications of studies of randomised enforcement

Overall, these studies suggest, at best, a modest effect of randomised police enforcement on reducing violence. Moreover, despite reminders to licensees of their legal obligations and the emphasis on relationship-building between licensees and police, none of these short-term interventions appeared to produce any stable reduction in violence, even for the period of one or two months following the intervention. The lack of any carry-over of the effects of policing can be contrasted with the *Safer Bars* program, where a modest impact was still detectable, with most observations conducted six or more months following participation in the program. The importance of a longer time frame is also illustrated by the results from the STAD project in Sweden (described in detail later in this chapter), which found that a sustained policing effort resulted in substantial reductions in serving to intoxication that increased over time. The findings from the STAD project suggest that, instead of conducting studies to assess the short-term impact of short-term enhanced policing, projects with longer time frames are needed to demonstrate (a) the stability of reductions in violence attributable to randomised enforcement, and (b) the extent that enforcement efforts can be lessened gradually over time while maintaining the impact.

Targeted police enforcement – interventions focused on problem establishments

The Alcohol Linking Program

The Alcohol Linking Program (Wiggers *et al.* 2004), conducted over a nine-year period in New South Wales (NSW), Australia, provides an excellent model of the development, implementation and evaluation of a sustainable form of targeted police enforcement. The initiative included a range of strategies to facilitate the adoption of enhanced police enforcement relating to licensed premises, including a 'research into practice' team that was responsible for conducting each sequence of the process of the project. Thus, unlike the short-term focus of most other evaluated interventions, this project was designed first and foremost to change police practices permanently.

Data regarding the location in which the last drink had been consumed by offenders who had been drinking at the time of contact with the police were collected both in order to target high-risk premises and for evaluating outcomes. Therefore, before conducting the outcome evaluation, the team worked with the NSW Police to develop and refine a data collection protocol for monitoring 'last drink' data and to establish the feasibility of this protocol as a system for ongoing use by police (Daly *et al.* 2002). The randomised control evaluation involved about 400 premises. Licensees assigned to the control group received usual policing, while those in the experimental group received the following:

1 A feedback report describing the number and details of alcohol-related crime incidents associated with their premises over the previous four months, and comparison of their performance with all other premises in the study, and informational materials to assist them with making changes in alcohol service and management practices.

2 In the week after sending the report, police visited all premises that had at least one incident attributed to them to conduct a 30-item audit focused on responsible service relating to the following 'eight policy domains: display required signage; responsible host practices to prevent intoxication and underage drinking; written policies and guidelines for responsible service; discouraging in-appropriate promotions; safe transport; responsible management issues; physical environment and entry conditions' (Wiggers 2003: 5). Assistance in improving practices was also offered.

3 About one month later, licensees who had been visited were invited to attend a follow-up workshop conducted by the police where they could discuss progress and problems in improving alcohol service and management practices.

The project resulted in a high rate of adoption of the program, with an increase in the recording of alcohol involvement in incidents, feedback distributed to all 1,413 premises included in the study area over a 12-month period, and audits implemented with the top 8 per cent of premises. In terms of impact, over a three-month period there was a reduction of 36 per cent in alcohol-related incidents in the experimental group compared with a reduction of 21 per cent in the control group (with the statistical significance of the difference between the two groups of $p = .08$, which is just short of the conventional cutoff of $p < .05$ but definitely indicating a positive trend). The difference for assault-related arrests was slightly smaller: 32 per cent in the experimental group versus 25 per cent in the control group (Wiggers 2003; Wiggers *et al.* 2004).

Unlike most other evaluated interventions, the Alcohol Linking Program did not end when the effectiveness information was obtained. The project included research showing the acceptability of the program and compiled evidence demonstrating how the procedures could be adopted into routine policing. Acceptability was measured with surveys of all police (n = 298, response rate = 77 per cent) and licensees (n = 239, response rate = 76 per cent) involved in the intervention, as well as with a survey of randomly selected households in the area (n = 864, response rate = 70 per cent). These surveys found high acceptability by all three groups. Interestingly, 92 per cent of responding licensees found the audit visit acceptable, and about half reported that the feedback report and audit were useful in helping them to change practices (Wiggers *et al.* 2004).

A final stage of the research was to document the factors that led to the successful implementation of the Alcohol Linking Program into routine policing by analysing the various contributing factors within the police organisation specifically and in the broader community generally, including:

1 Obtaining organisational leadership and policy support ...
2 Providing supportive organisational infrastructure ...
3 Developing police knowledge and skills ...
4 Implementing data quality assurance and performance feedback strategies. (Wiggers *et al.* 2004: 360)

The report by Wiggers *et al.* (2004) described other issues relevant to implementation, such as the key role of the research-into-practice team of forming partnerships and maintaining ongoing funding. Based on the evidence accumulated over the various stages of the project, a decision was made by the New South Wales Police to adopt the program state-wide, and by late 2007, the approach was being adopted in other Australian states and in New Zealand (Evans and Green 2007).

Tackling Alcohol-related Street Crime (TASC)/Cardiff Violence Prevention Group intervention
The TASC project (Maguire and Nettleton 2003) – described in more detail later in this chapter under licensing accords – was a multi-component project focused on reducing street crime in Cardiff. One component of this project was targeted enforcement based on emergency department (ED) data identifying licensed premises in which assaults occurred, as well as the street addresses of assaults in nearby streets (Warburton and Shepherd 2006). The police used these data to intervene in premises in a variety of ways, depending on the assessed level of risk. Tactics included regular contact with and monitoring of premises, checks on door staff to ensure that they were licensed and ongoing visits by a local community constable as

deemed necessary. Police also used injury data to oppose applications for new licenses.

The findings suggested that the targeted enforcement alone was not effective. However, an additional intervention involving both intensive police enforcement and a shock tactic by medical staff from the hospital (the 'ED intervention') did appear to show an impact (Warburton and Shepherd, 2006). Two large venues with a high rate of ED assault-related admissions were selected (71 ED admissions in Club 1 and 27 in Club 2). The intervention involved two medical consultants presenting graphic details of injuries sustained at the two clubs to the club managers and informing them that the ED was auditing violence in their premises and would be sending a published report of this audit to the media in six months time. Club 1 also received high-level police intervention, involving, amongst other things, a one-day covert operation and an eight-week high-visibility program along two nearby roads identified as trouble hotspots. Club 2 received only 'low level' police intervention, involving regular monitoring and visits by police as deemed necessary. Comparison with similar ED admissions related to clubs in similar locations found a greater reduction in assaults in Clubs 1 and 2 than in comparison establishments (significant for Club 1). These findings are promising, but the fact that the intervention was carried out in only two establishments and that these two were selected because of their high number of ED admissions suggests caution in interpretation.

Evaluated accords

Australian accords

As described in Chapter 7, alcohol accords are voluntary agreements among licensees and police, local government, community groups, health agencies and other interested parties. Stockwell (2001: 262) observed that in the 1990s alcohol accords emerged in Australia as a 'new model for regulating licensed premises' and were quickly 'applied to innumerable local areas' in that country. By 2007, the largest state, New South Wales, had 141 such accords (McCarthy 2007). As described in the following sections, a number of the Australian accords were evaluated, including those in Geelong, Fremantle and Kings Cross.

The Geelong Local Industry Accord

This police-led accord focused on reducing excessive drinking and problems in the streets, lanes and open spaces surrounding licensed premises in Geelong, a city near Melbourne in the state of Victoria. The agreement included strategies such as imposing minimum entry charges after 11 p.m. and eliminating drink promotions and passes that allowed patrons to leave and re-enter the premises without paying. The core of the accord was a code of practice, negotiated between police and licensees, the aim of which was to 'ensure and maintain proper and ethical conduct within all licensed premises ... and promote the responsible service of alcohol philosophy within the Geelong Region' (Kelly 1994, cited in Lang and Rumbold 1997). A special feature was the preparedness of the police to get tough on non-compliant licensees through strict enforcement of even minor infringements observed on regular visits.

Evaluations (Felson *et al.* 1997; Rumbold *et al.* 1998) suggested a reduction in the rate of assaults and improvements in terms of responsible drinking promotions, amenities, and responsible serving practices; however, interpretation of the reduction in assaults is hampered by the lack of a comparison community, by the failure to disaggregate assault statistics according to location (home, inside venues, in the near vicinity of venues) and time of day (Stockwell 2001), and by analyses that used a baseline year that probably reflected a time when problems had peaked in Geelong. There was also no supporting evidence of reductions in factors likely to be associated with assaults, such as crowding or intoxication.

The Fremantle Police–Licensee Accord

A second Australian accord initiated in Fremantle in Western Australia in March 1996 included some of the Geelong elements, such as the imposition of a late-night entrance fee at nightclubs and the prohibition of discounting. In addition, a 'Better Practices Committee' was established, and the Police and Health Departments provided training to managers and bar staff in responsible serving practices. This accord was evaluated using more rigorous methods than were used in Geelong. It included the use of a comparison community and extensive data collection from various sources twelve months before and twelve months after implementation. The data included risk assessments of individual premises completed by the researchers; observed responses of serving staff to pseudo-drunk and pseudo-underage actors; surveys of residents, businesses, taxi drivers, police and patrons; statistics on drink-driving offences and crashes; and police statistics on assaults occurring in or near licensed premises (Hawks *et al.* 1999). The study found no evidence of effectiveness of the accord on any measure. The evaluators concluded that most elements were ineffectively implemented because market competition eroded any positive benefits of the voluntary agreements that were the key components of the accord.

The Kings Cross Accord

The third evaluated Australian accord was developed in 1997 in Kings Cross, Sydney, an entertainment and high-density residential area renowned for many decades for its numerous pubs, nightclubs, strip clubs, brothels, and gambling establishments. The accord involved police, liquor licensing, local government, state government departments, and industry and business associations, and was built around a structured forum that focused on safety issues and reminding licensees of their legal obligations (McCarthy 2007). The evaluation showed no statistically significant improvement in police-recorded alcohol-related incidents or in incidents recorded by the local hospital emergency department.

Accord-like projects in countries other than Australia

Tackling Alcohol-Related Street Crime (TASC), Cardiff, Wales

The TASC project in Cardiff (Maguire and Nettleton 2003), already discussed briefly in the context of police enforcement, was a police-led, multi-agency program developed in 2000 in response to the city's rapid growth as a leading centre for leisure and entertainment industries, including a big increase in the number of licensed drinking venues and a related increase in violence and disorder. The partnership included the South Wales Police, Cardiff County Council, Safer Cardiff, the Accident and Emergency Unit of the University Hospital of Wales, and the Cardiff Licensees Forum. The involvement of the hospital group built on the active program of research and interventions on violence carried out by Shepherd and his colleagues over a number of years (Shepherd 1994; Warburton and Shepherd 2002).

Even though the project involved additional components that are not typically part of Australian accords, TASC was similar to these accords in that the Licensees Forum was considered a key component of the project (Maguire and Nettleton 2003: 13). Although initiated and supported by the TASC project, the Forum was envisaged as a permanent industry association that would facilitate dialogue between the licensees as a group and regulatory agencies, particularly the police. Discussions focused on issues such as location of fast food outlets, the availability of taxis, and joint planning with police to reduce the impact of major sporting events on violence.

Other components of the TASC project included: targeted police operations directed at areas with numerous drinking establishments and a high rate of street problems; attempts to influence licensing policy and practice through the local council; media releases relating to the problem of alcohol and violence; cognitive behavioural therapy (CBT) for repeat offenders (which had minimal impact because only a small number received the therapy during the project); implementation of a training program in responsible beverage service ('Servewise', which was implemented late in the project, and like the CBT, involved too few participants before the evaluation was completed to have a measurable impact); a school education program; and support for victims who were treated at hospital for alcohol-related assaults.

The intervention also included:

1 Visits by the TASC sergeant to licensed premises to conduct assessments and provide advice about security. These visits were initially random but became increasingly focused on problem premises over the course of the project. Recommendations included ensuring that closed circuit TV cameras were recording at all times, refusing admission to persons who were drunk or underage, and training and registering all door staff.

2 Dialogue with senior managers of major leisure companies and breweries to address problems related to company policies such as drink promotions.

3 Enforcement of the requirement that all door staff be trained and registered for entertainment and dancing venues.

4 Replacement of the existing training for security staff (which was less than one day) with a two-day training program that incorporated an 'innovative conflict model and encouraged a sense of professionalism' (Maguire and Nettleton 2003: 18).

5 Creation of a database showing penalty points for violations received by each registered security staff member in the system.

Measures used for evaluation included: incidents recorded by the police classified either as violence or disorder on the streets or in licensed premises or fast food outlets; custody records; crime records; and Accident and Emergency admissions (described earlier in this chapter under targeted police enforcement (Warburton and Shepherd 2006). The project also included careful and detailed monitoring of a number of other data sources, including capacities of drinking establishments in the area.

A strong feature of the evaluation was the development of a database that combined police and hospital ED data; however, this was specific to the study areas and could not therefore be used for comparison purposes to the control area. Estimation of project effects was also made difficult by the 10 per cent increase in licensed premises during the study period. In addition, only about half of the project's efforts were directed toward licensed premises, and the relative contribution of the various program elements to outcomes was not clear.

Overall, there was some evidence of a decline in violence on some measures when the increase in capacity was taken into consideration (Maquire and Nettleton 2003; Warburton and Shepherd 2006); however, given the weak pre-post design of the study and inconsistent effects depending on the data source, the evidence was far from conclusive. Problems included a time frame for the project that was probably unrealistically short, delays in implementing the security staff training program, and the uncooperative stance of the County Council in taking disciplinary measures against unsatisfactory or violent door staff and in developing broader planning and licensing policies. As noted by Maguire and Nettleton:

> ... despite the high profile of TASC, and despite using information from the database to support their argument, the police were largely unsuccessful in convincing licensing magistrates that granting such licences increased the potential for serious disorder in the area. They were also unsuccessful in an appeal to the Crown Court against the granting of a licence to open a new club in the location. The judge decided that it was not a properly brought case and commented that the police should 'get on with the job' of policing the area (2003: 23).

Implications of the evaluations of accords

Despite their promise, the biggest weakness of accord-type partnerships may be their reliance on voluntary compliance with good management practices by licensees. The importance of consistent and comprehensive enforcement of the Liquor Act was noted by both Lang and Rumbold (1997), with regard to the Geelong Accord, and Hawks and colleagues regarding the Fremantle Accord. The cooperative approach is attractive to local residents, police and other regulatory agencies because it promises a way to avoid non-productive confrontational encounters, and is attractive to licensees because it provides an opportunity for their perspective to be heard and, in principle, for win-win strategies to be implemented. However, cooperation risks the possibility of 'regulatory capture' (that is, where the regulator becomes unduly influenced by those being regulated) and has the potential for displacement of goals from violence reduction and other improvements in community wellbeing to an emphasis on process and compliance issues that are of secondary importance.

Thus, the lack of strong evidence of the effectiveness of accords suggests that partnerships that emphasise purely voluntary compliance with good practices do not generally produce strategies that are sufficiently powerful or focused to reduce violence. To address this weakness, community action approaches have been developed that focus on changes in the community, regulatory agencies and industry structures, as well as on drinking establishments, and that rely on a broader range of incentives for compliance by staff and management of drinking establishments. In addition, some community action approaches have involved more solid and carefully implemented evidence-based strategies. The descriptions of evaluated community action projects in the next section may, therefore, assist in the identification of regulatory approaches that put partnerships and licensee compliance into a more sophisticated and effective framework.

Community action projects

We are aware of only two community approaches that included comprehensive evaluations of quantitative outcomes relating to violence in and around licensed premises: the four Queensland Safety Action Projects in the 1990s (Hauritz *et al.* 1998a; Homel *et al.* 2004; Homel *et al.* 1997); and the STAD project (Stockholm Prevents Alcohol and Drug Problems) implemented between 1997 and 2006 (Wallin, Norström and Andréasson 2003; Wallin, Lindewald and Andréasson 2004; Wallin and Andréasson 2005; Wallin, Gripenberg and Andréasson 2005).

An earlier community intervention study in Rhode Island in the United States (Putnam, Rockett and Campbell 1993; Stout *et al.* 1993) also showed an impact on violence. The project appears to have been a comprehensive community intervention that involved server training as well as publicity campaigns, local task force activities, and community forums, supported by training of police and increased levels of enforcement with respect to alcohol-related accidents and crimes. The results indicated a 21 per cent reduction in Emergency Room assault injury rates in the intervention site compared with a 4 per cent increase for a comparison community. However, these results were described as preliminary and we were unable to find further published information about the project to include a more analytic review of it here.

The Queensland Safety Action Projects

Communities ready to take action

Problems of alcohol-related disorder and violence were very evident in the 1990s throughout Australia, particularly in the entertainment areas of the sub-tropical and tropical cities strung along 2000 kilometres of the Queensland coastline. These cities include the Gold Coast, Mackay, Townsville, and Cairns, each of which were large and growing urban centres that attracted tens of thousands of tourists and locals each year. Problems were especially intense in Surfers Paradise, the centre of Gold Coast city, and the largest of the four cities (with a population of more than 500,000). The attractions in 'Surfers' include one of the highest concentrations of bars and nightclubs in a small area of any region in Australia. Surfers tends to serve as a destination for young people seeking to experience a 'rite of passage' of drinking and early adulthood, involving many of the major issues associated with aggression in drinking establishments identified in other chapters of this book, including macho issues, sexual and romantic mating and drinking to intoxication. In the words of one young man who visited Surfers Paradise with 20 mates from his football team in order to experience this rite of passage:

> You wouldn't want to return to Melbourne without a black eye, a couple of sheilas' [girls'] phone numbers for next year's holiday, and mainly being so pissed each night that you threw up. (McIlwain 1994: 3)

In the 1990s, these problems were exacerbated by competition among the bars and clubs in the four Queensland cities to cut the price of alcohol and even give it away. Managers of drinking establishments seemed to lack experience and management skills, and appeared to have little sense of responsibility for the kind of drinking environment they were collectively creating. They were also poorly regulated by police and licensing authorities. The community was especially ready to engage in organised action due to the negative publicity about crime and safety problems in Surfers Paradise and the widespread view of the business community, other local leaders and residents that 'something had to be done'. This sense of readiness for change was crucial in getting the Queensland projects off the ground and influenced how these projects evolved.

A partnership to implement a modified version of the Melbourne West End Forum Project (described in Chapter 7) in Surfers Paradise in 1993 was established between Griffith University and Gold Coast Council, the Queensland Department of Health, community groups such as the Chamber of Commerce, and – eventually – the venue managers. Links with police and liquor licensing were also critical but were more difficult to establish (as described below). The interventions in the other Queensland cities were implemented two years later on the basis of the perceived success of the Surfers initiative.

Framework and strategies
The four central strategies of the intervention design in all sites were:

(a) the creation of a community forum leading to the development of community-based task groups and implementation of a safety audit;

(b) the development and implementation of risk assessments in licensed premises by project personnel, followed by the development and implementation of a code of practice by nightclub managers;

(c) various training programs for the community-based project steering committee, the project officer, managers, bar and security staff, and police; and

(d) improvements in the external regulation of licensed premises by police and liquor licensing inspectors, with a particular emphasis on preventive rather than reactive strategies, and a focus on the prevention of assaults by security staff as well as compliance with provisions of the Queensland Liquor Act prohibiting the serving of intoxicated persons.

Building initially on the qualitative and quantitative data on risk factors for aggression and violence in licensed premises identified in a series of observational studies in Sydney (Homel, Tomsen and

Thommeny 1992; Homel and Clark 1994), strategies were developed to address the core problem of management practices that allowed or encouraged serving to intoxication, the employment of aggressive crowd controllers (doormen and security staff), the dumping of large numbers of inebriated patrons onto the street with no safe transport options, and the creation of a generally permissive environment in which there were no clear rules about behavioural limits and respect for the rights of patrons. The theoretical bases of these strategies were situational prevention and responsive regulation, and the theory of change behind the strategies was to reduce these risk factors and hence observed rates of aggression and violence.

The strategies were designed to bring about change by combining pressure for better self-regulation by licensees (strategies b and c above) with improved methods of formal enforcement by state agencies, namely police and liquor licensing (strategies c and d), supported by new forms of informal regulation based on licensee accountability to each other and to the local community through the creation of new organisational structures (strategy a). The exact form and content of these three kinds of regulatory levers evolved with the projects. In practice, the first three strategies were implemented effectively in all four sites, but only partial success was obtained with regard to the fourth strategy (formal enforcement).

Community mobilisation and training

Community mobilisation yielded tangible outcomes in a short period. An average of 12 organisations and 17 individuals participated in the steering committees in each city, and hundreds of residents, local business people, public servants and others participated in the community forums and the Venue Management and other task groups. Most of these groups met once or twice a month for the duration of funding. In addition, extensive training was carried out in all sites, including: half-day courses run by project officers for the steering committees on structure, content, process and accountability; five-day courses by research staff for the project officers in project theory, structure, responsibilities and processes; seven-day training in liquor licensing law and investigations, mainly run by specialist police, for police and project officers; two-day courses for security staff on security legislation and best practice conducted by the Queensland Hotels Association; and courses of variable length run by project staff and external specialists for licensees in management practices, development of house policies, responsible serving practices and management of security staff.

Evaluation

Extensive evaluation data collected in the four cities included systematic observations by trained researchers, incident recording by security staff, and police data. Given the unreliability of police data for small areas, however, the core outcome variables for all the studies were the number and severity of incidents of violence inside the licensed premises (mainly nightclubs) observed by small teams of trained observers before and after the intervention. Environmental data were also collected on a wide range of variables, including patron characteristics, the social and physical environment, serving and drinking practices, and physical and non-physical aggression. Detailed results from the evaluations are presented in Hauritz *et al.* (1998abc), Homel *et al.* (1997), and Homel, Carvolth *et al.* (2004). Because interventions in the three North Queensland cities occurred at approximately the same time with similar results, we report combined findings for these cities.

As shown in Figure 8.2 (Homel *et al.* 2004: reproduced with permission), the intervention was associated with a significant decrease in observed aggression in both Surfers and the North Queensland cities. Police data on assaults showed a similar decline in violence in all cities except Mackay. The high rate of violence in Surfers Paradise at the inception of the project in 1993 is striking compared with the

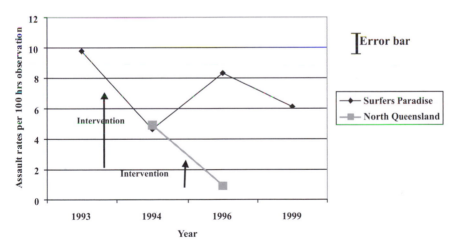

Note: The error bar is the approximate standard error for each point.

Figure 8.2 Number of assaults per 100 hours of observation in drinking establishments before and after interventions in Queensland Safety Action Projects

level of violence in the northern cities in 1994 when the interventions began in those locations. However, by 1994, physical aggression in Surfers had decreased to the pre-intervention level of the northern cities, making Surfers Paradise a useful comparison, although not a completely satisfactory control area, for evaluating the impact of the replication projects.

Results of the evaluations indicated that not only were the interventions associated with a reduction in violence, there was also evidence of improvement in environmental risk factors, supporting the underlying theory of change. These improvements, which did not vary greatly between cities, included reductions in the levels of perceived permissiveness in venues, increases in sociability, cheerfulness and friendliness, a range of significant improvements in host responsibility practices, and a marked decline in levels of male drunkenness. The geographical location of licensed premises in all four cities, especially in the north, was such that displacement of incidents to venues in adjoining areas could not have accounted for the observed declines. Patronage (and crowding) increased and prices stayed the same, suggesting no decline in levels of profitability.

The most encouraging feature of the results was the consistency with which observed aggression and violence declined in the four sites immediately after the interventions (concomitant with a range of observed improvements within and around the premises), suggesting that the Safety Action model is effective at least in the short term, and is also replicable with fairly predictable results. However, the later increase in violence in Surfers Paradise in 1996 indicated that sustainability could be a key problem.

Although funding was not available for follow-up observations in the three North Queensland cities to assess sustainability formally, extensive efforts were made through Queensland Health and Griffith University to promote and document government, community, and industry capacities for system change and to maintain and extend project achievements in the four cities and across Queensland (Centre for Crime Policy and Public Safety 1996; Homel *et al.* 2003; Queensland Health 1998). A key informant survey was developed to map the maintenance of structures, mechanisms and impacts in the four cities (Carvolth 1997). The survey revealed a higher level of persistence in both structures and investment of effort in the immediate post-intervention phase than had previously been recognised in the formal evaluation (Hauritz *et al.* 1998a).

Analysis some years later of system changes directly or indirectly associated with the Queensland approach (Homel *et al.* 2003) revealed significant increases in the capacity of the formal regulatory system, including the following:

1 Responsible policy and practices were specified more clearly in legislation.
2 A sounder practical knowledge base and guides for action for licensees and licensing officers had been developed.
3 Licensing officers were better supported to engage effectively with community stakeholders in informal community regulatory support.
4 The formal powers of local government to comment on licence renewals were clarified.
5 Most local councils established permanent community safety officer positions with particular responsibility for licensed premises.

What went right? What went wrong?

There were many lessons learned by researchers, project staff, and government partners from the design, implementation, evaluation and attempted mainstreaming of the project model. The following sum-marises these lessons according to the interrelationships between the processes of self-regulation, informal regulation, and formal regulation (at least in terms of the policing aspects of formal regulation).

Self-regulation. The Venue Management Task Groups resolved major professional conflicts between police and licensees, integrated groups of licensees who were previously alienated from each other and organised training for licensees. Soon, licensees themselves took the initiative and formed venue managers' associations. These associations, which continued after the project ended, gave the licensees a common voice, allowed them to work together in positive ways, such as in the development of the code of practice, and helped to give them standing as a legitimate business group.

Informal regulation. The essence of the Safety Action Model is to use a variety of methods to pressure licensees to address problems and improve their practices. These methods included fostering public forums and media publicity, using managers committed to the reform process from another city to bring pressure to bear on local licensees, and employing project officers who had the interpersonal skills necessary to persuade managers to implement improved practices. A critically important strategy involved regulating managers through an informal community-based monitoring committee. Monitoring committees provided a forum for the discussion and resolution of problems in the venues, specifically failures by licensees to comply with their own codes of practice. The committees oversaw, regulated and arbitrated the code of practice and came together to address such issues as free drinks, inappropriate sexual behaviour in public by patrons following a nightclub strip show, advertising of specials on alcohol, and overcrowding.

Licensees lacked any formal incentives to improve their practices because police or liquor licensing officers rarely took action against them even when serious problems emerged. Therefore, the committees relied on the moral authority of members who were local business people, the project officer or the representatives of public service departments, such as the health department, rather than on police enforcement, to obtain compliance with the code of practice. Licensees also distrusted the police and liquor licensing authority (despite the lack of enforcement) and would not have worked with any monitoring committee that included these officials as members. One important reason for the committees' effectiveness was the willingness of some licensees to work with the committee (effectively through the venue managers' association) to apply pressure to their colleagues in certain situations. However, when the projects ceased in each city, the committees either lapsed or their role was taken over by police (as in Surfers Paradise: Blazevic 1996). When police took over, the pre-existing problem of licensees' distrust of police reasserted itself. Thus, the eventual collapse of the informal monitoring and regulatory work of the committee in Surfers Paradise may have been an important factor in the subsequent rise in violence.

Formal regulation: the role of the police. Police enforcement in each city was mainly limited to sweeps of the streets on weekend nights to round up troublemakers and people who were drunk. The original plan was to have police engage in random and highly visible visits to premises; however, this goal was not achieved in any of the cities because it proved impossible to implement this strategy in the limited time permitted by funding. Nevertheless, police were supportive of the safety action projects in each city and participated regularly in meetings, provided data, and responded to incidents of violence and disorder inside and outside licensed premises. These activities could be seen, however, as part of business as usual, representing the kind of support that police regularly provide to inter-agency projects and not reflective of an enhanced police role outside the established paradigm of 'professional law enforcement', the hallmarks of which are rapid responses to incidents, routine car-based patrols and criminal investigation (Moore 1995). The police in Surfers Paradise, nevertheless, became much more actively involved once the intervention was perceived as a success by the community. Although the experience with the community monitoring committee indicated that not all aspects of police involvement were necessarily positive, their later commitment to the project demonstrated the potential value of police-community engagement. Police in Australia and most developed countries have become far more aware than they were in the mid-1990s of the limitations of the professional law enforcement model, and of the power of preventive and cooperative approaches to address problems such as violence in the licensed environment. Indeed, the emphasis on collaboration in both the official police report on the second stage of the Surfers project (Blazevic 1996) and in an inaccurate but, nevertheless, very positive promotional police video about the project (Queensland Police Service 1997) were important steps in the evolution of police attitudes.

The Queensland experience highlights the need for community action projects to adopt a time frame long enough to allow for organisational changes of the kind demonstrated by the police and to build in strategies for long-term sustainability, as described in the earlier discussion of targeted enforcement through the Alcohol Linking Program in New South Wales (Wiggers *et al.* 2004). The importance of the longer time frame is reinforced by results of the other evaluated community action project, STAD, described below.

The Stockholm Prevents Alcohol and Drug Problems (STAD) project

Context, project framework and strategies

Alcohol consumption in Sweden has increased considerably in recent years, paralleled by a marked increase in the number of licensed premises. These changes are partly explained by Swedish membership of the European Union, which has led to the dismantling of most aspects of the old system of strict controls through government monopolies over the production, distribution and sale of alcohol. Although the retail monopoly remains, the overall policy environment is, as in many other countries, one of liberalisation and increased ease of access to alcohol (Wallin *et al.* 2005).

In this context, the Stockholm Prevents Alcohol and Drug Problems (STAD) Project (http://www.stad.org/default.aspx?id=4andepslangua ge=EN), probably the most successful evaluated project of its type to date, was launched by the Stockholm County Council in 1995, inspired by experiences elsewhere, with multicomponent interventions based on local mobilisation, training in responsible beverage service (RBS), and stricter enforcement of licensing laws regulating the service of alcohol to minors and intoxicated persons (Wallin *et al.* 2004).

The project was implemented in the northern part of central Stockholm with the southern part serving as the control area. Although there were more licensed premises (550) in the project area than in the control area (270), the two areas had similar entertainment districts and outlet density. However, the proximity of the two areas could not rule out possible spillover of program effects (which would serve to make the comparison more conservative). Displacement of violence from the intervention area to the comparison area was also a possibility, although the authors suggested that the distance between the two areas was sufficient to make this unlikely.

An early and important task was to conduct a survey of owners of licensed premises. The survey revealed a notable disjunction between the views of owners and those of the licensing authorities, with owners of the view that alcohol service to intoxicated or underage persons was not a problem. The issue became of more concern to owners, however, when the project revealed low rates of refusal of service to actors ('pseudo patrons') hired to simulate drunkenness and order beer.

The next stage in the project was to identify key persons and form an action group consisting of 'representatives from the county council, the licensing board, police officers from the task force for restaurant-related crimes, local police officers, the county administration, the National Institute of Public Health (NIPH), the Organization for Restaurant Owners, the union of restaurant employees, and the specially selected owners of popular nightclubs/restaurants' (Wallin *et al.* 2004: 398) ('restaurant' is used as a generic term for licensed premises). The goals of the action group were to develop strategies to prevent alcohol service to underage patrons and intoxication. Primary strategies included:

1 A two-day training course in responsible beverage service for servers, security staff and owners. The course covered not only Swedish alcohol law and the effects of alcohol but also methods for managing conflict. By the year 2000, about 570 staff from 50 licensed premises had been trained.

2 New forms of enforcement, including 'notification letters' to premises identified by police or other authorities as exhibiting problems such as overserving, and 'mutual controls' of licensed premises conducted by the licensing board and the police. These

mutual controls, based on analyses by both agencies of the nature of problems in specific venues, were suggested by the head of the licensing board as a way of improving communication between the two authorities. Both forms of enforcement were introduced gradually from 1997.

A critical step in the project's evolution was the signing of a written agreement by high-ranking officials in June 2001. The agreement specified how responsibilities for different parts of the intervention were to be distributed among participating organisations. After this agreement, the action group transformed into a more formal steering group, with the head of the licensing board replacing the project coordinator as chair. Although restaurant owners were not initially included in the re-formed group because they were not signatories to the agreement, they were quickly included in the membership and began to send high-ranking representatives. Comprehensive documentation of the sequence of the project and the issues addressed is provided in Wallin, Lindewald and Andréasson (2004).

The STAD project provides an excellent example of a carefully planned and implemented program of prevention that included a time frame that was sufficiently long to allow sustained change. In addition, Wallin produced a series of papers on the project as part of her PhD program (Wallin 2004), providing critical information and reinforcing feedback to the project in a timely and critical manner.

Evaluation

The intervention was evaluated primarily in terms of police-reported violence occurring indoors and outdoors between 10 p.m. and 6 a.m. (closing time was 5 a.m.). Rates of refusal of service to actors ('pseudo patrons') simulating intoxication were also recorded. The violence data were analysed using interrupted time series methods, with allowance in the model for the gradual introduction of the training and enforcement components. The reduction in violent crimes was estimated at 29 per cent for the intervention area compared to a slight increase in the control area (Wallin *et al.* 2003).

An alternate time series model that that did not model the gradual nature of the interventions did not fit the data as well, suggesting that there was a cause-effect relationship that grew in intensity as the intervention components gained momentum. Extraneous factors, such as a water festival that took place in the years 1994–98 in the intervention area, were also ruled out as feasible explanations for the observed changes. In addition, the observed increase in rates of refusal of service, from 5 per cent in 1996 to 47 per cent in 1999 and 70 per cent in 2001, suggest that real changes took place in licensed premises as a result of the project (Wallin *et al.* 2002; Wallin *et al.* 2005). Although improvements in refusal of service also occurred in the control area (possibly reflecting some spillover of the intervention), the refusal rate was higher for RBS-trained licensed premises in the intervention area. The authors suggest that violence did not decline in the control area despite improvements in serving practices because synergies between program components, such as training of doormen in conflict management techniques and responsible serving practices, occurred only in the intervention area.

Why did STAD work so well?

As with the Queensland projects, the STAD project coordinator created a very strong collaborative climate, high levels of participation, successful recruitment of participants for the training, and the formation of working parties within the action group to facilitate the development of training. Action group members became proponents of the project and actively lobbied for the support of politicians and others in the community. These efforts were supported by extensive media coverage and were reinforced by evaluation data that began to show the positive effects of the project. This, in turn, spurred police to greater levels of enforcement activity that involved not only the specialist officers that participated from the beginning, but also police with more general duties. Other action/steering group members began to provide active support for the training and to disseminate the project more widely. Institutionalisation of the project was greatly assisted by the willingness of action group members to provide financial support for the training and other project activities (Wallin *et al.* 2004).

In addition to the effective working relationship among various groups involved in STAD, the role of the head of the licensing board as chair of the steering group was extremely important. She 'attended almost every action group meeting, took part in many of the smaller working groups, and conducted lobbying for politicians and key leaders' (Wallin *et al.* 2004: 415). That she was unanimously elected chair after the written agreement suggests a level of respect and practical cooperation between licensees and their regulators that has not been as evident in projects in other jurisdictions.

Police in the STAD project appeared to take a strongly cooperative approach that increased over time. It is noteworthy that there was no increase during the project in prosecutions of wayward licensees, suggesting that the letters and control orders, albeit gentle tactics, were sufficient to encourage compliance. The strong and continued participation of restaurant owners and employees in the change process undoubtedly helped in this regard, providing powerful industry pressure for compliance that undergirded and helped legitimise enforcement.

Perhaps the most important characteristic of STAD, compared to other programs such as the Queensland Safety Action Projects and the TASC project in Cardiff, was the length of time allowed for the project. With the 10-year time frame, STAD was given much more time to develop than most other interventions. For example, efforts to ensure sustainability were implemented only after sufficient time had elapsed to allow growth in the demand for programs such as the RBS training. In addition, the program was implemented in a country with highly developed public services and a long history of strong government controls on access to alcohol. This culture and history facilitated an action approach that, over time, resulted in a powerful partnership between formal regulation by police and licensing officials and informal regulatory processes at the local level and the level of industry associations. This combination of formal and informal pressures created a powerful incentive for restaurant owners and other licensees to engage in an effective and sustained process of self-regulation. By contrast, although the Queensland projects effectively brought into alignment self-regulation and informal, community-based regulation, this combination proved unstable because it was not reinforced and legitimated during the life of the project by the police or other regulatory authorities.

Tools used in community prevention often focus on community empowerment and typically include mass mobilisation, social action, citizen participation, public advocacy, popular education and local services development (Checkoway 1995; Lander 1995). However, the STAD project appeared to achieve its substantial and sustained benefits using a more 'top-down' approach and without the involvement, at least to any discernible extent, of local residents and local business people who were not involved directly in the sale of alcohol, although the project did include a general population survey that showed strong support for responsible service and stricter enforcement (Wallin and Andréasson 2005). This is in contrast to the Queensland projects, where the community forum and the various task groups succeeded in mobilising significant numbers of citizens who were unconnected with the hospitality industry or its regulation. The success of STAD compared to the initial but only partly sustained success of the

Queensland projects suggests that, while all three levels of regulation (self-regulation, formal regulation, informal regulation) are important, the strong commitment of formal regulators, underpinned by a high degree of legitimacy achieved through cooperative action and the acceptance of shared goals by key organisations, is necessary for community action initiatives to achieve lasting effects. Wallin and colleagues (2004) also noted the importance of the formal regulatory roles being reinforced by a written agreement making explicit that the cooperating organisations, independent of specific persons within those organisations, would take responsibility for the continuing work.

In summary, although the most powerful forces for sustained change lie in the hospitality industries themselves and in local communities, these forces are unlikely to be applied effectively without leadership from official bodies and the sensitive and intelligent use of the powers that reside in regulatory institutions. Thus, community approaches need to involve an appropriate balance between self-regulation, informal regulation and formal regulation, with the nature of this balance customised to fit the local context.

The evidence base for the effective prevention of aggression and violence in the licensed environment

The following sections provide a brief summary of the main findings for each type of prevention approach.

Voluntary programs for individual drinking establishments

The need to improve staff and management attitudes, skills and knowledge is a clear implication of the evidence we have assembled throughout this book. *Safer Bars* is the only freestanding training and risk assessment program focused specifically on preventing and managing violence in drinking establishments for which outcome evaluation results are available. The program is based on detailed research into environmental factors and social processes related to aggression and is one of the few prevention programs evaluated using a randomised control design – the most rigorous method available for establishing causal relationships between interventions and outcomes.

The impact of *Safer Bars* on rates of aggression demonstrated the potential of goodwill, quality resources and training materials, and modest financial incentives to effect modest but statistically and practically significant improvements in staff practices. The impact could probably be increased if the training were of longer duration, provided on an ongoing basis and combined with pressures from police or regulatory bodies. The fact that small reductions in violence were achieved through a voluntary training program makes comprehensive, evidence-based training a priority for further research and development. Although the *Safer Bars* evaluation did not find a mediating role of environmental change, such a role was evident in some of the Queensland intervention studies, suggesting the potential for improving self-regulation through modification of environmental factors that have been consistently identified as risk factors across a number of studies (described in Chapter 5).

Police enforcement

The results from the police enforcement experiments suggest that a mixture of targeted and randomised models may be desirable, but there is simply not enough evidence to make any recommendations about the optimal balance. The most successful of all the policing approaches, the Alcohol Linking Program in New South Wales, demonstrated the success of using place of last drink data as the basis for targeted enforcement, as well as the potential for implementing enhanced policing as a long-term strategy.

The review of enforcement experiments suggested a number of other conclusions:

1 While there are good reasons for believing that randomised enforcement methods if properly implemented will have substantial deterrent effects (Jeffs and Saunders 1983), the effects on crime, disorder and violence that have actually been observed in published studies are small and do not appear to have been sustained beyond the period of enforcement.

2 Neither randomised nor targeted enforcement demonstrated large reductions in assaults; therefore, more research is needed to assess whether enhanced police enforcement is a cost-effective method for preventing violence in the licensed environment, and, if so, how this can best be accomplished.

3 Most enforcement experiments have the weakness that they concentrate on alcohol serving practices and ignore the other types of environmental, staff and patron risks that we have identified in earlier chapters; the impact of broadening the focus for policing to include addressing other risk factors needs to be evaluated.

4 Experience with police enforcement in related fields such as drinking and driving (Homel 1988) strongly suggests that to be effective, enforcement (like training) must be maintained at enhanced levels indefinitely. The development of the Alcohol Linking Program in New South Wales (Wiggers *et al.* 2004) is a model for how to plan research so that it leads to the adoption of increased levels of enforcement and effective prevention practices by police and other regulatory bodies on an ongoing basis.

Local accords

We have identified community partnerships, in particular, as key aspects of a number of the police enforcement projects, with alcohol or licensing accords and similar partnerships comprising one method of local governance that attempts to embed police enforcement in a larger framework that is able to draw on a range of non-enforcement resources. Although accords have been embraced with great enthusiasm by police, politicians and the community in some jurisdictions (for example, New Zealand Department of Prime Minister and Cabinet 2000), there is scant evidence for their effectiveness. The Australian studies reviewed above either used weak evaluation methods or showed no effects on injuries or incidents of crime and violence. The Cardiff project (Maguire and Nettleton 2003), which had an accord in the form of a Licensees Forum as a key component, produced evidence of a small reduction in violence on some measures, but results from the different data sources were inconsistent.

Community action projects

Community action models of the type implemented in Queensland and Stockholm also depend heavily on partnerships, but have demonstrated more success than accords because they draw on a wider range of regulatory levers and focus on the capacities of communities and regulatory agencies as well as on licensed premises. The strengths of the Queensland model include the theory of change that is explicit in its design, its capacity to synthesise formal and informal regulation with self-regulation by drinking establishments, its capacity to mobilise licensees and the community and to involve a large number of stakeholders, and – especially – its reproducibility despite its complexity. In its operationalisation in four Queensland cities, the model succeeded in all components except for the sustained and effective involvement of the police and the liquor licensing authority. This failure partly reflected the inadequate time allowed for planning enforcement strategies and for building relationships with the regulators, an error not made by the designers of STAD.

The success of the STAD project suggests more strongly than the Queensland projects that partnership and community action approaches can indeed bring about sustained reductions in violence under the right conditions. STAD had a 10-year time frame, so there was time to undertake detailed research on the nature of the problem and to establish a broadly based action group that initiated training for servers, security staff and owners and introduced new forms of enforcement. These new enforcement methods were based on careful problem analysis, required action both by police and the licensing board, were tailored to specific local conditions and evolved over time. The whole process was eventually solidified by a written agreement that became a catalyst for more active participation by key groups. The Stockholm STAD model, of all the studies we have reviewed, provides the strongest evidence for substantial and permanent reductions in violence, and should be studied carefully with a view to adapting and testing it in other countries.

The need for ongoing research on the prevention of violence in drinking establishments

In this chapter, we have described in detail preventive programs that have been subjected to at least minimal outcome evaluation. We have tried to identify how successful results were achieved but also how things went wrong, because failures can be as instructive as successes in planning and evaluating improved prevention strategies. We have reviewed the impact of preventive interventions, ranging from staff training, through various forms of police enforcement, to partnerships based on licensing accords or community action, and have concluded that all approaches – with the possible exception of voluntary accords – have demonstrated some promise. However, even when effects on violence or aggression have been found, these effects have generally been small and often only temporary.

The tentative nature of the conclusions that can be drawn from the limited evaluation research underscores the urgent need for research leading to improved strategies for preventing bar violence. The use of unproven programs that may be ineffective or even harmful is all too common. While randomised controlled trials for most programs would not be possible or necessarily appropriate, especially in the context of large scale community projects (Graham and Chandler-

Coutts 2000), it is important that at least minimal evaluation standards be used so that small-scale evaluations at the local level can provide interpretable results. For example, it is not meaningful to demonstrate a reduction in violence following implementation without being able to show (a) that the rate of violence prior to the program reflected a stable pattern rather than a chance increase that was part of normal fluctuations where a reduction would have occurred anyway, and (b) that the reduction also reflected a stable pattern rather than a chance fluctuation. These criteria do not rule out other competing explanations for a reduction in violence (Cook and Campbell 1979), but they at least provide some scientific basis for claiming an impact of a particular strategy or program.

When possible, a theoretical or logic model for the prevention program should be developed prior to adopting strategies in order to (a) identify the goals for change, (b) understand the mechanisms necessary for achieving these changes, and (c) select the kinds of programs that will trigger these mechanisms and ultimately the desired outcomes. Design for evaluation should be seriously considered at the time that programs are being developed, such as a phased implementation in different communities to allow for appropriate comparisons, a focused attempt at rigorous data collection that is conducted consistently before and after the program, and collection of implementation data that provide evidence of plausible mechanisms for program impact. Often, data on implementation are collected to demonstrate that a funded project was successfully completed, but much more could be learned with a well thought-out model and solid measures of outcomes, including linking specific implementation processes to specific outcomes.

Despite the relatively small evaluation literature on preventing aggression in and around licensed premises, the variety of promising results we have reviewed provides an encouraging basis for planning 'the next generation' of prevention initiatives. As we describe in more detail in Chapter 9, next generation approaches need to:

(a) address known risk factors and processes;
(b) use multi-component approaches based on components with demonstrated effectiveness; and
(c) incorporate flexible, multi-agency partnerships that can adapt effectively to local conditions and social changes.

Chapter 9

Violence prevention: towards sustainable evidence-based practices

There surely are good reasons to be pessimistic about the capacity of regulatory agencies to stand up to powerful industries. Yet the pathologically pessimistic might consider the regulatory power of a creature more socially accomplished than ourselves – the dog. How is it that a single Australian sheep-dog or cattle-dog can exercise unchallenged command over a large flock of sheep or herd of cattle every member of which is bigger than herself?

(Ayres and Braithwaite 1992: 44)

The central message of this book is that bar violence is a serious social problem that requires a serious societal response. A serious response means going beyond reactive policing or public education programs that construe the problem solely in terms of individual patron choice and responsibility. It also means understanding the problem in system terms (Holder 1998), including how a deregulated night-time economy affects the social purposes, culture and environments of drinking establishments, as well as the role of legislative and institutional systems that shape regulatory policies and practices. Finally, it means building new policies and practices on the firm foundation of research evidence.

The aim of this chapter is to integrate the findings of earlier chapters in terms of developing better strategies for reducing bar violence. We first synthesise the key factors that research shows are linked to violence in drinking establishments and the main approaches that have been developed for addressing these factors. We then discuss how a responsive regulatory framework can be used to incorporate effective strategies for prevention into routine practices. We conclude with a discussion of future directions for prevention and the prospects for raising the bar on standards for preventing bar violence.

Key factors associated with violence in and around drinking establishments and approaches to addressing these factors

The ambiguous and contested nature of acceptable behavioural boundaries is fundamental to understanding the causes of aggression and violence in and around drinking establishments. 'Normal trouble' happens – but what is regarded as normal and acceptable varies greatly from patron to patron, from one staff member to another, and from place to place. Certain establishments and geographic areas gain a reputation over time for being places where the boundaries can really be stretched and 'time out' becomes an epic experience. Nevertheless, boundaries are needed, and owners and managers who wish to maintain a safe environment that will remain profitable over the long run will aim to set limits on normal trouble. At the same time, these limits must allow an environment in which the positive and time-out effects of alcohol can be enjoyed in the context of prolonged social contact and open socialising. Controls that undermine these basic functions will not succeed, which means that a certain amount of conflict and aggression is probably inevitable. The challenge is to minimise the frequency and seriousness of such aggression.

Table 9.1 highlights the key factors that have emerged from research described in earlier chapters relating to the cultural context, the role of alcohol, patron characteristics, the barroom environment, staff behaviour, and spaces around drinking establishments. The table also lists approaches, interventions and programs that relate to each of these aspects of the drinking environment, including evaluated approaches described in Chapter 8, strategies reported in the literature but not yet evaluated, and hypothetical approaches that could potentially be developed based on consideration of routine activity theory and situational prevention.

Cultural expectations

A theme that permeates every chapter in this book is the need to modify cultural attitudes and practices that legitimate or trivialise bar violence, in some settings even celebrating it as an acceptable form of entertainment. We have given numerous examples of how these attitudes play out in practice and have suggested a range of ways in

Table 9.1. Key factors linked to violence in drinking establishments and examples of approaches, interventions and programs addressing these factors

	Key factors	Approaches, interventions and programs
Cultural expectations	• Bar violence is normative and largely acceptable in many countries, and cultural expectations are widespread that violence will occur at least in some drinking establishments	• Legislative, licensing, educational and regulatory approaches that communicate clearly to patrons, staff, management, regulators, politicians and the community that bar violence is not acceptable.
Effects of alcohol consumption	• The risk of aggression is increased by the effects of alcohol on thinking, problem-solving, perceptions, time orientation and emotions. However, whether these effects lead to aggression depends on characteristics of the drinker, the drinking environment and the culture of drinking. • Effects of alcohol such as perseveration and poor problem-solving make intoxicated patrons difficult to handle.	• Training staff in responsible beverage service (RBS) to prevent serving to intoxication (Buka and Birdthistle 1999; Geller et al. 1987; Gliksman et al. 1993; Lang et al. 1998; Saltz 1987); RBS has also been included as part of multi-component programs (Hauritz et al. 1998a; Homel et al. 1997; Maguire and Nettleton 2003; Wallin et al. 2002, 2003, 2004, 2005). • Formal regulations that prohibit serving to intoxication and enforcement of these regulations (Burns et al. 1995; Jeffs and Saunders 1983; Levy and Miller 1995; McKnight and Streff 1994; Sim et al. 2005; Stewart 1993; Wiggers et al. 2004).

Table 9.1 continues overleaf

Table 9.1 continued

Key factors	Approaches, interventions and programs
	• Training staff in techniques for dealing with intoxicated persons (included as part of the Safer Bars training (Graham, Osgood *et al.* 2004; Graham, Jelley and Purcell 2005) as well as in some RBS programs).
	• Some aspects of local accords such as agreements to ban drink promotions (Felson *et al.* 1997; Hawks *et al.* 1999; McCarthy 2007; Rumbold *et al.* 1998).
	• Promoting voluntary house policies to reduce service to intoxicated patrons (Toomey *et al.* 2001); similar house policies are also part of many RBS programs and multi-component community approaches cited above.
	• Reducing environmental irritants that provoke emotional or impulsive responses by intoxicated individuals.
Patron characteristics	• Patrons of drinking establishments are more likely to have characteristics associated with increased risk of aggression (for example, male, young, heavy drinker, marginalised subculture) compared with persons who drink in other
	• Patron or public education that may be done as a stand-alone strategy or as part of enforcement and multi-component approaches.
	• Focusing on eliminating the presence of the most trouble-making patrons by:

locations such as at home or at a restaurant.

- These characteristics are linked to the main functions of drinking establishments, including participating in the young male macho culture, meeting sexual or romantic partners, and socialising.
- While patron characteristics and the functions of drinking establishments increase the risk of aggression, environmental controls and staff behaviour can reduce this risk.

Risk factors in the environment

- There is now consistent evidence from a number of studies conducted in different countries linking aggression to specific aspects of the barroom environment.
- Although these associations are consistent, it is not known whether changes on any particular environmental risk factor or factors will result in measurable changes in aggression because: (a) the mechanism by which each environmental factor is linked to aggression has

– Pubwatch/pub-ban arrangements among licensees/managers to warn one another and police about a person causing problems (Hadfield et al. 2005a; MCM Research 1993).

– Environmental risk assessments that include banning patrons who repeatedly engage in aggression (Graham 1999).

– Door screening to keep out trouble-makers (included as part of a number of policy/training approaches).

- House policies and staff practices that encourage patrons to assume a guardian role (in routine activity terms) in preventing incidents between patrons.

- *Safer Bars* risk assessment booklet for managers to rate environmental risks (Graham 1999).

- Environmental aspects addressed in multi-component programs, including codes of practice and informal regulation through community monitoring committees (Homel et al. 1997).

- Addressing aspects of the physical features of the exterior or interior of a bar (including

Table 9.1 continues overleaf

Table 9.1 continued

	Key factors	Approaches, interventions and programs
	not been confirmed for many risk factors, (b) interactions, cumulative effects and synergies among risk factors are not well understood.	cleanliness, ventilation and temperature) that might signal that aggression is expected or accepted. • Physical design modifications that reduce intersecting pedestrian flows within establishments. • House policies that establish minimum dress standards for female servers and ban the playing of sexually explicit music with violent overtones.
Staff behaviour	• Evidence suggests that staff play a crucial role in preventing, managing and sometimes even causing aggression. • The role and importance of security staff has increased dramatically in recent years. There is an increased presence of personnel from private, specialised security firms performing a security role inside and outside licensed premises. • The culture of security staff and the framing of staff roles as confrontational rather than focused on safety and protection of patrons may be serving to increase rather than prevent violence.	• Staff training: – Training all staff in preventing violence and managing problem behaviour (Graham *et al.* 2004). – Security staff training (Hobbs, Hadfield, Lister and Winlow 2002; Lister, Hadfield, Hobbs and Winlow 2001; MCM Research 1993). – Various training programs for staff done as part of multi-component community interventions (Hauritz *et al.* 1998a; Homel *et al.* 1997; Maguire and Nettleton 2003; Wallin *et al.* 2002, 2003, 2004, 2005). • Licensing of security staff (Lister *et al.* 2001; Prenzler and Hayes 1998) supported by

- effective and prompt administration.
- House policies that make all staff (not just security) responsible for minimising aggression.
- Regulation and training that supports a culture of security staff as guardians not enforcers, including reducing environmental precipitators of aggression related to staff behaviour.

- Local accords and Licensing Forums (Felson et al. 1997; Hawks et al. 1999; Maguire and Nettleton 2003; McCarthy 2007; Rumbold et al. 1998).
- Community action programs (Homel et al. 1997; Wallin and Andreasson 2005).
- Safety audits including improving public transport to remove patrons quickly (Hauritz et al. 1998a), street lighting (Farrington and Welsh 2002) and the effective use of closed circuit TV (Sivarajasingam et al. 2003).
- Minimising the number of patrons waiting in queues and managing queues fairly and non-aggressively.
- Regulating the flow of patrons between establishments.
- Identifying, preventing and targeting hot spots and critical times.

Spaces around drinking establishments

- There is less systematic research on risk factors regarding problems outside versus inside establishments, but there is at least some evidence that problems are associated with density or clustering of drinking establishments.
- Although problems outside drinking establishments are clearly linked to problems within, there is a lack of clarity regarding the extent that drinking establishments *vs* other community agencies have formal responsibility for safety outside.
- In different jurisdictions, different agencies (for example, police, community groups, hospitality associations) have led partnerships to reduce these problems.

which the culture can be modified, including some of the strategies listed in other sections of Table 9.1. A promising population-level approach, based on the experience in some countries with drinking and driving (Babor *et al.* 2003; Homel, Carseldine and Kearns 1988), is for government to set the standard through legislation and effective regulation supported by public education, coercing a degree of behaviour change among all players that might contribute over time to reducing societal tolerance of bar-related violence.

The effects of alcohol consumption and the role of intoxication

As described in Chapter 3, there are a number of ways that the effects of alcohol can increase the likelihood that aggression will occur. Studies of barroom violence have consistently found a positive association between level of violence and level of intoxication of patrons. Both individual-level consumption and being in an environment in which a large proportion of patrons are intoxicated have been shown to be associated with increased aggression. As described in Chapter 5, factors that may contribute to intoxication and hence the increase in violence include a fast rate of drinking, round buying, cheap drinks and drinks specials. Recent evidence (Hughes *et al.* 2007) suggests that pre-drinking prior to going to the club or bar may also play a role in the intoxication-aggression link.

Evaluation of programs focused on serving practices suggests that these programs can sometimes have a modest impact on intoxication levels. However, effects of these programs on aggression and violence have not been assessed, although training in responsible beverage service has been included as one component of broader programs that have shown an impact on reducing violence (Felson *et al.* 1997; Homel *et al.* 1997; Putnam *et al.* 1993; Wallin *et al.* 2003).

Studies of enhanced enforcement of laws prohibiting serving to intoxication (Levy and Miller 1995; McKnight and Streff 1994; Putnam *et al.* 1993) suggest that enforcement has a significant effect on intoxication/serving practices, and one study (Putnam *et al.* 1993) showed a link between the enforcement of responsible serving practices and reduced injuries from assault. As described in Chapter 8, some police enforcement programs focused on serving practices have also shown a short-term decrease in violence or public disorder (Jeffs and Saunders 1983; Sim *et al.* 2005).

Banning drink promotions and cheap drinks may be a useful regulatory response for stopping a large proportion of patrons within an establishment from drinking to intoxication (Babor *et al.* 1980) – to the extent that such a strategy does not contravene competition

246

legislation. However, given recent evidence of the prevalence of drinking prior to going out to clubs (Forsyth 2006; Hughes *et al.* 2007), banning drinking promotions may be less effective in contemporary drinking establishments than was found to be the case in previous research.

Patron characteristics

Although much of what is written in the popular press blames individual troublemakers for bar violence, no studies were found which evaluated patron education programs designed to reduce aggressive behaviour, such as the 'Enjoy the night, not the fight' campaign in Queensland, Australia or the 'Cage Your Rage' public education campaign in Alberta, Canada (http://www.aglc.gov. ab.ca/responsibleliquorservice/cageyourrage.asp). The one existing evaluation of the effectiveness of an educational approach directed towards patrons of drinking establishments (related to drinking and driving not violence) did not show any measurable impact on behaviour (McLean *et al.* 1994). Moreover, educational approaches have generally not been found to be effective prevention strategies (Babor *et al.* 2003).

Although attempts at prevention using educational approaches or strategies focused on defining the problem as the behaviour of a few troublesome individuals (such as pubwatch/pub-ban agreements) are unlikely to be effective, understanding the relationship between aggression and the characteristics of patrons needs to be a key factor in policy and training programs for staff and management of licensed premises, as well as in accords and broader community approaches. For example, we have described how aspects of the macho culture, such as men engaging in aggression to support a buddy or to protect a female, can escalate the severity of conflict situations. While changing the characteristics and culture of patron populations may be difficult to effect in the short-term, we have provided examples throughout this book of interventions by third parties or by staff that have prevented or defused conflicts despite the macho concerns of the antagonists. The pattern of masculinity norms among young male drinkers and security staff that supports disengagement from serious violence, found recently by Tomsen (2005), reinforces the contention that a masculine culture need not inevitably lead to aggression.

Similarly, knowledge of other high-risk patron characteristics or functions of drinking establishments (for example, establishments that serve as a home base for marginalised or aggressive subcultures or as a place to meet sexual/romantic partners) can be used to ensure that environmental and staff training approaches are appropriate for specific target populations.

Environmental risk factors

Recurring patterns or associations between violence and the environment are obvious targets for prevention, especially if they are evident in different countries over time, as has been found for many of the environmental risk factors discussed in Chapter 5. One such factor is the expectation held by patrons and staff about acceptable behaviour in and around particular establishments. As we observed in Chapter 5, many features of the physical and social environments can mould expectations, including what a building looks like outside and inside, signage, and the experiences of patrons as they enter. Similarly, previous experience at a particular establishment where, for example, aggression was unchecked or made worse by staff may set up an expectation that aggression will be tolerated in that establishment.

Many other examples of the ways that expectations are created and moulded have been presented in earlier chapters. These examples highlight the need for owners and management to understand the kinds of signals that they are sending to patrons (and to their staff) and to take responsibility for creating a physical environment and a social milieu that promotes non-aggressive interactions and sets clear rules for acceptable behaviours. In addition to making specific changes based on a comprehensive risk assessment, one way of setting clear expectations might be to have a prominently displayed code of practice for staff, as used in accords and community actions approaches.

We also presented analyses in Chapter 5 that suggested that poor physical design, such as intersecting traffic flows (through, for example, the inappropriate location of toilets, serving areas and dance floors), combined with generally permissive or poor management practices, greatly increased the risk of aggressive encounters. Although more research is needed, these findings suggest that consideration should be given to the physical design of drinking establishments in order to facilitate smooth pedestrian flow and minimise points of intersection.

Numerous publications have reiterated the importance of environmental risks in drinking establishments (Doherty and Roche 2003; Graham and Homel 1997; Hadfield 2006; MCM Research 1993), and risk assessments and house policies have often been included as part of prevention efforts (Graham 2000). Although addressing environmental risks has been included as a component of programs shown to reduce violence (Graham, Osgood *et al.* 2004; Hauritz *et al.* 1998; Homel *et al.* 1997; Wiggers *et al.* 2004), evaluation of the impact of making specific changes to the environment on reducing violence has not yet been conducted. The overall conclusion is that, while the consistent patterns linking violence to environmental characteristics point to the environment as a powerful controller of patron behaviour, we still do not know the full potential for using modification of barroom environments to reduce and minimise violence in drinking establishments.

Staff behaviour

The role of staff appears to be critical in preventing and reducing violence. Many aggressive incidents involve escalation from minor or trivial irritants or provocations, and staff can often prevent escalation by intervening early in arguments, horseplay, unprovoked shoves, swearing, finger pointing, and similar behaviours. Although it may be impossible to monitor the early stages of all such incidents in a large crowded bar, staff can maintain a general alertness to incipient problems, especially if all staff, not just security staff, have an explicit mandate to prevent violence.

Other methods identified in Chapter 6 to aid staff in preventing problem behaviours, based on existing knowledge of staff roles in bar aggression and the application of situational crime prevention theory, include: ensuring that macho, competitive and confrontational behaviour is not elicited by staff behaviour, attitudes or demeanour; controlling pressures that encourage patrons to react aggressively, such as fostering an environment where manliness is not defined by fighting; reducing permissibility by setting clear rules and enforcing them fairly; and reducing provocation by treating patrons with courtesy and respect, even when faced with frustrating situations. A fundamentally important strategy that we proposed is to redefine the staff role as guardians in routine activity terms, rather than as enforcers or guards.

Training bar staff in methods for preventing and managing problem behaviours and aggression was the key component of the *Safer Bars* program (Graham, Jelley and Purcell 2005) and appeared to be largely responsible for the program's impact. Staff training has also been part of larger community-based initiatives that have been effective in reducing violence (Hauritz *et al.* 1998a; Homel *et al.* 1997; Wallin *et al.* 2003).

Licensing and regulation of staff, particularly security staff, has been adopted in many jurisdictions over the past 15 to 20 years

(Arnold and Laidler 1994; Hobbs *et al.* 2003; Lister *et al.* 2001; MCM Research 1993). There have been no evaluations of the effectiveness of these programs, although there is some evidence that their effects are probably weak, partly because of inconsistent implementation (Lister *et al.* 2001).

Spaces around drinking establishments

As we described in Chapter 6, there are clear links between what takes place inside establishments and the extent of violence outside. Many licensing accords have included strategies such as reducing traffic between different establishments by prohibiting passes for free re-entry (Felson *et al.* 1997; Hawks *et al.* 1999; McCarthy 2007; Rumbold *et al.* 1998) in order to address problems and violence in the areas outside drinking establishments. However, as described in Chapter 8, the impacts of accords have been modest at best, possibly because of their reliance on voluntary compliance. Community action approaches (Hauritz *et al.* 1998a; Homel *et al.* 1997; Wallin *et al.* 2003) have achieved some success in terms of the broader areas around drinking establishments, but because these partnership models always involve the implementation of a range of programs and techniques, it is not easy to isolate the effects of specific components, such as community mobilisation, safety audits, codes of practice, or crime prevention through environmental design (CPTED) initiatives, such as improved transport options or closed circuit TV monitoring. Thus, like the environment inside drinking establishments, the potential for reducing violence by addressing systematically factors in the areas around drinking establishments remains largely unknown.

Responsive regulation as a framework for incorporating evidence-based prevention into routine practices

We observed in Chapter 1 that the regulatory agenda should be based on a clear understanding of the processes implicated in aggression and violence, enhanced by an analysis of situational risk factors and by scientific evidence on the most effective strategies for minimising the effects of these risk factors. In the previous section, we presented a brief overview of key issues, risk factors and possible preventive responses (including both evidence-based strategies and some approaches that are as yet untried or unevaluated). Because, as we have emphasised, so many of the processes that give rise to aggression and violence are connected with each other (such as macho culture, patron intoxication, the physical and social environment, and the attitudes and behaviour of security staff), it seems likely that effective preventive responses will need to include more than one approach. For example, establishing clear norms that promote non-aggressive interactions is a priority, but achieving this outcome is likely to involve attention to the physical environments of drinking establishments, as well as an investment in staff selection and training and improvements in management practices.

In addition, the specific approaches that will be most successful are likely to vary by drinking establishment, community and culture, and each type of establishment is likely to pose different regulatory challenges. Neighbourhood bars, for example, tend to have a loyal clientele and operate according to well-established informal norms that have evolved over many years. On the other hand, nightclubs and bars crowded together in city centre entertainment areas may operate as discrete and highly competitive business entities, lack any sense of tradition, and aim to package excitement and glamour for hundreds or even thousands of young adults who may have trouble remembering where they were the night before.

In summary, prevention of aggression and violence in the licensed environment needs to be based on knowledge about core risk factors and interactional processes, build on scientific evidence of strategies that actually reduce aggression and violence, and be carefully tailored to the specific circumstances of each establishment and community. Prevention also needs to be responsive to processes already put in place by the industry and other players in each situation. A broad, heavy-handed enforcement approach, for example, will not be effective when problems are due to a small number of uncooperative high-risk premises and where most licensees have been cooperating effectively for some time with local government, community groups and police. On the other hand, prevention programs that emphasise voluntary involvement in codes of practice and staff training may make little progress in a situation where there is a culture of confrontation between licensees and the authorities, or where short-term competition is the major concern among drinking establishments.

Another consideration for prevention is the broader social and regulatory context in which drinking establishments function. As we noted in Chapter 1 and elsewhere in this book, liberalisation of liquor licensing laws, deregulation of the sale of alcohol and the growth of the night-time economy have been occurring in many parts of the world. Therefore, in developing effective strategies for reducing bar violence, it is important to keep in mind that prevention requires not only a solid understanding of the types of factors that influence the risk of violence in and around drinking establishments and the various policy, training and other options available for reducing or managing risks, but also a detailed knowledge of the specific types of drinking establishments in the target area, the characteristics of the clientele who patronise these establishments, and the culture and community to which prevention is being directed.

The theory of responsive regulation as applied to preventing bar violence

The theory of responsive regulation that we introduced in Chapter 2 provides the conceptual tools for thinking through the challenges involved in choosing evidence-based strategies and balancing persuasion with punishment in complex and rapidly changing situations (Ayres and Braithwaite 1992; Braithwaite 2002). The ideal, of course, is perfect and universal self-regulation by patrons, staff and licensees, with compliance made as easy as possible through support from clear laws, helpful licensing officials and industry associations, and the availability of extensive resources including affordable training programs. As we described in earlier chapters, self-regulation in drinking establishments is indeed the norm. Most places are not violent most of the time, patrons frequently walk away from trouble or intervene effectively to defuse or divert potential conflicts, staff often exercise great skill and subtlety and show remarkable restraint in dealing with troublemakers, and managers and licensees more often than not strive to create a peaceful but enjoyable environment.

On the other hand, there are many clear examples of the failure of self-regulation in our research and the literature generally. Braithwaite (2002) makes the important observation that non-compliance with laws and industry best practice is not primarily because of rational business calculations by operators, but because management does not have the competence to comply. If this is true for big business and for the large service industries discussed by Braithwaite, one would expect it to be even more true for an industry that employs mostly casual, young and inexperienced staff, dealing with persons whose reason and emotions are affected by alcohol in a culture where aggression, at least between males, is typically seen as normative. If supporting or facilitating self-regulation is the ideal, then providing training such as *Safer Bars*, and other resources such as risk assessment protocols to create a greater capacity for compliance and self-regulation, become of fundamental importance.

One problem with simply making resources available, however, is that not all owners and managers see spending money on assessment and training as a priority. It is likely, therefore, that the regulatory environment will have to be structured in a way that creates incentives for licensees and managers to introduce assessment and training and to engage in other evidence-based practices that will minimise the risks of violence. There are many possible ways of creating incentives. One basic approach is to emphasise the regular provision of information and educational resources, relying on dialogue, persuasion and appeals to operators to establish their reputations as good corporate citizens. When this fails, a regulator might make a friendly visit to an establishment, pointing out the effects of poor management practices on the risks of injuries to patrons and staff, and leaving behind an application form for a training program – similar to the procedures adopted as part of the Alcohol Linking Program. Pressure could be increased where necessary to include warning letters, 'name and shame' articles in the local paper using data publicly available from the regulatory agency, public forums organised by local residents and business groups and supported by the regulator, civil penalties such as 'polluter pays' levies imposed by government or even an industry association, fines and other criminal penalties and, ultimately, licence suspension or revocation.

These examples, most of which have some basis in the evidence we reviewed in Chapter 8, comprise the elements of a basic enforcement pyramid – a central tool of the responsive regulator. A simple hypothetical pyramid relating to responsive regulation of drinking environments is depicted in Figure 9.1. The cooperative base of the pyramid is where most action takes place, with transition by the regulator to higher and more coercive levels only when the cooperative approach fails.

Conversely, when a more punitive measure has been necessary and has achieved success, the regulator would move down the pyramid again to the least invasive level needed. If managers and staff quickly improve their practices after a more than usually rigorous period of enforcement, for example, it may be appropriate to ease back and emphasise capacity building options such as training, or to offer support to the local industry association to help rein in renegade operators. Just as one can almost certainly enhance the effects of voluntary approaches by using incentives and deterrents through enforcement strategies, pure enforcement may be more effective and more acceptable, and hence more sustainable, if it is combined with measures from lower down the pyramid. This approach can include educative visits by health and licensing officials, as in the Wellington study (Sim *et al.* 2005), encouragement to take advantage of voluntary training programs such as *Safer Bars*, or even shock tactics using

Figure 9.1 An example of a simple enforcement pyramid for drinking establishments

photographs of disfigured victims of violence, as employed by medical specialists in the Cardiff study (Warburton and Shepherd 2006).

A related feature of the enforcement pyramid is the idea of the 'benign big gun' (Ayres and Braithwaite 1992: 40). This means that 'the greater the heights of punitiveness to which an agency can escalate, the greater its capacity to push regulation down to the cooperative base of the pyramid'. In terms of the application of this principle to drinking establishments, the most effective regulatory agencies are likely to be those that clearly have both the authority and the will to follow-up with fines or other sanctions if voluntary agreements are violated. A problem with a number of the approaches to prevention that we discussed in Chapter 8 was that, although local police and licensing authorities apparently had the power, their behaviour suggested that they were unlikely to use it. For example, no licensees were prosecuted in the Sydney police enforcement project (Burns *et al.* 1995) and only two were prosecuted in the Wellington study (Sim *et al.* 2005), suggesting that the threat of a 'big gun' was not seen as credible by those being regulated (that is, the licensees). Similarly, in the TASC project (Maguire and Nettleton 2003), the country council had the power to implement disciplinary measures and prevent new licences being issued, but refused to exercise this power, thereby greatly weakening the potential impact of the licensees forum.

The involvement of third parties in the regulatory process, such as the role of the monitoring committees in the Queensland projects, is desirable, although the success of the STAD project suggests that third parties may not always be necessary. However, as noted in Chapter 8, the risks of regulatory capture are minimised and the regulatory armoury expanded if residents and community and business groups are empowered to participate in regulatory processes by performing an effective monitoring and advocacy role. What Ayres and Braithwaite (1992) call 'tripartism' fosters the participation of community associations by giving them full access to all the information available to the regulator, a seat at the negotiating table and (ideally) the same standing to sue or prosecute as the regulator.

In summary, responsive regulation theory provides a powerful, practical and flexible framework within which to locate evidence-based preventive practices. Equally important, a responsive regulation framework provides a model for institutionalising or mainstreaming prevention programs that have been developed as demonstration projects by researchers, making it possible to determine how the mix and intensity of preventive components may be varied over time in response to changing industry conditions. For example, a heavy emphasis may be required at the beginning on capacity building through training, but as the market becomes more competitive the incentives for compliance may need to be increased through more active monitoring by local businesses and community groups or through a short period of intense police enforcement directed at non-compliant licensees. The exact mix of elements, and their duration, will depend on local conditions as they vary over time and are moulded by the actions and reactions of all the players involved.

Future directions for enhancing prevention of bar violence

As described in Chapter 8, evaluations of approaches to preventing violence in drinking establishments provide some basis for optimism that bar violence can be reduced. There is evidence for the effectiveness of intervention techniques at all levels of the enforcement pyramid, ranging from facilitated self-regulation through the provision of training and risk assessment resources, to cooperative methods based on persuasion and warnings, to community action approaches that build industry, community and institutional capacities, and to enforced self-regulation using various forms of police enforcement and regulatory measures. However, the evidence base is far too small to support strong recommendations, and many questions remain regarding even the most successful initiatives in terms of their long-term effects and replicability in other countries or contexts. The following sections outline some basic strategies to enhance the current knowledge base of approaches for reducing violence related to licensed premises.

Further development of evidence-based policies and practices

The body of scientific research is thin, and the field is replete with unproven approaches. As we noted in Chapter 8, there is an urgent need for research to assess the effects on aggression of specific types of changes in the environment or regulatory strategies, holding other factors constant. Such assessments are necessary in order to build powerful multi-component strategies, and are essential for regulators who need to know the effectiveness of specific strategies such as warning letters or licence suspensions. Small-scale but rigorous studies could be undertaken to address more systematically the potential for reducing the contribution of specific environmental risk factors to bar violence and to assess the effects of specific regulatory techniques.

We also need to know more about the preventive effects of general regulatory options, such as limits on the number of premises within a particular geographic area. Several studies have demonstrated a relationship between changes in density of alcohol outlets and changes in violence (Livingston *et al.* 2007), but the effect of controlling density as a strategy to reduce violence has not been evaluated, and issues such as thresholds and other contextual factors have not been addressed. Similarly, there is evidence, primarily from the US and Canada (as described in reviews by Babor *et al.* 2003; Graham 2000), that holding owners and staff liable under civil or criminal law for damages and injury resulting from the violence perpetrated by persons whom they have served alcohol may be effective in persuading licensees to ensure that there are ample numbers of well-trained staff, appropriate policies and reduced environmental risks. However, there is currently no systematic evaluation evidence of the effect of planned strategic increases in liability related to bar violence, although the reduction in incidents of driving after drinking achieved by increasing the legal liability of servers and owners (Sloan *et al.* 2000) suggests that similar effects on violence are possible.

Not only do we need more research on the effects of specific measures, we need research that compares the effects of different mixes of strategies in comprehensive prevention models. We simply do not have enough evidence to know, for example, what kind of balance is desirable between measures at the broad base of the enforcement pyramid and measures at the top. For example, experimentation is required to determine whether relatively gentle enforcement measures, such as the notification letters used in the alcohol linking program, would be sufficient to induce reluctant licensees to participate in risk assessments and training, or whether the effects of this approach could be enhanced by combining it with other strategies such as community monitoring or local industry associations. Similarly, because accords have been promoted so uncritically, there is insufficient evidence to identify the kinds of formal enforcement that could be implemented to further reduce violence while still maintaining any effects achieved through the cooperation of licensees or industry associations.

Balancing targeted versus universal prevention

The appropriate balance of targeted and universal prevention approaches is another issue of fundamental importance not only for prevention of bar violence but for prevention generally. Considerations in this balance include the risk of stigmatisation caused by targeted strategies, the efficient use of resources, public acceptability, the extent of cooperation of a targeted population, the general failure of targeted approaches to focus on social context, and a host of related concerns (Homel 2005; Offord *et al.* 1999). One important consideration is the possible applicability of the 'prevention paradox', a term coined to describe a situation where the net gain for society of broad-based preventive approaches is greater than would be gained by targeted approaches, even though most people in society are not at risk of the problem. In terms of how this might apply to drinking establishments, it is possible that a small reduction in risk amongst the large number of low-to-moderate risk premises may produce a larger population reduction in violence and injury than would be accomplished by large risk reductions in the small number of high-risk premises. In other words, because relatively low-risk establishments are so numerous, even though they individually produce few problems, collectively over time they may contribute a larger proportion of the total number of violent incidents than do high-risk premises.

The evidence we have reviewed in this book does not permit any clear conclusions with regard to the relative effectiveness of targeted versus universal approaches. Enforcement experiments based on both methods showed some promise, with both the Torquay (universal) and the Alcohol Linking (targeted) enforcement studies yielding reductions in alcohol-related crime. Moreover, to some extent, the contrast of the randomised model with the intelligence-led targeted approach is artificial, since police often include targeted enforcement as part of universal approaches, as in the Wellington experiment. Conversely, the Alcohol Linking Program in New South Wales involved feedback *via* letters on several occasions to all licensed premises, illustrating that police will include universal enforcement tactics as part of targeted approaches if these can be implemented cheaply and easily. The experience of the STAD project, where feedback to errant licensees based on data was also used, suggests that, whether targeted or not, the feedback strategy is likely to be useful. In addition, the information collected as part of the Alcohol Linking Program in order to target specific premises has the added benefit of providing quick feedback to police of crime data related to specific premises, thereby allowing police to intensify or modify their enforcement strategies as appropriate (Wiggers *et al.* 2004).

Although the optimal balance between targeted and universal approaches is unknown and likely to vary depending on the circumstances, universal strategies may be generally more appropriate for certain types of approaches to preventing bar violence. For example, because licensed premises are part of a larger industry with numerous interconnections among owners, managers and staff, there are practical difficulties in concentrating regulatory policies solely on high-risk premises or in imposing special conditions on some premises but not on others. In this context, it is challenging to target restrictions, even if supported by statistical evidence of a higher risk of certain premises, when the managers of the targeted establishments know that identical practices are being used in non-targeted premises. In sum, it is likely that the decision between targeted versus universal focus in any particular context will depend on a number of factors, including costs, opportunities and political and social conditions.

Incorporating responsiveness to local conditions

One of the most important lessons from the STAD program in Stockholm is that effective prevention takes time and must be carefully moulded to fit local conditions. STAD was developed in a country that has a long history of government services and controls on access to alcohol, and under these circumstances involvement of the broader community did not appear to be necessary. The STAD approach may be a less effective vehicle for change, however, in countries such as Australia and the United States where there are strong traditions of grassroot involvement in community partnerships.

Even within one country, the situation can vary markedly between different cities and regions or different sectors of the market. There are a variety of local conditions that need to be taken into consideration including: the level and nature of violence, crime and injuries; the particular features of local drinking establishments that attract patrons; the safety, noise and other issues associated with particular establishments; applicable legislation related to the regulation of licensed premises and the night-time economy generally; the extent of existing cooperative relationships between owners/managers and regulators and local authorities; the key issues from the perspectives of local regulators and policy makers; and the characteristics of the broader community context in which the drinking establishments are located. For example, although entertainment areas have been the focus of most public concern related to bar violence, violence is not confined to entertainment districts. The suburban tavern or bar can be another high-risk type of venue (Block and Block 1995; Daly, Campbell, Wiggers and Considine 2002; Graham, Bernards *et al.* 2006), depending on how it is managed and the type of patrons it attracts. Thus, while entertainment areas have been the focus of many interventions, a comprehensive approach to bar violence would address problems throughout the community. Adopting a model of responsive regulation would help to ensure that strategies are quickly modified in the light of industry reactions.

Finally, researchers, or at least those who understand research, need to be part of local planning groups. The empirical research of Nutley and her colleagues (2007: 306) on how research influences practice emphasises the social and collective nature of research and stresses that successful dissemination strategies focus on 'mechanisms of interaction, social influence and local facilitation'.

Building sustainability into policies and practices

To be of value, preventive strategies must not just be effective in the short term; they also need to be sustainable. The Alcohol Linking Program and the STAD project put particular effort into ensuring sustainability over time and appear to have been successful. As we have noted elsewhere in this book, sustainability and effective regulation are likely to rely on the interaction of:

(a) formal regulation and enforcement, that is efforts at the political or governmental level;

(b) informal regulation, such as mobilising civil society through residents' action and through community and business groups; and

(c) self-regulation, in the form of voluntary good practices by staff and management of drinking establishments and liquor industry associations.

Taking these three levels into consideration, the *Safer Bars* program, for example, while showing a reasonably durable effect of at least a few months, would likely need to be combined with other strategies (such as informal or formal regulation) in order to have a broad and sustainable effect beyond that obtained through voluntary participation of some drinking establishments. The community action approach of the Queensland projects showed a reliable and replicable reduction in violence but was less successful at achieving stable changes. The Queensland approach, however, demonstrated the powerful role that could be played by informal regulation in the form of community monitoring committees even though this role diminished over time. The STAD project, as well as recent research in New Zealand on reducing alcohol-related harm to young people (Conway *et al.* 2007), supports the view that the outcomes of community action approaches need not be temporary but can include, at least, limited structural changes (which in the New Zealand case was a reorientation of service providers to more evidence-based practice and the building of an intersectoral capacity for change).

Holder and Moore (2000) identified some important strategies related to sustainability of community action approaches generally, such as honouring community values, obtaining key leader support, flexibility, developing local resources, leveraging prior success and planning for policy and structural changes. Table 9.2 shows related examples of approaches to sustainability at the level of self-regulation and formal regulation relating to reducing bar violence, drawing on effective approaches identified in Chapter 8. The table is not intended to provide a recipe for action, but rather to stimulate thought about some of the dimensions, such as reinforcers and institutional mechanisms, for achieving sustainable change.

Prospects for raising the bar

In this book, we have drawn on our own research and that of others to describe the many facets of bar violence and its prevention.

Table 9.2 Illustrative strategies for the institutionalisation of positive change and good practices

Level of regulation	Reinforcers of positive change and good practices	Institutional mechanisms to safeguard good practices
Government (national, state, provincial, local) Formal regulation and law enforcement	Reliable and timely data to police about incidents related to specific establishments (STAD and Alcohol Linking) Police and other regulators given resources to take responsibility for ongoing implementation (STAD and Alcohol Linking)	Written commitment of key government agencies (STAD) Written policies that ensure that preventive practices are built into organisational routines (Alcohol Linking)
Licensees, owners, managers, staff and industry associations Standard setting and self-regulation	Evidence-based training programs accessible and affordable on a continuing basis (*Safer Bars*) Continued profitability of drinking establishments with responsible serving practices (STAD and Queensland)	Industry associations given standing by regulators so they have a responsibility for the maintenance of responsible practices (STAD and Queensland)

Although we still know too little about the dynamics of violence in the licensed environment and far too little about effective strategies for reducing such violence, current knowledge suggests that a shift in policy thinking is needed, towards a public health perspective that emphasises empirical evidence, and away from punitive, individualistic and unevaluated criminal justice approaches. The sensitivity of human beings to environmental contingencies and the amenability of environmental factors to modification through planning and regulation mean that the prospects for preventing violence are quite good, especially if staff attitudes and skills can be improved through training or through realistic incentives for the responsible management of patrons.

The transition of social problems to public problems – that is, as problems that governments and society generally believe they need to do something about – involves a mysterious process that depends partly on scientific evidence but mostly on what Joseph Gusfield (1981) called 'the symbolic order'. In the last few decades, child abuse, drinking and driving, and family violence have been transformed from the private to the public realm. This has been achieved largely through the efforts of activists who have captured the public imagination, often by highlighting the injustice of persons being injured or killed by the negligence or malevolence of the killer drunk or the predatory male.

Although victims of bar violence are unlikely to evoke the same level of public sympathy and outrage as do victims of family violence and drunk driving, there are, nevertheless, compelling reasons for taking public action to reduce bar violence, and lessons to be learned from the success of previous movements. The frequency of bar-related injuries and deaths, especially among young men, bears witness to the human, financial and social costs of bar violence. Just as societal intolerance has led to important reductions in injurious behaviour including drinking and driving, smoking, and child and wife abuse, public intolerance combined with research-informed strategies can be used to reduce aggression, violence and injury associated with commercial drinking establishments. We would argue, therefore, that it is well and truly time to 'raise the bar' by using the promulgation of scientific evidence to improve the standards of operations of drinking establishments, to raise community expectations regarding safe drinking establishments, and to increase the effective use of regulatory policies and practices.

References

Albrecht, S. and Morrison, J. (1992) *Contact and cover: Two officer suspect control*. Springfield, Illinois: Charles Thomas Publishing.

Anderson, C. A. (1989) 'Temperature and aggression: Ubiquitous effects of heat on occurrence of human violence', *Psychological Bulletin*, 106: 74–96.

Ardizzone, E. and Gorham, M. (1939), *Back to the Local*. London: Cassell and Co.

Armstrong, A., Francis, R., Bourne, M. and Dussuyer, I. (2006) 'Towards developing an evidence based database for the evaluation of the community governance of crime prevention and community safety', in A. Armstrong (ed.) *Evaluating the community governance of crime prevention and community safety project papers*. Melbourne: Centre for International Corporate Governance Research, Victoria University, pp. 11–34.

Arnold, M. J. and Laidler, T. J. (1994) *Situational and environmental factors in alcohol-related violence*. Canberra: Government Publishing Services.

Ayres, I. and Braithwaite, J. (1992) *Responsive regulation: Transcending the deregulation debate*. New York: Oxford University Press.

Babb, P. (2007) *Drug data update*, Research Development and Statistics Directorate, Home Office.

Babor, T. F., Mendelson, J. H., Uhly, B. and Souza, E. (1980) 'Drinking patterns in experimental and barroom settings', *Journal of Studies on Alcohol*, 41: 635–51.

Babor, T., Caetano, R., Casswell, S., Edwards, G., Giesbrecht, N., Graham, K., Grube, J., Gruenewald, P., Hill, L., Holder, H., Homel, R., Osterberg, E., Rehm, J., Room, R. and Rossow, I. (2003) *Alcohol: No ordinary commodity. Research and public policy*. Oxford: Oxford University Press.

Baron, R. A. and Richardson, D. (1994) *Human Aggression*. Plenum: New York.

Baum-Baicker, C. (1987) 'The psychological benefits of moderate alcohol consumption: a review of the literature', *Drug* and *Alcohol Dependence*, 15: 305–22.

Bellis, M. A., Hughes, K. and Lowey, H. (2002) 'Healthy nightclubs and recreational substance use from a harm minimisation to a healthy settings approach', *Addictive Behaviors*, 27: 1025–35.

Ben-Porath, D. D. and Taylor, S. P. (2002) 'The effects of diazepam (valium) and aggressive disposition on human aggression: An experimental investigation', *Addictive Behaviors*, 27: 167–77.

Benson, D. and Archer, J. (2002) 'An ethnographic study of sources of conflict between young men in the context of the night out', *Psychology, Evolution and Gender*, 4: 3–30.

Berk, B. (1977) 'Face-saving at the singles dance', *Social Problems*, 24: 530–44.

Blazevic, G. R. (1996) *Surfers Paradise Safety Action Project: Creating a culture of collaboration for addressing alcohol related violence*. Queensland: Queensland Police.

Block, R. L. and Block, C. R. (1995) 'Space, place, and crime: Hot spot areas and hot places of liquor-related crime', in J. E. Eck and D. Weisburd (eds) *Crime prevention studies* (vol. 4). Monsey, New York: Criminal Justice Press, pp. 145–84.

Boles, S. M., and Miotto, K. (2003) 'Substance abuse and violence: A review of the literature', *Aggression and Violent Behavior*, 8: 155–74.

Braithwaite, J. (2002) *Restorative justice and responsive regulation*. Oxford: Oxford University Press.

Brantingham, P. L. and Brantingham, P. J. (1993) 'Nodes, paths, and edges: Considerations on the complexity of crime and the physical environment', *Journal of Environmental Psychology*, 13: 3–28.

Brantingham, P. L. and Brantingham, P. J. (1999) 'A theoretical model of crime hot spot generation', *Studies on Crime and Crime Prevention*, 8: 7–26.

Brantingham, P. L. and Brantingham, P. J. (2003) 'Computer Simulation as a Tool for Environmental Criminologists', unpublished paper presented at *Eleventh International Symposium on Environmental Criminology and Crime Analysis*, Cincinnati, Ohio.

Brennan, T. (2005) 'Taverns and the Public Sphere in 18th Century Paris', *Contemporary Drug Problems*, 32: 29–43.

Briscoe, S. and Donnelly, N. (2001) 'Temporal and regional aspects of alcohol-related violence and disorder', *Alcohol Studies Bulletin*, 2: 1–15.

Buddie, A. M. and Parks, K. A. (2003) 'The role of the bar context and social behaviors on women's risk for aggression', *Journal of Interpersonal Violence*, 18: 1378-93.

Buka, S. L. and Birdthistle, I. J. (1999) 'Long-term effects of a community-wide alcohol server training intervention', *Journal of Studies on Alcohol*, 60: 27–36.

Burns, L. and Coumarelos, C. (1993) *Policing pubs: Evaluation of a licensing enforcement strategy*. Sydney: NSW Bureau of Crime Statistics and Research.

Burns, L., Flaherty, B., Ireland, S. and Frances, M. (1995) 'Policing pubs: What happens to crime?', *Drug and Alcohol Review*, 14: 369–75.

Burns, T. F. (1980) 'Getting rowdy with the boys', *Journal of Drug Issues*, 10: 273–286.

Burrell, A. and Erol, R. (2006) *Violence in the night-time economy: Tracking hot spots over time*. London: UCL Jill Dando Institute of Crime Science.

Burrows, S., Nicholas, C. and Waites, J. (2004) 'Strategies and outcomes in translating alcohol harm reduction research into practice: The Alcohol Linking Program', *Drug and Alcohol Review*, 23: 355–64.

Bushman, B. J. (1997) 'Effects of alcohol on human aggression: Validity of proposed explanations', in M. Galanter (ed.) *Recent developments in alcoholism: Alcohol and violence*, vol. 13. New York, New York: Plenum Press, pp. 227–43.

Byrne, N. (1978) 'Sociotemporal considerations of everyday life suggested by an empirical study of the bar milieu', *Urban Life*, 6: 417–37.

Caceres, C. F. and Cortinas, J. I. (1996) 'Fantasy island: An ethnography of alcohol and gender roles in a Latino gay bar', *Journal of Drug Issues*, 26: 245–60.

Campbell, M. A. (1991) 'Public drinking places and society', in D. J. Pittman and H. Raskin White (eds) *Society, culture and drinking patterns reexamined*. New Brunswick: Rutgers Center of Alcohol Studies, pp. 361–81.

Carvolth, R. (1997) 'Key Informant Questionnaire: Safety Action Projects in Central Business Districts – Where are they at?' Brisbane: Alcohol, Tobacco & Other Drugs Service, Queensland Health.

Carvolth, R., Homel, R., Hauritz, M., Wortley, R., Clark, J. and McIlwain, G. (1996) 'Swilling in Surfers: Responsible Hospitality Practice', *Community Quarterly: Community Development in Action*, 38: 22–8.

Casswell, S., Zhang, J. F. and Wyllie, A. (1993) 'The importance of amount and location of drinking for the experience of alcohol-related problems', *Addiction*, 88: 1527–34.

Cavan, S. (1966) *Liquor license: An ethnography of a bar*. Chicago: Aldine.

Chandler Coutts, M., Graham, K., Braun, K. and Wells, S. (2000) 'Results of a pilot program for training bar staff in preventing aggression', *Journal of Drug Education*, 30: 171–91.

Chatterton, P. and Hollands, R. (2002) 'Theorising urban playscapes: Producing, regulating and consuming youthful nightlife city spaces', *Urban Studies*, 39: 95–116.

Checkoway, B. (1995) 'Six strategies of community change', *Community Development*, 3: 2–20.

Chikritzhs, T. and Stockwell, T. (2002) 'The impact of later trading hours for Australian public houses (hotels) on levels of violence', *Journal of Studies on Alcohol*, 63: 591–99.

Clark, W. B. (1966) 'Demographic characteristics of tavern patrons in San Francisco', *Quarterly Journal of Studies on Alcohol*, 27: 316–27.

Clark, W. B. (1981) 'The contemporary tavern', in Y. Israel, F. B. Glaser, H. Kalant, R. E. Popham, W. Schmidt and R. G. Smart (eds) *Research advances in alcohol and drug problems*, vol. 6. Toronto: Addiction Research Foundation.

Clarke, R. V. (ed.) (1997) *Situational crime prevention: Successful case studies* (2nd edn). Guilderland, New York: Harrow and Heston.

Clarke, R. V. and Eck, J. E. (2003) *Become a problem-solving crime analyst in 55 small steps*. London: Jill Dando Institute of Crime Science, University College London.

Clarke, R. V. and Homel, R. (1997) 'A revised classification of techniques of situational crime prevention', in S. P. Lab (ed.) *Crime prevention at a crossroads*. Cincinnati, Ohio: Anderson, pp. 21–35.

Clinard, M. B. (1962) 'The public drinking house and society', in D. J. Pittman and C. R. Snyder (eds) *Society, culture, and drinking patterns*. New York; John Wiley and Sons, pp. 270–92.

Cloyd, J. W. (1976) 'The market-place bar: The interrelation between sex, situation, and strategies in the pairing ritual of Homo Ludens', *Urban Life*, 5: 293–312.

Cohen, D. and Nisbett, R. E. (1994) 'Self-protection and the culture of honor: Explaining southern homicide', *Personality and Social Psychology Bulletin*, 20: 551–67.

Cohen, D., Nisbett, R. E., Bowdle, B. F. and Schwartz, N. (1996) 'Insult, aggression, and the southern culture of honor: An "experimental ethnography"', *Journal of Personality and Social Psychology*, 70: 945–60.

Cohen, L. E. and Felson, M. (1979) 'Social change and crime rate trends: A routine activity approach', *American Sociological Review*, 44: 588–608.

Collins, R. L., Quigley, B. M. and Leonard, K. E. (2007) 'Women's physical aggression in bars: An event-based examination of precipitants and predictors of severity', *Aggressive Behavior*, 33: 304–13.

Conway, K., Greenaway, S., Casswell, S., Liggins, S. and Broughton, D. (2007) 'Community action – challenges and constraints – implementing evidence-based approaches within a context of reorienting services', *Substance Use and Misuse*, 42: 1867–82.

Cook, T. D. and Campbell, D. T. (eds) (1979) *Quasi-experimentation: design and analysis issues for field settings*. Chicago: Rand McNally College Publishing Co.

Cornish, D. B. and Clarke, R. V. (2003) 'Opportunities, precipitators and criminal decisions: A reply to Wortley's critique of situational crime prevention', in M. J. Smith and D. B. Cornish (eds) *Theory for practice in situational crime prevention*, vol. 16. Monsey, NY: Criminal Justice Press, pp. 41–96.

Cornish, D. B. and Clarke, R. V. (eds) (1986) *The reasoning criminal: Rational choice perspectives on offending*. New York: Springer Verlag.

Craze, L. and Norberry, J. (1994) 'The objectives of liquor-licensing laws in Australia, in T. Stockwell (ed.) *An examination of the appropriateness and efficacy of liquor-licensing laws across Australia*, vol. 5. Canberra: Australian Government Publishing Service, pp. 35–56.

Crowe, T. (1991) *Crime Prevention Through Environmental Design: Applications of Architectural Design and Space Management Concepts.* Boston: National Crime Prevention Institute, Butterworth-Heinemann.

Cusenza, S. (1998) 'Organizing to reduce neighborhood alcohol problems: A frontline account', *Contemporary Drug Problems,* 25, pp. 99–111.

Daly, J. B., Campbell, E. M., Wiggers, J. H. and Considine, R. J. (2002) 'Prevalence of responsible hospitality policies in licensed premises that are associated with alcohol-related harm', *Drug and Alcohol Review,* 21: 113–120.

Day, K., Gough, B. and McFadden, M. (2003) 'Women who drink and fight: A discourse analysis of working-class women's talk', *Feminism Psychology,* 13: 141–58.

de Crespigny, C., Vincent, N. and Ask, A. (2000) 'Young women's social drinking in context – pub style: A study of decision-making and social drinking of young women in South Australia', *Contemporary Drug Problems,* 26: 439–56

Demers, A., Kairouz, S., Adlaf, E. M., Gliksman, L., Newton-Taylor, B. and Marchand, A. (2002) 'Multilevel analysis of situational drinking among Canadian undergraduates', *Social Science and Medicine,* 55: 415–24.

Doherty, S. J. and Roche, A. M. (2003) *Alcohol and licensed premises: Best practice in policing.* Payneham, S.A: Australasian Centre for Policing Research.

Donnerstein, E., and Wilson, D. W. (1976) 'Effects of noise and perceived control on ongoing and subsequent behavior', *Journal of Personality and Social Psychology,* 34: 774–81.

Dowds, L. (1994) 'Victim surveys: Exploring the nature of violent crime', *Psychology, Crime & Law,* 1: 125–32.

Duailibi, S., Ponicki, W., Grube, J., Pinsky, I., Laranjeira, R. and Raw, M. (2007) 'The effect of restricting opening hours on alcohol-related violence', *American Journal of Public Health,* 97: 2276–80.

Dyck, N. (1980) 'Booze, barrooms and scrapping: Masculinity and violence in a western Canadian town', *Canadian Journal of Anthropology,* 1: 191–98.

Eck, J. E. and Weisburd, D. (1995) 'Crime places in crime theory', in J. E. Eck and D. Weisburd (eds) *Crime and place. Crime Prevention Studies* (vol. 4). Monsey, NY: Criminal Justice Press, pp. 1–34.

Elvins, M. and Hadfield, P. (2003) *West End 'stress area' night-time economy profiling: A demonstration project.* Durham: University of Durham.

Evans, S. and Green, J. (2007) 'Law enforcement – using intelligence to target drink-drivers – a collaborative partnership', *Australian and New Zealand Society of Criminology Annual Conference,* Adelaide.

Farrington, D. P. and Welsh, B. C. (2002) 'Effects of improved street lighting on crime: A systematic review', *Home Office Research Study,* 251: 1–52.

Felson, R. (1978) 'Aggression as impression management', *Social Psychology,* 41: 205–13.

Felson, M. (1995) 'Those who discourage crime', in J. E. Eck and D. Weisburd (eds) *Crime and place. Crime Prevention Studies* (vol. 4). Monsey, NY: Criminal Justice Press, pp. 63–6.

Felson, M., Berends, R., Richardson, B. and Veno, A. (1997) 'Reducing pub hopping and related crime', in R. Homel (ed.) *Policing for prevention: Reducing crime, public intoxication and injury* (vol. 7). Monsey, New York: Criminal Justice Press, pp. 115–132.

Felson, R. B. (1993) 'Predatory and dispute-related violence: A social interactionist approach', in R. V. Clarke and M. Felson (eds) *Routine activity and rational choice* (vol. 5). New Brunswick, USA: Transaction Publishers, pp. 103–25.

Felson, R. B., Baccaglini, W. and Gmelch, G. (1986) 'Bar-room brawls: Aggression and violence in Irish and American bars', in A. Campbell and J. Gibbs (eds) *Violent transactions. The limits of personality*. New York: Basil Blackwell, pp. 153–66.

Fennelly, L. (2004) *Effective physical security* (3rd edn). Burlington and Oxford: Elsevier Butterworth-Heinmann.

Ferris, J. (1997) 'Courtship, drinking and control: A qualitative analysis of women's and men's experiences', *Contemporary Drug Problems*, 24: 667–702.

Fielding, N. (2005) *The police and social conflict* (2nd edn). London: Cavendish.

Fields, S. (1992) 'The effect of temperature on crime', *British Journal of Criminology*, 32: 340–52.

Fillmore, M.T. and Weafer, J. (2004) 'Alcohol impairment of behavior in men and women: a reply to the commentaries', *Addiction*, 99: 1252–4.

Fleming, J. (2006) 'Working through networks: The challenge of partnership policing', in J. Fleming and J. Wood (eds) *Fighting crime together: The challenge of policing and security networks*. Sydney: UNSW Press, pp. 87–115.

Forsyth, A. J. M. (2006) *Assessing the relationships between late night drinks marketing and alcohol-related disorder in public space*. Glasgow: Alcohol Education Research Council (AERC).

Forsyth, A. and Cloonan, M. (2008) 'Alco-pop? The use of popular music in Glasgow pubs', *Popular Music and Society*, 31: 57–78.

Forsyth, A. J. M., Cloonan, M. and Barr, J. (2005) *Factors associated with alcohol-related problems within licensed premises*. Glasgow: NHS Board.

Fox, J. and Sobol, J. (2000), 'Drinking patterns, social interaction, and barroom behavior: A routine activities approach', *Deviant Behavior: An Interdisciplinary Journal*, 21: 429–50.

Fromme, K., Katz, E. and D'Amico, E. (1997) 'Effects of alcohol intoxication on the perceived consequences of risk taking', *Experimental and Clinical Psychopharmacology*, 5: 14–23.

Garlick, R. (1994) 'Male and female responses to ambiguous instructor behaviors', *Sex Roles*, 30: 135–58.

Garner, G. W. (1998) *Surviving the street: Officer safety and survival techniques.* Springfield, Illinois: Charles Thomas Publishing.

Geller, E. S., Russ, N. W. and Delphos, W. A. (1987) 'Does server intervention training make a difference?', *Alcohol Health and Research World*, 11: 64–69.

Gerson, L. W. (1978) 'Alcohol-related acts of violence: Who was drinking and where the acts occurred', *Journal of Studies on Alcohol*, 39: 1294–96.

Giancola, P. R. (2000) 'Executive functioning: A conceptual framework for alcohol-related aggression', *Experimental and clinical psychopharmacology*, 8: 576–97.

Giancola, P. R. (2002) 'Alcohol-related aggression during the college years: Theories, risk factors and policy implications', *Journal of Studies on Alcohol*, Supplement No. 14: 129–139.

Glass, D. and Singer, J. (1972) *Urban stress*. New York, NY: Academic Press.

Gliksman, L., Single, E., McKenzie, D., Douglas, R., Brunet, S. and Moffat, K. (1993) 'The role of alcohol providers in prevention: An evaluation of a server intervention programme', *Addiction*, 88: 1189–97.

Goldstein, H. (1990) *Problem-oriented policing*. New York: McGraw-Hill.

Grabosky, P. (1995) 'Using non-governmental resources to foster regulatory compliance', *Governance: An International Journal of Policy and Administration*, 8: 527–550.

Graham, K. (1980) 'Theories of intoxicated aggression', *Canadian Journal of Behavioural Science*, 12: 141–58.

Graham, K. (1985) 'Determinants of heavy drinking and drinking problems: The contribution of the bar environment', in E. Single and T. Storm (eds) *Public drinking and public policy*. Toronto, Canada: Addiction Research Foundation, pp. 71–84.

Graham, K. (1999) *Safer Bars: Assessing and reducing risks of violence*. Toronto: Centre for Addiction and Mental Health.

Graham, K. (2000) 'Preventive interventions for on-premise drinking. A promising but underresearched area for prevention', *Contemporary Drug Problems*, 27: 593–668.

Graham, K. (2003) 'The Yin and Yang of alcohol intoxication: Implications for research on the social consequences of drinking', *Addiction*, 98: 1021–23.

Graham, K. (2005) 'Public drinking then and now', *Contemporary Drug Problems*, 32: 45–56.

Graham, K., Bernards, S., Osgood, D. W. and Wells, S. (2006) 'Bad nights or bad bars? Multilevel analysis of environmental predictors of aggression in late-night large-capacity bars and clubs', *Addiction*, 101: 1569–80.

Graham, K., Bernards, S., Osgood, D. W., Homel, R. and Purcell, J. (2005) 'Guardians and handlers: The role of bar staff in preventing and managing aggression', *Addiction*, 100: 755–66.

Graham, K. and Chandler-Coutts, M. (2000) 'Community action research: who does what to whom and why? Lessons learned from local prevention efforts (International Experiences)', *Substance Use and Misuse*, 35: 87–110.

Graham, K., Jelley, J. and Purcell, J. (2005) 'Training bar staff in preventing and managing aggression in licensed premises', *Journal of Substance Use*, 10: 48–61.

Graham, K., LaRocque, L., Yetman, R., Ross, T. J. and Guistra, E. (1980), 'Aggression and barroom environments', *Journal of Studies on Alcohol*, 41: 277–292.

Graham, K., Osgood, D. W., Wells, S. and Stockwell, T. (2006) 'To what extent is intoxication associated with aggression in bars? A multilevel analysis', *Journal of Studies on Alcohol*, 67: 382–90.

Graham, K., Osgood, D. W., Zibrowski, E., Purcell, J., Gliksman, L., Leonard, K., Pernanen, K., Saltz, R. F. and Toomey, T. L. (2004) 'The effect of the *Safer Bars* programme on physical aggression in bars: Results of a randomized controlled trial', *Drug and Alcohol Review*, 23: 31–41.

Graham, K., Tremblay, P. F., Wells, S., Pernanen, K., Purcell, J. and Jelley, J. (2006), 'Harm and intent and the nature of aggressive behavior: Measuring naturally-occurring aggression in barroom settings', *Assessment*, 13: 280–96.

Graham, K. and Wells, S. (2001a) '"I'm okay. You're drunk!" Self–other differences in the perceived effects of alcohol in real-life incidents of aggression', *Contemporary Drug Problems*, 28: 441–62.

Graham, K. and Wells, S. (2001b) 'Aggression among young adults in the social context of the bar', *Addiction Research*, 9: 193–219.

Graham, K. and Wells, S. (2003) '"Somebody's gonna get their head kicked in tonight!" Aggression among young males in bars – A question of values', *The British Journal of Criminology*, 43: 546–66.

Graham, K., Wells, S. and Jelley, J. (2002) 'The social context of physical aggression among adults', *The Journal of Interpersonal Violence*, 17: 64–83.

Graham, K., Wells, S. and West, P. (1997) 'A framework for applying explanations of alcohol-related aggression to naturally-occurring aggressive behavior', *Contemporary Drug Problems*, 24: 625–66.

Graham, K. and West, P. (2001) 'Alcohol and crime: examining the link', in N. Heather *et al. International Handbook of Alcohol Dependence and Problems*. New York, Brisbane, Toronto: John Wiley and Sons.

Graham, K., West, P. and Wells, S. (2000) 'Evaluating theories of alcohol-related aggression using observations of young adults in bars', *Addiction*, 95: 847–63.

Graves, T. D., Graves, N. B., Semu, V. N. and Sam, I. A. (1981) 'The social context of drinking and violence in New Zealand's multi-ethnic pub settings', in T.C. Harford and L. S. Gaines (eds) *Research Monograph No. 7: Social drinking contexts*. Rockville, MD: NIAAA, pp. 103–20.

Graves, T. D., Graves, N. B., Semu, V. N. and Sam, I. A. (1982) 'Patterns of public drinking in a multiethnic society: a systematic observational study', *Journal of Studies on Alcohol*, 43: 990–1009.

Grazian, D. (2008) *On the Make*. Chicago: University of Chicago Press.

Green, Micheael (2001) *The Art of Coarse Drinking*. London: Robson Books.

Gruenewald, P. and Remer, L. (2006) 'Changes in outlet densities affect violence rates', *Alcoholism: Clinical and Experimental Research*, 30: 1184–1193.

Gruenewald, P., Freisthler, B., Remer, L., LaScala, E. A. and Treno, A. (2006) 'Ecological models of alcohol outlets and violent assaults: Crime potentials and geospatial analysis', *Addiction*, 101: 666–77.

Grupp, L. A. (1980) 'The influence of some neurotransmitter agonists and antagonists on the response of hippocampal units and the cortical EEG to ethanol in the awake rat', *Psychopharmacology*, 75: 327–34.

Gusfield, J. (1981) *The Culture of Public Problems: Drinking-Driving and the Symbolic Order*. Chicago: The University of Chicago Press.

Gussler-Burkhardt, N. L., and Giancola, P. R. (2005) 'A further examination of gender differences in alcohol-related aggression', *Journal of Studies on Alcohol*, 66: 413–22.

Haak, M., Coase, P. and Tranjic, S. (2003) *Alcohol Accords: Stakeholder review. Report to Alcohol Accords Stakeholder Review Steering Committee*, NFO Donovan Research Marketing and Communications Research Consultants.

Hadfield, P. (2006) *Bar wars: Contesting the night in contemporary British cities*. Oxford, England: Oxford University Press.

Hadfield, P., Collins, J., Doyle, P., Flynn, R. and Kolvin, P. (2005a) 'The operation of licensed premises', in P. Kolvin (ed.) *Licensed premises: Law and practice* (rev edn). Haywards Heath, West Sussex, UK: Tottel Publishing, pp. 567–617.

Hadfield, P., Collins, J., Doyle, P. and Mackie, K. (2005b) 'The prevention of public disorder', in P. Kolvin (ed.) *Licensed premises: Law and practice* (rev edn). Haywards Heath, West Sussex, UK: Tottel Publishing, pp. 618–682.

Haggård-Grann, U., Hallqvist, J., Långström, N. and Möller, J. (2006) 'The role of alcohol and drugs in triggering criminal violence: a case-crossover study', *Addiction*, 101: 100–8.

Harford, T. C. (1983) 'A contextual analysis of drinking events', *The International Journal of the Addictions*, 18: 825–34.

Hauritz, M., Homel, R., McIlwain, G., Burrows, T. and Townsley, M. (1998a) 'Reducing violence in licensed venues through community safety action projects: The Queensland experience', *Contemporary Drug Problems*, 25: 511–51.

Hauritz, M., Homel, R., Townsley, M., Burrows, T. and McIlwain, G. (1998b) *Reducing Violence in Licensed Venues: Community Safety Action*. Brisbane: Griffith University, Centre for Crime Policy and Public Safety; School of Justice Administration, p. 139.

Hauritz, M., Homel, R., Townsley, M., Burrows, T. and McIlwain, G. (1998c) *An evaluation of the Local Government Safety Action Projects in Cairns, Townsville and Mackay: A report to the Queensland Department of Health, the Queensland Police Service and the Criminology Research Council*. Brisbane: Griffith University, Centre for Crime Policy and Public Safety.

Hawks, D., Rydon, P., Stockwell, T., White, M., Chikritzhs, T. and Heale, P. (1999) *The evaluation of the Fremantle police – licensee accord: Impact on serving practices, harm and the wider community*. Perth: National Drug Research Institute, Curtin University of Technology.

Heath, D. B. (2000) *Drinking Occasions: comparative perspectives on alcohol and culture*. New York: International Center for Alcohol Politics.

Herzog, T. A. (1999) 'Effects of alcohol intoxication on social inferences', *Experimental and Clinical Psychopharmacology*, 7: 448–53.

Hewitt, D. B., Levin, P. F. and Misner, S. T. (2002) 'Workplace homicides in Chicago: Risk factors from 1965 to 1990', *AAOHN Journal*, 50: 406–12.

Hey, V. (1986) *Patriarchy and pub culture*. London: Tavistock Publications.

Hoaken, P. N. S. and Stewart, S. H. (2003) 'Drugs of abuse and the elicitation of human aggressive behavior', *Addictive Behaviors*, 28: 1533–54.

Hobbs, D. (2003) 'The night-time economy', *Alcohol Concern Research Forum Papers*. Durham: Durham University.

Hobbs, D., Hadfield, P., Lister, S. and Winlow, S. (2002) '"Door loor" The art and economics of intimidation', *British Journal of Criminology*, 42: 352–70.

Hobbs, D., Hadfield, P., Lister, S. and Winlow, S. (2003) *Bouncers: Violence and governance in the night-time economy*. Oxford, England: Oxford University Press.

Hobbs, D., Hadfield, P., Lister, S. and Winlow, S. (2005) 'Violence and control in the night-time economy', *European Journal of Crime, Criminal Law and Criminal Justice*, 13: 89–102.

Hobbs, D., Lister, S., Hadfield, P., Winlow, S. and Hall, S. (2000) 'Receiving shadows: Governance and criminality in the night-time economy', *British Journal of Sociology*, 51: 701–17.

Hobbs, D., O'Brien, K. and Westmarland, L. (2007) 'Connecting the gendered door: Women, violence and doorwork', *The British Journal of Sociology*, 58: 21–38.

Holder, H. (1998) *Alcohol and the community: A systems approach to prevention*. Cambridge, UK: Cambridge University Press.

Holder, H. D. and Moore, R. S. (2000) 'Institutionalization of community action projects to reduce alcohol-use related problems: Systematic facilitators', *Substance Use and Misuse*, 35: 75–86.

Homel, P. (2007) 'Who says crime prevention hasn't worked?', paper presented at the *Proceedings of the International Centre for the Prevention of Crime (ICPC) Annual Colloquium: Communities in action for crime prevention*, Montreal, Canada.

Homel, R. (1988) *Policing and punishing the drinking driver: A study of general and specific deterrence*. New York: Springer-Verlag.

Homel, R. (1994) 'Can police prevent crime?', in K. Bryett and C. Lewis (eds) *Contemporary policing: Unpeeling tradition*. Australia: Macmillan, pp. 7–34.

Homel, R. (2004) 'Drivers who drink and rational choice: Random breath testing and the process of deterrence', in R. V. Clarke and M. Felson (eds) *Routine activity and rational choice. Advances in criminological theory*, vol. 5. New Brunswick, NJ: Transaction Publishers, pp. 59–84.

Homel, R. (2005) 'The puzzles and paradoxes of youth crime prevention', *Safer Society*, 27: 2–4.

Homel, R. and Clark, J. (1994) 'The prediction and prevention of violence in clubs and pubs', in R. V. Clarke (ed.) *Crime prevention studies* (vol. 3). New York: Criminal Justice Press, pp. 1–46.

Homel, R. and Tomsen, S. (1991), 'Pubs and violence: Violence, public drinking, and public policy', *Current Affairs Bulletin*, December: 20–7.

Homel, R., Carseldine, D. and Kearns, I. (1988) 'Drink-driving countermeasures in Australia', *Alcohol, Drugs and Driving*, 4: 113–44.

Homel, R., Carvolth, R., Hauritz, M., McIlwain, G. and Teague, R. (2004) 'Making licensed venues safer for patrons: What environmental factors should be the focus of interventions?', *Drug and Alcohol Review*, 23: 19–29.

Homel, R., Carvolth, R., Hauritz, M., McIlwain, G. and Teague, R. (2003) 'Cleaning up the nightclub act through problem-focussed, responsive regulation', *International Research Symposium: Preventing substance use, risk use and harm: what is evidence-based policy?* Fremantle, Western Australia: National Drug Research Institute.

Homel, R., Freiberg, K., Lamb, C., Leech, M., Hampshire, A., Hay, I., *et al.* (2006) *The Pathways to Prevention project: The first five years, 1999–2004*. Sydney, Australia: Griffith University and Mission Australia.

Homel, R., Hauritz, M., McIlwain, G., Wortley, R. and Carvolth, R. (1997) 'Preventing drunkenness and violence around nightclubs in a tourist resort', in R. V. Clark (ed.) *Situational crime prevention: successful case studies*. Guilderland, New York: Harrow and Heston, pp. 263–82.

Homel, R., Hauritz, M., Wortley, R., McIlwain, G. and Carvolth, R. (1997) 'Preventing alcohol-related crime through community action: The Surfers Paradise Safety Action Project', in R. Homel (ed.) *Policing for prevention: Reducing crime, public intoxication and injury* (vol. 7). Monsey, New York: Criminal Justice Press, pp. 35–90.

Homel, R., McIlwain, G. and Carvolth, R. (2004) 'Creating safer drinking environments', in N. Heather and T. Stockwell (eds) *The essential handbook of treatment and prevention of alcohol problems*. West Sussex, UK: John Wiley & Sons Ltd.

Homel, R., Tomsen, S. and Thommeny, J. (1992) 'Public drinking and violence: Not just an alcohol problem', *Journal of Drug Issues*, 22: 679–97.

Hope, T. (2001) 'Community crime prevention in Britain: A strategic overview', *Criminal Justice*, 1: 421–439.

Hughes, K., Anderson, Z., Morleo, M. and Bellis, M. A. (2007) 'Alcohol, nightlife and violence: The relative contributions of drinking before and during nights out to negative health and criminal justice outcomes. *Addiction*, 103: 60–5.

Indermaur, D. (1998) 'Violent crimes in Australia: Interpreting the trends', *Trends and Issues in Crime and Criminal Justice*, 61. Sydney: Australian Institute of Criminology.

Ireland, C. S. and Thommeny, J. L. (1993) 'The crime cocktail: Licensed premises, alcohol and street offences', *Drug and Alcohol Review*, 12: 143–50.

Israelstam, S. and Lambert, S. (1984) 'Gay bars', *Journal of Drug Issues*, 14: 637–53.

Jeffs, B. W. and Saunders, W. M. (1983) 'Minimizing alcohol related offences by enforcement of the existing licensing legislation', *British Journal of Addiction*, 78: 67–77.

Josephs, R. A. and Steele, C. M. (1990) 'The two faces of alcohol myopia: Attentional mediation of psychological stress', *Journal of Abnormal Psychology*, 99: 115–26.

Kelly, W. M. (1994) *Local industry accord – A partnership in crime prevention*. Geelong, Victoria: Barwon Police Community Consultative Committee.

Kolvin, P. (ed.) (2005a) *Licensed premises: Law and practice*. Haywards Heath, West Sussex: Tottel Publishing.

Kolvin, P. (2005b) 'Challenges', in P. Kolvin (ed.), *Licensed premises: law and practice*. Haywards Heath, West Sussex: Tottel Publishing, pp. 1–27.

Konecni, V. J. (1975) 'The mediation of aggressive behavior: Arousal level versus anger and cognitive labeling', *Journal of Personality and Social Psychology*, 32: 706–12.

Kümin, B. (2005) 'Drinking and public space in early modern German lands', *Contemporary Drug Problems*, 32: 9–27.

Lander, A. (1995) *Preventing alcohol-related violence: A manual for community action*. Sydney: Social Change Media.

Lang, E. and Rumbold, G. (1997) 'The effectiveness of community-based interventions to reduce violence in and around licensed premises: A comparison of three Australian models', *Contemporary Drug Problems*, 24: 805–26.

Lang, E., Stockwell, T., Rydon, P. and Beel, A. (1998) 'Can training bar staff in responsible serving practices reduce alcohol-related harm?', *Drug and Alcohol Review*, 17: 39–50.

Lang, E., Stockwell, T., Rydon, P. and Gamble, C. (1992) *Drinking settings, alcohol related harm, and support for prevention policies*. New South Wales, Australia: National Centre for Research into the Prevention of Drug Abuse.

Langley, J., Chalmers, D. and Fanslow, J. (1996) 'Incidence of death and hospitalization from assault occurring in and around licensed premises: a comparative analysis', *Addiction*, 91: 985–993.

Leary, J. P. (1976) 'Fists and foul mouths: Fights and fight stories in contemporary rural American bars', *The Journal of American Folklore*, 89: 27–39.

Leather, P. and Lawrence, C. (1995), 'Perceiving pub violence: The symbolic influence of social and environmental factors', *British Journal of Social Psychology*, 34: 395–407.

Leonard, K. E., Collins, R. L. and Quigley, B. M. (2003) 'Alcohol consumption and the occurrence and severity of aggression: An event-based analysis of male to male barroom violence', *Aggressive Behavior*, 29: 346–65.

Leonard, K. E., Quigley, B. M. and Collins, R. L. (2002) 'Physical aggression in the lives of young adults: Prevalence, location, and severity among college and community samples', *Journal of Interpersonal Violence*, 17: 533–50.

Leonard, K. E., Quigley, B. M. and Collins, R. L. (2003) 'Drinking, personality, and bar environmental characteristics as predictors of involvement in barroom aggression', *Addictive Behaviors*, 28: 1681–700.

Levy, D. T. and Miller, T. R. (1995) 'A cost-benefit analysis of enforcement efforts to reduce serving intoxicated patrons', *Journal of Studies on Alcohol*, 56: 240–47.

Lincoln, R. and Homel, R. (2001) 'Alcohol and youthful rites of passage', in P. Williams (ed.) *Alcohol, young persons and violence*. Canberra: Australian Institute of Criminology, pp. 47–60.

Lister, S., Hadfield, P., Hobbs, D. and Winlow, S. (2001) 'Accounting for bouncers: Occupational licensing as a mechanism for regulation', *Criminology and Criminal Justice*, 1: 363–384.

Lister, S., Hobbs, D., Hall, S. and Winlow, S. (2000) 'Violence in the night-time economy. Bouncers: The reporting, recording and prosecution of assaults', *Policing and Society*, 10: 383–402.

Livingston, M., Chikritzhs, T. and Room, R. (2007) 'Changing the density of alcohol outlets to reduce alcohol-related problems', *Drug and Alcohol Review*, 26: 557–66.

Loeber, R. and Farrington, D. P. (eds) (1998) *Serious and violent juvenile offenders: Risk factors and successful interventions*. Thousand Oaks, CA: Sage Publications.

Ludbrook, A., Godfrey, C., Wyness, L., Parrott, S., Haw, S., Napper, M. and van Teijlingen E. (2002) *Effective and cost-effective measures to reduce alcohol misuse in Scotland*. Edinburgh: Scottish Executive Health Department.

Luke, L. C., Dewar, C., Bailey, M., McGreevy, D., Morris, H. and Burdett-Smith, P. (2002) 'A little nightclub medicine: the healthcare implications of clubbing', *Emergency Medicine Journal*, 19: 542–5.

MacAndrew, C. and Edgerton, R. B. (1969) *Drunken comportment. A social explanation*. Chicago: Aldine.

Macdonald, S., Wells, S., Giesbrecht, N. and Cherpitel (1999) 'Demographics and substance use factors related to violent and accidental injuries: Results from an emergency room study', *Drug and Alcohol Dependence*, 55: 53–61.

MacIntyre, S. and Homel, R. (1997) 'Danger on the dance floor: A study of interior design, crowding and aggression in nightclubs', in R. Homel (ed.) *Policing for prevention: Reducing crime, public intoxication and injury* (vol. 7). Monsey, New York: Criminal Justice Press, pp. 91–113.

Macrory, B. E. (1952) 'The tavern and the community', *Quarterly Journal of Studies on Alcohol*, 13: 609–37.

Maguire, M. and Nettleton, H. (2003) *Reducing alcohol-related violence and disorder: An evaluation of the 'TASC' project* (Home Office Research Study No. 265). London: Home Office.

Malbon, B. (1999) *Clubbing: Dancing, ecstasy, and vitality*. London, UK: Routledge.

Marsh, P. and Kibby, K. (1992) *Drinking and public disorder*. London, England: Portman Group.

Martin, C., Wyllie, A. and Casswell, S. (1992) 'Types of New Zealand drinkers and their associated problems', *Journal of Drug Issues*, 22: 773–96.

Mazerolle, L. and Ransley, J. (2006) *Third party policing*. Melbourne: Cambridge University Press.

McCarthy, P. (2007) *Accords: Are they an effective means of mitigating alcohol-related harm?* Melbourne, Victoria: DrinkWise Australia.

McClelland, D. C., Davis, W. N., Kalin, R. and Wanner, E. (1972) *The drinking man. Alcohol and human motivation*. Toronto, Canada: Collier-Macmillan.

McIlwain, G. (1994) *Paradise saved – community enforcement in the sun*, paper presented at the *Perspectives for change 1994 conference*, Rotorua, New Zealand.

McKnight, A. J. and Streff, F. M. (1994) 'The effect of enforcement upon service of alcohol to intoxicated patrons of bars and restaurants', *Accident Analysis and Prevention*, 26: 79–88.

McLean, S., Wood, L., Montgomery, I., Davidson, J. and Jones, M. (1994) 'Promotion of responsible drinking in hotels', *Drug and Alcohol Review*, 13: 247–55.

MCM Research (1993) *Keeping the peace: A guide to the prevention of alcohol-related disorder*. London, England: Portman Group.

Melbourne City Council West End Forum. (1991) *Interim status report April 1991 for the Good Neighbourhood Program Ministry of Police and Emergency Services*. Melbourne, Victoria: Government of Victoria.

Miczek, K. A., DeBold, J. F., van Erp, A. M. M. and Tornatzky, W. (1997) 'Alcohol, GABAa-benzodiazepine receptor complex, and aggression', in M. Galanter (ed.) *Recent developments in alcoholism* (vol. 13). New York: Plenum Press, pp. 139–72.

Monaghan, L. F. (2002) 'Regulating "unruly" bodies: work tasks, conflict and violence in Britain's night-time economy', *British Journal of Sociology*, 53: 403–29.

Monaghan, L. F. (2003) 'Danger on the doors: Bodily risk in a demonised occupation', *Health, Risk and Society*, 5: 11–31.

Monaghan, L. F. (2004) 'Doorwork and legal risk: Observations from an embodied ethnography', *Social and Legal Studies*, 13: 453–480.

Moore, M. H. (1995) 'Public health and criminal justice approaches to prevention', in M. Tonry and D. P. Farrington (eds) *Strategic approaches to crime prevention: Building a safer society* (vol. 19). Chicago: The University of Chicago Press, pp. 237–62.

Moore, T. M. and Stuart, G.L. (2004) 'Illicit substance use and intimate partner violence among men in batterers' intervention', *Psychology of Addictive Behaviors*, 18: 385–9.

Morojele, N. K., Kachieng, M. A., Mokoko, E., Nkoko, M. A., Parry, C. D. H., Nkowane, A. M., Moshia, K. M. and Saxena, S. (2006) 'Alcohol use and sexual behaviour among risky drinkers and bar and shebeen patrons in Gauteng province, South Africa', *Social Science and Medicine*, 62: 217–27.

Morris, S. (1998) *Clubs, drugs and doormen*, Crime Detection and Prevention Series (B. Webb, ed.), Paper 86. London, England: Police Policy Directorate, Home Office.

Murdoch, D., Pihl, R.O. and Ross, D. (1990) 'Alcohol and crimes of violence: present issues', *The International Journal of the Addictions*, 25: 1065–81.

Nelson, A. L., Bromley, R. D. F. and Thomas, C. J. (2001) 'Identifying micro-spatial and temporal patterns of violent crime and disorder in the British city centre', *Applied Geography*, 21: 249–74.

New Zealand Department of Prime Minister and Cabinet (2000) *Alcohol accords: Getting results – A practical guide for accord partners*. New Zealand: Crime Prevention Unit Department of the Prime Minister and Cabinet; Alcohol Advisory Council of New Zealand (ALAC); New Zealand Police.

Newman, O. (1972) *Defensible space: Crime prevention through urban design*. New York, NY: USGPO.

Newton, A., Sarker, S. J., Pahal, G. S., van den Bergh, E. and Young, C. (2007) 'Impact of the new UK licensing law on emergency hospital attendances: A cohort study', *Emergency Medicine Journal*, 24: 532–4.

Norstrom, T. (2000) 'Outlet density and criminal violence in Norway, 1960–1995', *Journal of Studies on Alcohol*, 61: 907–11.

Nutley, S. M., Walter, I. and Davies H. (2007) *Using evidence: How research can inform public services*. Bristol, UK: The Policy Press.

Offord, D. R., Kraemer, H. C., Kazdin, A. E., Jensen, P. S., Harrington, R. and Gardner, J. S. (1999) 'Lowering the burden of suffering: Monitoring the benefits of clinical, targeted, and universal approaches', in D. P. Keating and C. Hertzman (eds) *Developmental health and the wealth of nations: Social, biological and educational dynamics*. New York: Guilford Press.

Oldenburg, R. (1999) *Great good place: Cafes, coffee shops, bookstores, bars, hair salons, and other hangouts at the heart of a community*. New York: Marlowe.

Oliver, W. (1993) 'Violent confrontations between Black males in bars and bar settings', Ph. D Dissertation. Albany: School of Criminal Justice, State University of New York, p. 395.

Palk, G. R., Davey, J. D. and Freeman, J. E. (2007) 'Policing and preventing alcohol-related violence in and around licensed premises', in *Proceedings 14th International Police Executive Symposium*, Dubai.

Parker, H. and Williams, L. (2003) 'Intoxicated weekends: Young adults' work hard-play hard lifestyles, public health and public disorder', *Drugs: Education, Prevention and Policy*, 10: 345–67.

Parks, K. A. and Miller, B. A. (1997) 'Bar victimization of women', *Psychology of Women Quarterly*, 21: 509–25.

Parks, K. A. and Scheidt, D. M. (2000) 'Male bar drinkers' perspective on female bar drinkers', *Sex Roles*, 43: 927–41.

Parks, K. A. and Zetes-Zanatta, L. M. (1999) 'Women's bar-related victimization: Refining and testing a conceptual model', *Aggressive Behavior*, 25: 349–64.

Parks, K. A., Miller, B. A. Collins, R. L. and Zetes-Zanatta, L. (1998) 'Women's descriptions of drinking in bars: Reasons and risks', *Sex Roles*, 38: 701–17.

Pease, K. (1999) 'A review of street lighting evaluations: Crime reduction effects', in K. Painter and N. Tilley (eds) *Surveillance of public space: CCTV, street lighting and crime prevention* (vol. 10). Monsey, New York: Criminal Justice Press, pp. 47–76).

Pernanen, K. (1976) 'Alcohol and crimes of violence', in B. Kissin and H. Begleiter (eds) *The biology of alcoholism*. New York: Plenum Press, pp. 351–444.

Pernanen, K. (1991) *Alcohol in human violence*. New York: The Guilford Press.

Peterson, J. B., Rothfleisch, J., Zelazo, P. D. and Pihl, R. O. (1990) 'Acute alcohol intoxication and cognitive functioning', *Journal of Studies on Alcohol*, 51: 114–22.

Pettigrew, S. (2006) 'Symbolic double-coding: The case of Australian pubs', *Qualitative Market Research: An International Journal*, 9: 157–69.

Phillips, C., Jacobson, J., Prime, R., Carter, M. and Considine, M. (2002) *Crime and disorder reduction partnerships: Round one progress*. London: Home Office Policing and Reducing Crime Unit: Research, Development and Statistics Directorate.

Pihl, R. O. and Peterson, J. B. (1993) 'Alcohol/drug use and aggressive behaviour', in S. Hodgins (ed.) *Mental Disorder and Crime*. Newbury Park: Sage, pp. 263–83.

Pihl, R. O. and Ross, D. (1987) 'Research on alcohol related aggression: A review and implications for understanding aggression', *Drugs and Society*, 1: 105–26.

Pihl, R. O., Peterson, J. B. and Lau, M. A. (1993) 'A biosocial model of the alcohol-aggression relationship', *Journal of Studies on Alcohol*, 11: 128–39.

Pihl, R. O., Zeichner, A., Niaura, R., Nagy, K., and Zacchia, C. (1981) 'Attribution and alcohol-mediated aggression', *Journal of Abnormal Psychology*, 5: 468–75.

Plant, E. J. and Plant M. A. (2005) 'A "leap in the dark?" Lessons for the United Kingdom from past extensions of bar opening hours', *International Journal of Drug Policy*, 16: 363–8.

Plant, M. A. and Plant, M. L. (2001) 'Heavy drinking by young British women gives cause for concern', (letter) *British Medical Journal*, 323: 1183.

Plant, M. L., Miller, P. and Plant, M. A. (2005) 'The relationship between alcohol consumption and problem behaviours: Gender differences among British adults', *Journal of Substance Use*, 10: 22–30.

Pliner, P. and Cappell, H. (1974) 'Modification of affective consequences of alcohol: A comparison of social and solitary drinking', *Journal of Abnormal Psychology*, 83: 418–25.

Prenzler, T. and Hayes, H. (1998) 'Nightclub managers and the regulation of crowd controllers', *Security Journal*, 10: 103–10.

Prus, R. (1978) 'From barrooms to bedrooms: Towards a theory of interpersonal violence', in M. Beyer (ed.) *Violence in Canada*. Toronto: Gammon, pp. 51–73.

Purcell, J. and Graham, K. (2005) 'A typology of Toronto nightclubs at the turn of the millennium', *Contemporary Drug Problems*, 32: 131–67.

Putnam, S. L., Rockett, I. R. and Campbell, M. K. (1993) 'Methodological issues in community-based alcohol-related injury prevention projects: Attribution of program effects', in T. K. Greenfield and R. Zimmerman (eds) *Experiences with community action projects: New research in the prevention of alcohol and other drug problems*. Rockville, MD: US Department of Health and Human Services, pp. 31–39.

Queensland Health, Alcohol, Tobacco and Other Drug Services (1998) *Partnerships to reduce intoxication, violence and injury in the licensed environment*. Brisbane: Queensland Health.

Queensland Liquor Licensing Division (2007) *Brisbane City Safety Action Plan*. Brisbane: Queensland Liquor Licensing Division.

Queensland Police Service. (1997) *Surfers Paradise Safety Action Project*, video 17. Brisbane, Queensland: QPS.

Quigley, B. M., Leonard, K. E. and Collins, R. L. (2003) 'Characteristics of violent bars and bar patrons', *Journal of Studies on Alcohol*, 64: 765–72.

Rawson, H. (2002) *Unwritten laws. The unofficial rules of life as handed down by Murphy and other sages*. Edison, New Jersey: Castle Books.

Reilly, D., Van Beurden, E., Mitchell, E., Dight, R., Scott, C. and Beard, J. (1998) 'Alcohol education in licensed premises using brief intervention strategies', *Addiction*, 93: 385–98.

Responsible Hospitality Institute (2006) *Planning, managing and policing hospitality zones: A practical guide*. Santa, Cruz, California: Responsible Hospitality Institute.

Rigakos, G. S. (2004) 'Nightclub security and surveillance', *Canadian Review of Policing Research*, 1: 54–60.

Roberts, J. C. (1998) *Alcohol-related aggression in the barroom environment: A study of drinking establishments at the Jersey shore*, Unpublished master's thesis, Rutgers University School of Criminal Justice, Newark, New Jersey.

Roberts, J. C. (2002) *Serving up trouble in the barroom environment* (Doctoral dissertation, Rutgers University, 2002). *Dissertation Abstracts International*, 63: 3367.

Roberts, J. C. (2007) 'Barroom aggression in Hoboken, New Jersey: Don't blame the bouncers!' *Journal of Drug Education*, 37: 429–45.

Roche, A. M., Watt, K., McClure, R., Purdie, D. M. and Green, D. (2001) 'Injury and alcohol: A hospital emergency department study', *Drug and Alcohol Review*, 20: 155–66.

Roebuck, J. and Spray, S. L. (1967) 'The cocktail lounge: A study of heterosexual relations in a public organization', *American Judicature Society*, 72: 388–95.

Roebuck, J. B. and Frese, W. (1976) *The rendezvous: A case study of an after-hours club*. New York and London: Collier Macmillan Publishers.

Romanus, G. (1992) 'EU strategy on alcohol lobbied by the alcohol industry – but the Council conclusions are better than the Commission's', *Nordic Studies on Alcohol and Drugs*, 23: 513–17.

Roncek, D. W. and Bell, R. (1981–82) 'Bars, blocks and crimes', *Journal Environmental Systems*, 11: 35–47.

Roncek, D. W. and Maier, P. A. (1991) 'Bars, blocks and crimes revisited: Linking the theory of routine activities to the empiricism of "hot spots"', *Criminology*, 29: 725–53.

Roncek, D. W. and Pravatiner, M. A. (1989) 'Additional evidence that taverns enhance nearby crime', *Social Science Research*, 73: 185–188.

Room, R. (2004) 'Disabling the public interest: alcohol strategies and policies for England', *Addiction*, 99: 1083–89.

Room, R. (2005) 'Alcohol control and the public interest: international perspectives', in P. Kolvin (ed.) *Licensed premises: Law and practice*. Haywards Heath, West Sussex: Tottel Publishing.

Rossow, I. (1996) 'Alcohol-related violence: The impact of drinking pattern and drinking context', *Addiction*, 91: 1651–61.

Rotundo, M., Nguyen, D.-H. and Sackett, P.R. (2001) 'A meta-analytic review of gender differences in perceptions of sexual harassment', *Journal of Applied Psychology*, 86: 914–23.

Rumbold, G., Malpass, A., Lang, E., Cvetkovski, S. and Kelly, W. M. (1998) *An evaluation of the Geelong Local Industry Accord*. Fitzroy, Victoria: Turning Point Alcohol and Drug Centre and the Victoria Police.

Russell, B. L. and Trigg, K. Y. (2004) 'Tolerance of sexual harassment: An examination of gender differences, ambivalent sexism, social dominance, and gender roles', *Sex Roles*, 50: 565–73.

Sabic, I., Walker, A., McNamara, J., Smith, C. and Kolvin, P. (2005), 'Door supervision', in P. Kolvin (ed.) *Licensed premises: Law and practice* (rev. edn). Haywards Heath, West Sussex, UK: Tottel Publishing, pp. 819–38.

Saltz, R. F. (1987) 'The roles of bars and restaurants in preventing alcohol-impaired driving: An evaluation of server intervention', *Evaluation and the Health Professions*, 10: 5–27.

Saltz, R. F. (1997) 'Evaluating specific community structural changes. Examples from the assessment of Responsible Beverage Service', *Evaluation Review*, 21: 246–67.

Sanders, M. R., Markie-Dadds, C., Tully, L. and Bor, W. (2000), 'The Triple P-Positive Parenting Program: A comparison of enhanced, standard, and self directed behavioral family intervention', *Journal of Consulting and Clinical Psychology*, 68: 624–40.

Sayette, M. A., Wilson, T. and Elias, M. J. (1993) 'Alcohol and aggression: A social information processing analysis', *Journal of Studies on Alcohol*, 54: 399–407.

Schmutte, G., Leonard, K. and Taylor, S. (1979) 'Alcohol and expectations of attack', *Psychological Reports*, 45:163–7.

Scott, M. S. (2001) *Assaults in and around bars.* Problem-oriented guides for police series, Guide No. 1. Washington, DC: US Department of Justice, Office of Community Oriented Policing Services, p. 45.

Sears, D., Paplau, L. A. and Taylor, S. E. (1991) *Social Psychology* (7th edn). New Jersey: Prentice Hall.

Shepherd, J. (1994) 'Violent crime: The role of alcohol and new approaches to the prevention of injury', *Alcohol and Alcoholism*, 29: 5–10.

Sherman, L. W., Gartin, P. R. and Buerger, M. E. (1989) 'Hot spots of predatory crime: Routine activities and the criminology of place', *Criminology*, 27: 27–55.

Sim, M., Morgan, E. and Batchelor, J. (2005) *The impact of enforcement on intoxication and alcohol related harm.* Wellington, New Zealand: Accident Compensation Corporation.

Single, E. (1985) 'Studies of public drinking: An overview', E. Single and T. Storm (eds) *Public drinking and public policy.* Toronto, Canada: Addiction Research Foundation, pp. 5–34.

Single, E. and Wortley, S. (1993) 'Drinking in various settings as it relates to demographic variables and level of consumption: Findings from a national survey in Canada', *Journal of Studies on Alcohol*, 54: 590–99.

Sivarajasingam, V., Shepherd, J. P. and Matthews, K. (2003) 'Effect of urban closed circuit television on assault injury and violence detection', *Injury Prevention*, 9: 312–16.

Sloan, F., Stout, E., Whetten-Goldstein, K. and Liang, L. (2000) *Drinkers, drivers and bartenders: Balancing private choices and public accountability.* Chicago: The University of Chicago Press.

Smith, K. L., Wiggers, J. H., Considine, R. J., Daly, J. B. and Collins, T. (2001) 'Police knowledge and attitudes regarding crime, the responsible service of alcohol and a proactive alcohol policing strategy', *Drug and Alcohol Review*, 20: 181–91.

Smith, M. A. (1985) 'A participant observer study of a "rough" working-class pub', *Leisure Studies*, 4: 93–306

Snow, D. A., Robinson, C. and McCall, P. L. (1991) '"Cooling out" men in singles bars and nightclubs: Observations on the interpersonal survival strategies of women in public places', *Journal of Contemporary Ethnography*, 19: 423–49.

Spradley, J. P. and Mann, P. J. (1975) *The cocktail waitress: Women's work in a man's world.* New York: John Wiley and Sons.

Steele, C. M. and Josephs, R. A. (1990) 'Alcohol myopia: its prized and dangerous effects', *American Psychologist*, 45: 921–33.

Steele, C. and Southwick, L. (1985) 'Alcohol and social behavior I: The psychology of drunken excess', *Journal of Personality and Social Psychology*, 48: 18–34.

Steele, C., Critchlow, B. and Liu, T. (1985) 'Alcohol and social behavior II: The helpful drunkard', *Journal of Personality and Social Psychology*, 48: 35–46.

Stewart, L. (1993) *Police enforcement of liquor licensing laws: The UK experience*. Auckland, New Zealand: Alcohol and Public Health Research Unit; School of Medicine, University of Auckland.

Stockwell, T. (ed.) (1994) *Alcohol misuse and violence: An examination of the appropriateness and efficacy of liquor licensing laws across Australia* (vol. 5). Canberra: Australian Government Publishing Service.

Stockwell, T. (1997) 'Regulation of the licensed drinking environment: A major opportunity for crime prevention', in R. Homel (ed.) *Policing for prevention: Reducing crime, public intoxication and injury* (vol. 7). Monsey, New York: Criminal Justice Press, pp. 7–33.

Stockwell, T. (2001) 'Responsible alcohol service: Lessons from evaluations of server training and policing initiatives', *Drug and Alcohol Review*, 20: 257–65.

Stockwell, T. and Gruenewald, P. (2004) 'Controls on the physical availability of alcohol', in N. Heather and T. Stockwell (eds) *The essential handbook of treatment and prevention of alcohol problems*. West Sussex, UK: John Wiley and Sons Ltd., pp. 213–34.

Stockwell, T., Lang, E. and Rydon, P. (1993) 'High risk drinking settings: The association of serving and promotional practices with harmful drinking', *Addiction*, 88: 1519–26.

Stockwell, T., Rydon, P., Lang, E., and Beel, A. (1993) *An evaluation of the 'Freo Respects You' responsible alcohol service project*. Bentley, WA: National Centre for Research into the Prevention of Drug Abuse, Curtin University of Technology.

Storm, T. and Cutler, R. E. (1985) 'The functions of taverns', in E. Single and T. Storm (eds) *Public drinking and public policy*. Toronto, Canada: Addiction Research Foundation, pp. 35–47.

Stout, R. L., Rose, J. S., Speare, M. C., Buka, S. L., Laforge, R. G., Campbell, M. K. and Waters, W. J. (1993) 'Sustaining interventions in communities: The Rhode Island community-based prevention trial', in T.K. Greenfield and R. J. Zimmerman (eds) *Experiences with community action projects: new research in the prevention of alcohol and other drug problems*. Rockville, MD: U.S. Department of Health and Human Services, pp. 253–61.

Suggs, D. (2001) '"These young chaps think they are just men, too": redistributing masculinity in Kgatleng bars', *Social Science and Medicine*, 53: 241–50.

Sulkunen, P., Alasuutari, P., Natkin, R. and Kinnunen, M. (1985) *The Urban Pub*. Finland: Otava.

Sykes, G. M. and Matza, D. (1957) 'Techniques of neutralization: A theory of delinquency', *American Sociological Review*, 22: 664–70.

Tedeschi, J. T. and Felson, R. B. (1994) *Violence, aggression and coercive actions*. Washington, DC: American Psychological Association.

Thornton, S. (1995) *Club cultures: Music, media and subcultural capital*. Cambridge, UK: Polity Press.

Tierney, J. and Hobbs, D. (2003) *Alcohol-related crime and disorder data: Guidance for local partnerships*. London: Home Office: The Research Development and Statistics Directorate.

Tomsen, S. (1997) 'A top night out – Social protest, masculinity and the culture of drinking violence', *British Journal of Criminology*, 37: 990–02.

Tomsen, S. (2005) '"Boozers and bouncers": Masculine conflict, disengagement and the contemporary governance of drinking-related violence and disorder', *Australian and New Zealand Journal of Criminology*, 38: 283–97.

Tomsen, S., Homel, R. and Thommeny, J. (1991) 'The causes of public violence: Situational "versus" other factors in drinking related assaults', in D. Chappell, P. Grabosky and H. Strang (eds) *Australian Violence: Contemporary Perspectives*. Sydney, NSW: Australian Institute of Criminology, pp. 176–93.

Toomey, T. L., Kilian, G. R., Gehan, J. P., Perry, C. L., Jones-Webb, R. and Wagenaar, A. C. (1998) 'Qualitative assessment of training programs for alcohol servers and establishment managers', *Public Health Reports*, 113: 162–69.

Toomey, T. L., Wagenaar, A. C., Gehan, J. P., Kilian, G., Murray, D. M. and Perry, C. L. (2001) 'Project ARM: Alcohol risk management to prevent sales to underage and intoxicated patrons', *Health Education and Behavior*, 28: 186–99.

Treno, A. J., Gruenewald, P. J., Remer, L. G., Johnson, F. and LaScala, E. A. (2007) 'Examining multi-level relationships between bars, hostility and aggression: social selection and social influence', *Addiction*, 103: 66–77.

Tuck, M. (1989) 'Disorder in the paired towns', in *Drinking and Disorder: A study of Non-Metropolitan Violence*, Home Office Research Study 108: 11–103. London: Home Office.

Vaughan, S. (2001) 'Reducing alcohol-related harm in and around licensed premises: Industry accords – A successful intervention', in P. Williams (ed.) *Alcohol, young persons and violence* (vol. 35). Canberra: Australian Institute of Criminology, pp. 203–16.

Victorian Community Council Against Violence (1990) *Inquiry Into Violence in and around Licensed Premises*. Melbourne: Victorian Community Council Against Violence.

Wade, J. C. and Critelli, J. W. (1998) 'Narrative descriptions of sexual aggression: The gender gap', *Journal of Social and Clinical Psychology*, 17: 363–78.

Wall, A.-M., McKee, S. A. and Hinson, R. E. (2000) 'Assessing variation in alcohol outcome expectancies across environmental context: An examination of the situational-specificity hypothesis', *Psychology of Addictive Behaviors,* 14: 367–75.

Wallin, E. and Andreasson, S. (2005) 'Effects of a community action program on problems related to alcohol consumption at licensed premises', in T. Stockwell, P. Gruenewald, J. Toumbourou and W. Loxley (eds) *Preventing harmful substance use: The evidence base for policy and practice.* New York: John Wiley and Sons.

Wallin, E. and Andreasson, S. (2005) 'Public opinion on alcohol service at licensed premises: A population survey in Stockholm, Sweden 1999–2000', *Health Policy,* 72: 265–78.

Wallin, E., Gripenberg, J. and Andreasson, S. (2002) 'Too drunk for a beer? A study of overserving in Stockholm', *Addiction,* 97: 901–7.

Wallin, E., Gripenberg, J. and Andreasson, S. (2005) 'Overserving at licensed premises in Stockholm: Effects of a community action program', *Journal of Studies in Alcohol,* 66: 806–15.

Wallin, E., Lindewald, B. and Andreasson, S. (2004) 'Institutionalization of a community action program targeting licensed premises in Stockholm, Sweden', *Evaluation Review,* 28: 396–419.

Wallin, E., Norstrom, T. and Andreasson, S. (2003) 'Alcohol prevention targeting licensed premises: A study of effects on violence', *Journal of Studies on Alcohol,* 64: 270–77.

Warburton, A. L. and Shepherd, J. P. (2002) 'Alcohol-related violence and the role of oral and maxillofacial surgeons in multi-agency prevention', *International Journal of Oral and Maxillofacial Surgery,* 31: 657–63.

Warburton, A. L. and Shepherd, J. P. (2006) 'Tackling alcohol related violence in city centres: Effect of emergency medicine and police intervention', *Emergency Medical Journal,* 23: 12–17.

Washburne, C. (1956) 'Alcohol, self, and the group', *Quarterly Journal of Studies on Alcohol,* 17: 108–23.

Wells, S., and Graham, K. (1999) 'The frequency of third party involvement in incidents of barroom aggression', *Contemporary Drug Problems,* 26: 457–80.

Wells, S., Graham, K. and West, P. (1998) '"The good, the bad and the ugly": Responses by security staff to aggressive incidents in public drinking settings', *Journal of Drug Issues,* 28: 817–36.

Welsh, B. C. and Farrington, D. P. (1999) 'Value for money? A review of the costs and benefits of situational crime prevention', *British Journal of Criminology,* 39: 345–68.

Welsh, B. C. and Farrington, D. P. (2002) *Crime prevention effects of closed circuit television: A systematic review* (Home Office Research Study No. 252). London: Home Office.

Wikström, P. H. (1995) 'Preventing city-center street crimes', in M. Tonry and D. P. Farrington (eds) *Building a safer society: Strategic approaches to crime prevention* (vol. 19). Chicago, London: The University of Chicago Press, pp. 429–68.

Wiggers, J. (2003) *Problem-oriented policing: an alternative approach to reducing alcohol-related harm associated with alcohol consumption on licensed premises,* paper presented at an International Research Symposium on Preventing Substance Use, Risk, Use and Harm: What is Evidence and Based Policy?, Fremantle, Australia.

Wiggers, J. H., Jauncey, M., Considine, R. J., Daly, J. B., Kingsland, M., Purss, K., Burrows, S., Nicholas, C. and Waites, J. (2004) 'Strategies and outcomes in translating alcohol harm reduction research into practice: The Alcohol Linking Program', *Drug and Alcohol Review,* 23: 355–64.

Wilsnack, R. W., Vogeltanz, N. D., Wilsnack, S. C. and Harris, T. R. (2000) 'Gender differences in alcohol consumption and adverse drinking consequences: Cross-cultural patterns', *Addiction*, 95: 251–65.

Wilsnack, S. C. (1974) 'The effects of social drinking on women's fantasy', *Journal of Personality*, 42: 43-61.

Winlow, S. (2001) *Badfellas*: *Crime, tradition and new masculinities*. Oxford: Berg.

Winlow, S., Hobbs, D., Lister, S. and Hadfield, P. (2001), 'Get ready to duck: Bouncers and the realities of ethnographic research on violent groups', *British Journal of Criminology*, 41: 536–48.

Wood, J. and Shearing, C. (2007) *Imagining security*. Cullompton, Devon: Willan Publishing.

Wortley, R. (1997) 'Reconsidering the role of opportunity in situational crime prevention', in G. Newman, R. Clarke and S. Shoham (eds) *Rational choice and situational crime prevention*. Aldershot, Hampshire: Ashgate, pp. 65–82.

Wortley, R. (2001) 'A classification of techniques for controlling situational precipitators of crime', *Security*, 14: 63–82.

Wortley, R. (2002) *Situational prison control: Crime prevention in correctional institutions*. Cambridge, UK: Cambridge University Press.

Wortley, R. (2003) 'Situational crime prevention and prison control: Lessons for each other', in M. J. Smith and D. B. Cornish (eds) *Theory for practice in situational crime prevention* (vol. 16). Monsey, NY: Criminal Justice Press, pp. 97–117.

Wortley, R. and Smallbone, S. (2006) 'Applying situational principles to sexual offenses against children', in R. Wortley and S. Smallbone (eds) *Situational prevention of child sexual abuse. Crime Prevention Studies* (vol. 19). Monsey, NY: Criminal Justice Press, pp. 7–35.

Zeichner, A. and Pihl, R. (1979) 'Effects of alcohol and behavior contingencies on human aggression', *Journal of Abnormal Psychology*, 88: 153–60.

Index